W9-AXE-545

NEW YORK TIMES #1 BESTSELLING AUTHORS

WHY
WE WANT
YOU
TO BE
RICH

TWO MEN • ONE MESSAGE

DONALD J.
TRUMP | KIYOSAKI
ROBERT T.

NEW YORK TIMES #1 BESTSELLING AUTHORS

WHY
WE WANT
YOU
TO BE
RICH

TWO MEN • ONE MESSAGE

Donald J.
TRUMP | KIYOSAKI
Robert T.

PLATA®
PUBLISHING

If you purchase this book without a cover, or purchase a PDF, jpg, or tiff copy of this book, it is likely stolen property or a counterfeit. In that case, neither the authors, the publisher, nor any of their employees or agents has received any payment for the copy. Furthermore, counterfeiting is a known avenue of financial support for organized crime and terrorist groups. We urge you to please not purchase any such copy and to report any instance of someone selling such copies to Plata Publishing LLC.

This publication is designed to provide competent and reliable information regarding the subject matter covered. However, it is sold with the understanding that the author and publisher are not engaged in rendering legal, financial, or other professional advice. Laws and practices often vary from state to state and country to country and if legal or other expert assistance is required, the services of a professional should be sought. The author and publisher specifically disclaim any liability that is incurred from the use or application of the contents of this book.

Copyright ©2007, 2013 by Donald J. Trump and Robert T. Kiyosaki. All rights reserved. Except as permitted under the U.S. Copyright Act of 1976, no part of this publication may be reproduced, distributed, or transmitted in any form or by any means or stored in a database or retrieval system, without the prior written permission of the publisher.

Published by Plata Publishing, LLC

Trump and Trump Organization are trademarks of the Trump Organization. CASHFLOW, Rich Dad, and B-I Triangle are registered trademarks of CASHFLOW Technologies, Inc.

Some of the company and product names mentioned in this book are the trademarks or registered trademarks of their respective companies. They were used for identification purposes only.

  RICH DAD. are registered trademarks of CASHFLOW Technologies, Inc.

Plata Publishing, LLC
4330 N. Civic Center Plaza
Suite 100
Scottsdale, AZ 85251
(480) 998-6971

Visit our websites: PlataPublishing.com, Trump.com, RichDad.com
Printed in the United States of America
092013

First Edition: December 2007
First Plata Edition: September 2013

ISBN: 978-1-61268-091-0

TABLE OF CONTENTS

AUTHORS' NOTES
PREDICTIONS COME TRUE

There are three points I want to make. These three points will explain why this book, *Why We Want You To Be Rich,* is more relevant today than when it was first released in 2006.

Point #1:

In 2004, when Donald Trump and I first got together, we found out we shared the same concerns. These shared concerns caused us to write this book. Some of these concerns are:

1. A falling U.S. dollar and how a falling dollar would wipe out savers and the wealth of the middle class.

2. The rise in the price of oil. As world consumption of oil increases the price of oil keeps going up. Oil affects everything, which means everything becomes more expensive. Again, this affects savers and the middle class.

3. Excessive debt. Not only is the consumer in debt, so is the U.S. government. Today, the world is spinning from the fall out of the sub-prime credit mess.

4. 401(k) plans and mutual fund companies ripping off their investors. Soon after this book was first published, the *Wall Street Journal* wrote an article validating our concerns.

Point #2:

When *Why We Want You To Be Rich* was first published in 2006, the book was severely criticized by many people. This edition of the book points out why those critics weren't seeing the whole picture.

Point #3:

Donald and I joined forces as teachers…we both had rich dads who were our teachers. We wrote this book because we believe in financial education. We believe it is time to get smart with your money and become rich rather than to count on the government and politicians to care for you and your money.

– Robert T. Kiyosaki

The *Wall Street Journal* criticizes our book:
on October 11, 2006…

Wall Street Journal columnist Jonathan Clements criticized us regarding 401(k)s and mutual funds. The headline read:

Their Book is Hot, But Their Financial Tips Aren't
and challenged our position that mutual fund companies take
80% of the profits, leaving investors with only **20%.**

Less than a year later…in The *Wall Street Journal*:
on March 14, 2007 in a front page article by Eleanor Laise…

What Is Your 401(k) Costing You?
As Congress, Regulators Scrutinize Hidden Charges,
Employers Begin to Ditch High-Cost Plans, Negotiate Lower Fees

In summary: The little investor is being ripped off—legally. America is the best country if you are rich or if you want to become rich, but it's a horrible country if you are poor or—even worse—if you are working hard and then become sick. This is why we want you to be rich. And to get rich, you need to know good financial advice from poor financial advice.

WHY WE WANT YOU TO BE RICH
TWO MEN • ONE MESSAGE

The rich are getting richer, but are you?

"We are losing our middle class, and a shrinking middle class is a threat to the stability of America and to world democracy itself. We want you to be rich so you can be part of the solution…rather than part of the problem."

– Donald J. Trump and Robert T. Kiyosaki

Donald Trump and Robert Kiyosaki are both concerned. Their concern is that the rich are getting richer but America is getting poorer. Like the polar ice caps, the middle class is disappearing. America is becoming a two-class society. Soon you will be either rich or poor. Donald and Robert want you to be rich.

This phenomenon—the shrinking middle class—is a global problem, but predominantly in the richer G-8 nations (in countries such as England, France, Germany, Japan, etc.)

Former Federal Reserve Chairman Alan Greenspan said, "As I have often said, this is not the type of thing which a democratic society—a capitalist democratic society—can really accept without addressing." He went on to explain how the income gap between the rich and the rest of the U.S. population has become so wide, and is growing so fast, that it might eventually threaten the stability of democratic capitalism itself.

The Problem Is Education

What did the Federal Reserve Chairman state as the main cause of the problem? In one word, his answer was *education*. Mr. Greenspan points out that U.S. children test above the world average levels at the 4th grade level. But by the 12th grade level, they are far behind. He says, "We have to do something to prevent that from happening."

Donald Trump and Robert Kiyosaki also place the blame on the lack of *education*. But they focus on a different type of education, *financial education*. Both men are very concerned about the lack of quality financial education in America, at all levels. Both men blame the lack of financial education for the United States having gone from the richest country in the world to the biggest debtor nation in history, so quickly. A weak U.S. economy and a weak U.S. dollar (the reserve currency of the world) are not good for world stability. As is often said in other parts of the world, "When the United States sneezes, the world catches cold."

Both Men Are Teachers

Both Donald Trump and Robert Kiyosaki are successful entrepreneurs and investors. Both men do business and are recognized internationally. Both men are also teachers. Both men are best-selling authors, produce educational board games, speak at financial education events, and both have educational television programs. Donald Trump has his megahit network television show, *The Apprentice* and Robert Kiyosaki has his television show, *Rich Dad's Guide to Wealth,* on PBS, the highly acclaimed educational public television network.

Both men are teachers, not because they need more money. They are both teachers because they are concerned about the fate of you and your family, this nation and the world.

Rich people who want to make a difference typically give money to causes they believe in. But Donald and Robert are giving of both their time as well as their money. As the story goes, you can give a man a fish and feed him for a day or teach him to fish and feed him for a lifetime. Instead of just writing checks to help the poor and middle class, Donald and Robert are teaching them to fish.

Financial Advice

There are three levels of financial advice: advice for the poor, advice for the middle class, and advice for the rich. The financial advice for the poor is that the government will take care of them. The poor are counting on Social Security and Medicare. The financial advice for the middle class is: get a job, work hard, live below your means, save money, invest for the long term in mutual funds, and diversify. Most people in the middle class are passive investors—investors who work and invest *not to* lose. The rich are active investors who work and invest to win. This book is about becoming an active investor—expanding your means to live a great life by working and investing to win.

Donald Trump and Robert Kiyosaki are best-selling authors and popular speakers because they teach people to expand their means and improve the quality of their lives, rather than work hard to live below their means. They want people to work and invest to win.

A Little History

During the *Hunter-Gatherer Age* of human development, humans lived in tribes and, for the most part, all people were equal. If you were the chief of the tribe, you still lived pretty much like the rest of the tribe. Chiefs did not have Lear jets, multimillion-dollar estates, and golden parachutes.

In the *Agrarian Age,* there evolved a two-tiered society. The king and his rich friends on one tier and everyone else (peasants) working for the king on another tier. Generally, the king owned the land. The peasants worked the king's land, and paid the king a form of tax by giving the king a share of their harvests. The peasants owned nothing and royalty owned everything.

In the *Industrial Age,* the modern middle class was born in America and so was democracy.

The founding fathers of America were so impressed by the five tribes of the Iroquois Confederacy that lived in what is today known as New England that they used the tribal model as the model for our democracy. That model elected representatives, an upper and lower house, and a supreme court (made up of entirely women).

At the same time the founders of America were copying the Iroquois form of democracy, the idea of democracy and a middle class was still considered unrealistic in Europe—all while a powerful middle class and democratic society were blooming in the United States.

Today, in the *Information Age,* the middle class is slowly dying and so is democratic capitalism. Unlike any other time in history, there really is a very wide and growing gap between the haves and have-nots. Are we going backward, into the *Agrarian Age,* when there was no democracy and only two classes, or will we evolve into a new form of capitalism and democracy?

Problems on the Horizon

Just as we are only now becoming aware of the effects of global warming, we are also only now becoming aware of the effects of the loss of our middle class. Currently, most members of the middle class feel safe and secure.

They are content, even though most are aware that we have problems on the horizon.

They feel safe because they believe their government will step in and take care of them and protect them. Little do they know, there is little that government can do to protect them. Governments, even the U.S. government, cannot protect their people as they once could simply because the *problems are now global problems.* For example, the price of oil is determined by countries outside the control of the United States. Terrorism is not a war against nations. Terrorism is a war against ideas. A terrorist can strike anywhere and disappear into the populace. And globalization, causing the loss of so many American jobs, is the problem of multinational corporations becoming richer and more powerful than many countries. This globalization has also been made more possible through the World Wide Web making communication instantaneous anywhere in the world. Communication has become possible any time any where.

On the home front, just as *environmentalists* are noticing that some species of frogs are disappearing, *economists* are noticing that pensions and health care are disappearing for the middle class and poor. In a few years, the biggest baby boom generation in history begins to retire all over the world. Most governments do not have the financial resources to keep their promises.

Businessmen, Not Politicians

People expect their elected government officials to take care of the growing problems facing the poor and middle class. Donald Trump and Robert Kiyosaki are not politicians (although Donald has considered running for president). They write this book as entrepreneurs, investors, and educators.

Instead of promising to solve your problems, they want you to avoid becoming a victim of the problems. Do not expect your political and government officials to provide solutions. Do not think you are *entitled* to a secure, prosperous and healthy life. Instead Donald and Robert want you to become rich and become part of the solution to the problems we face as a nation and the world.

Not a How-To Book

When it comes to money, many people want to be told exactly what to do. They often ask specific questions, such as, "I have $25,000. What should I do with it?" When you tell people that you do not know what to do with your money, they are happy to tell you what to do…and their recommendation is that you give your money to them.

This book is not a how-to book. Donald and Robert will not be telling you what to invest in. They will share with you how they think, why they win financially, and how they see the world of money, business, and investing.

A Matter of Vision

Most rich people do not want you to know what they know or their secrets to becoming rich. But Donald and Robert are different. They want to share their knowledge with you.

One of the definitions of *leadership* is vision. This book is about vision, about seeing what most people never see through the eyes of two men who have won (and occasionally lost) at the game of money. *Why We Want You To Be Rich* is a book about *how* these two men think and why they think the way they do. Through their eyes you will gain additional insight into how you can improve your financial future.

A Word of Caution

In the world of money, there is another word often used—*transparency.* Transparency has many definitions. Three definitions applicable to this book are:

1. Free from pretence or deceit

2. Sheer enough to be seen through

3. Readily understood

People want greater vision so they can see with their own eyes and make their own decisions. Because our educational system does not really teach people to be financially literate, people cannot see. And if they cannot see, there is no transparency. Due to this lack of vision and transparency, people are simply investing by giving their money to someone else to invest. They blindly follow the advice of "work hard, save money, invest for the long term in mutual funds, and diversify." They work hard and follow this investment advice because they cannot see.

A word of caution: If you believe that working hard, saving money, investing for the long term in mutual funds, and diversifying is good advice then this book may not be for you.

Donald and Robert do not invest in mutual funds because mutual fund companies are not required to be transparent; they are not required to disclose their true expenses. Since most amateur investors cannot see, this fact does not bother them. Professional investors, as Donald and Robert are, require transparency in all their investments.

While the financial advice of saving money and investing in mutual funds may be good advice for the poor and middle class, it is not good advice for people who want to become rich. This book is about seeing through the eyes of two rich men and understanding a world of money very few people get to see.

How History Affects Today

This book will also discuss how history has brought us to this financial state of emergency. Some important dates are:

1971: Our money stopped being money and became a currency when it ceased being backed by gold. This is the year that "saving money" became obsolete and bad financial advice. Today, the middle class has very little in savings.

Could it be because they know that savings is an obsolete idea?

1973: The first oil shock was felt. It was a political problem. However, today the current oil shock is an actual supply and demand problem that will affect all of us. Some of us will get richer, but most of us will become poorer as a result of today's oil shortage.

How will the current oil crisis affect you?

1974: ERISA, the Employee Retirement Income Security Act was passed. ERISA eventually led to what we now know as 401(k) plans. Few law changes have affected so many of us as this one. The 401(k) was originally an arcane subparagraph in the U.S. Tax Code originally created only for high-income CEOs and executives looking for a way to shelter a few more dollars. It became a revolution in retirement savings after the IRS ruled in 1981 that workers could use the same rule. The problem is that the 401(k) is a savings plan and not a retirement plan. Many workers who have 401(k)s will not have enough money to retire on simply because the 401(k) was designed for very high-income executives, not lower wage workers. In simple terms, the 401(k) savings plan will not be adequate for approximately 80 percent of all workers, especially those making less than $150,000 a year. Millions of middle-class workers will be downgraded to the poor class even though they have a 401(k) plan today.

Do you have a 401(k)?

1989: The Berlin Wall came down and the World Wide Web went up. In other words, communism, an economic system designed to protect the workers, failed. At the same time, in the same year, we entered the Information Age. Suddenly young Internet millionaires and billionaires were being created while baby-boom workers were losing their jobs.

Many older workers have to work for younger workers simply because they are not technically current. Instead of receiving pay raises as they did in the Industrial Age, many older workers are receiving pink slips because their years of education and experience are obsolete.

Are your skills obsolete?

1996: The Telecom Reform Act was passed. This Act allowed the world to be connected via fiber optic cable, facilitating globalization. This meant that white-collar jobs could be exported. It now makes economic sense to hire a programmer, doctor, lawyer, and accountant in countries where the costs for these services are much lower due to the lower cost of living abroad.

Are you working in an area that fiber optic cable could change?

2001: China was admitted into the World Trade Organization (WTO). Today, America and many Western nations such as the G-8 nations have become consumers rather than producers. This sets up a huge balance-of-trade problem and also takes away our factories.

Many small businesses are not able to compete with companies like Wal-Mart, who has direct lines to China's factories.

Today in America and other Western nations, our middle class is shrinking as the middle class in China and India is growing.

Do you consume products manufactured overseas?

2004: During the Kerry-Bush debates, there was talk about the outsourcing of American jobs. But there is a bigger problem both parties avoided. There was little said about the outsourcing of American debt into the hands of foreigners.

While there is much discussion about illegal immigrants in our work force, there is a more serious immigration problem not being discussed: the amount of foreign capital that keeps the United States afloat. In 2004, 44 percent of our Treasury debt was owned by foreigners. No leading country in history has ever incurred this level of foreign debt. As a nation we cannot afford the payments to service this debt, and there is a limit to the amount of our debt the world will tolerate.

Are you able to service your own personal debt?

This book is not a political book. It will not blame Republicans or Democrats, Liberals or Conservatives. This book is about money, financial education, and the effects of a lack of financial education and money management. It is about protecting yourself from national money mismanagement. Today's problems are bigger than our government can handle. That may be why our politicians avoid discussing the real problems.

The United States has the highest standard of living in the world. We have attained that high standard of living by becoming the greatest debtor nation in the world. The U.S. dollar is also the world's reserve currency and so far, the world has allowed us to print as many dollars as we want. Is this a fairy tale scenario or a nightmare? Donald and Robert do not think this fantasy can last much longer. They expect a global correction on a massive scale. Unfortunately, the poor and middle class will be hurt the most. And this is why they want you to be rich.

This Book Is Not About Changing the World

This book is not about changing the world. *This book is about changing you so that you do not become a victim of a changing world.* The world is changing rapidly. Politicians and government bureaucracy cannot change fast enough or protect everyone from these shifts.

Bill Gates and Warren Buffett have joined forces to solve some of the world's most pressing problems. This is commendable as money does have the power to solve many of our world problems, such as hunger, affordable housing, and hopefully many diseases (such as cancer and AIDS).

Money Cannot Solve Poverty

The one problem money cannot solve is *poverty*. While there are many underlying causes of poverty, one of the causes is a lack of financial education. The problem with throwing money at the issue of poverty is that money only creates more poor people and keeps people poorer longer. This is why Donald and Robert are teachers. They know that the one true solution to worldwide poverty is financial education, not money. If money alone could solve poverty, they would donate their money. But since money cannot solve poverty, they donate their time.

As your financial education increases, you will start to recognize financial opportunities everywhere. Once you become rich, you may choose to help change the world as well. This is what Donald Trump and Robert Kiyosaki have done. This is why they have joined forces as teachers.

As you read this book you will see the voices of two men, from two different backgrounds, with two different perspectives, and two different voices. Robert is a story-teller and uses dialogue often in his writing. Donald is direct and to–the–point, using as few words as possible. We have used two different typefaces to emphasize their two voices (Adobe Garamond is used for Robert and Trebuchet is used for Donald).

Can you read this book with an open mind? If so, you will see the world through the eyes of these two successful men and you may expand your own mind-set about money and what is possible for your financial future.

"Yes, we did produce a near perfect Republic.
But will they keep it?
Or will they in their enjoyment of plenty,
lose the memory of freedom?
Material abundance without character is
the surest way to destruction.
Indeed, I tremble for my country when
I reflect that God is just."

– Thomas Jefferson

PART ONE

WHY DONALD TRUMP AND ROBERT KIYOSAKI WROTE THIS BOOK

For many reasons, Donald Trump and Robert Kiyosaki never should have met, much less written a book together. Donald Trump is from New York (the financial capital of the world), is from a wealthy family and is a billionaire who started making his money at a young age. Robert Kiyosaki grew up in Hawaii (the vacation capital of the world), is from a middle-class family and became a millionaire later in his life.

While both men are financially free and do not *have* to work anymore, they choose to continue to work harder than ever. While they do not run in the same circles, something brought them together: they share the same concerns.

Both Donald and Robert are internationally best-selling authors, and each could write another bestseller on his own.

Why would they choose to write a book together? You may have seen their books many times at the bookstore. Maybe you bought them, and maybe you didn't. But isn't it intriguing that these two superstars would join together to write one book? Maybe they are doing it to get your attention! It's that important.

Part One of this book contains Donald's and Robert's personal accounts of how they met and why they decided to write this book.

Chapter One

Millionaire
Meets Billionaire

Robert's View

Chicago: November 6, 2005

It is early Sunday afternoon. Tens of thousands of people are attending a large real estate expo in Chicago. The convention hall is filled with exhibits and displays of wealth-building investments and opportunities. In smaller classrooms, instructors are sharing their knowledge about how the attendees can build their own personal fortunes. The cavernous hall is filled with a buzz that is contagious. People are excited about what they are learning and how it can alter their financial destinies.

Backstage, in the large room where the production crews are working, there is a different excitement. It is a quiet, electric excitement. A long, black limousine has pulled up and people have begun to whisper, "He's here! Donald Trump has arrived."

I am standing in the green room, a private lounge where the main speakers wait before going onstage, so I do not see the limo arrive. But when I see two police officers go past the door of the green room, I know Donald Trump is about to enter.

From inside the green room I can see a tall, imposing figure stepping out of the limo. It could only be Donald Trump, his silhouette known to millions of *The Apprentice* viewers from around the world. Those of us with backstage passes spontaneously form two lines. Almost on cue, Donald Trump walks between the two lines of admirers, smiling and nodding. It is a greeting reserved for royalty or heads of state. If it had been Hollywood, a red carpet would have been ordered.

"Oh my God!" gasps a young woman. "He's even more impressive in real life." "I cannot believe how tall he is," says another young woman. "Did you see his hair?" asks another. For the most part, the men in the group are silent.

The door of the green room suddenly opens. Those who can peek in see that Donald is talking to reporters. The event promoter exits the room and walks over to me. "Are you ready to introduce Donald?" he asks. "Rich Dad's Robert Kiyosaki introducing The Donald. The crowd loves it."

Donald Trump emerges from the green room and walks over to where we are standing. After a few private words with the promoter, Donald turns to me and says, "Hello again. You're introducing me?" I nod in response.

"Great, I see you're still on *The New York Times* best seller list," says Donald. "That's amazing." Then he lowers his voice just a notch. "I want to talk to you about something. Have you got time right now?"

"Of course," I reply.

"You're the number one personal-finance author, and I'm the number one business author. We should do a book together. What do you think?"

Stunned by the offer, I am speechless.

I recover and reply, "Great idea. Let's do it."

I extend my hand to see if he's serious about this book idea. He is, and we shake. Donald then turns to Keith, his imposing bodyguard, and says, "Give Robert my card."

Keith, the six-foot-three bodyguard suddenly stops being an intimidating figure, smiles, breaks out a gold card case and hands me one of Donald Trump's personal business cards.

"Call me the next time you're in New York, and we'll begin putting the book together," says Donald. "I'll introduce you to Meredith. She'll help us on the project."

Soon it's show time, so I turn and head for the stage where more than 24,000 Chicago fans in the main hall and satellite rooms are waiting for Donald Trump. As soon as I am finished with my brief introduction, the theme song from the mega-hit television show, *The Apprentice*, comes on, thousands of gold balloons fall from the ceiling, and the crowd erupts with applause as Donald Trump walks onstage.

The Long Ride Home

Flying home from Chicago to Phoenix, the reality of that handshake set in. "Who am I to write a book with Donald Trump?" I kept asking myself. "And what would we write about?"

"Care for a blanket?" the flight attendant asked, snapping me out of my turmoil.

"No, thank you," I replied with a smile.

As soon as the flight attendant walked away an idea popped into my head: We could write about real estate.

With that thought, my personal critic chimed in, the critic who had been torturing me ever since the book idea was proposed. My critic cynically asked, "You and Donald Trump write a book on real estate? When it comes to real estate, Donald Trump is in the major leagues, and you're in the Little League. He builds skyscrapers in New York. And what do you own? A few apartment houses, a few low-rise commercial buildings, and some raw land. Besides, he's a billionaire, and you're only a millionaire."

Until now, I had been pretty satisfied with my accomplishments in life. But when considering a book with Donald Trump, my successes and accomplishments seemed very small and inconsequential. Instead of feeling honored to be asked to write a book with Donald Trump, I felt miserable. "What can we possibly write about?" I asked myself over and over again as the plane flew from Chicago to Phoenix.

The Boardroom

December 12, 2005

I was in New York to record a television program for PBS and to meet with Yahoo! Finance. Since I was to be in New York anyway, Meredith and I had agreed to meet to see if we could find the perfect book concept. On December 12th, my wife, Kim, and I took a cab to Donald Trump's office…not just his office, his office building.

For those of you who have seen *The Apprentice*, you are probably familiar with the gilded entrance to Trump Tower on New York City's famous Fifth Avenue. Standing on the sidewalk, I leaned back and let my gaze climb the heights, story after story until my eyes finally found the point where the building and the sky met. Trump Tower is definitely a lot bigger than any building Kim and I own. Although I had walked by the building many times, it looked much taller when I knew I was going inside for a meeting with Donald.

Being on Fifth Avenue brought back so many memories. I remembered looking up at buildings like this when I first came to New York to start school at the Merchant Marine Academy in 1965. I was a poor Hawaiian kid in the Big City for the first time.

And here I was, 40 years later, invited by Donald Trump to his office and his building. At that moment, I had a major reality check.

Most people consider me to be very successful. I have made and lost millions of dollars following the principles that I share in the Rich Dad books. But standing in front of Trump Tower, I suddenly realized how far I had come. It was an incredible feeling.

I remembered one of Donald's favorite sayings, "Think big!" Just by standing in front of his building, I realized how much bigger my thinking was that day than it was when I had first arrived in New York in 1965. "Wow!" I said aloud. Kim just squeezed my hand.

Taking a deep breath, we entered Trump Tower and proceeded to the elevators where security guards greeted us. Once cleared, we entered the elevator and rode it to one of the top floors from which Donald runs his empire.

If you have watched *The Apprentice*, you are familiar with the entrance to Donald Trump's office with the attractive receptionist guarding the door. (For those of you with inquiring minds, Donald had a replica of his office built a few floors below his office for the television show. Instead of walking into his real boardroom, he takes an elevator down and walks into the replica of his boardroom.) Although I had watched the program many times, never did I ever think that I might one day be walking into Donald Trump's world.

It was a strange experience to feel like I was on the set of the show. My mind continually flashed back and forth between the television show and real life.

The first person to greet us, once the receptionist had us take a seat, was Keith, Donald Trump's giant bodyguard. When he saw us, Keith took the time to greet us warmly as if we were old friends. He sat down next to us and made us feel completely at home. I could not believe how gracious he was as he told us about his previous career as a New York City detective and his current career as a personal bodyguard for Donald. He stayed with us, offered us water and kept us company until the door to the main office opened and Meredith walked in.

Meredith is the classic young New York City executive woman, an attractive woman who would be perfectly at home in London, Paris, Sydney, Tokyo, Toronto or Beijing. She extended her hand and offered us a warm smile as she said, "Great to finally meet you."

After thanking Keith for his graciousness, Kim and I followed Meredith through the glass doors and into the boardroom, the real boardroom. As we took our seats, my mind again began to flash to scenes from the television program, with male and female apprentice candidates sitting across the table Donald and his advisors. I silently asked myself, "What are you doing here? How did you get here?" (Actually, the words I really used were, "What the (bleep) am I doing here?" And, "How the (bleep) did I get here?").

After a few minutes of chatting, Meredith asked, "What would you like to write about?"

"Well, I am very concerned about poverty," I replied. "I believe we could write about what we would do to end it. The title could be *Ending Poverty*."

Meredith nodded. "That could be a possible subject."

"Or, I'm concerned about how the rich are getting richer, but America as a nation gets poorer. We could write about the demise of the middle class and the poor; how high-paying jobs are being exported to China and India. I've also been concerned for a long time about pensions disappearing and Social Security and Medicare going broke just as baby boomers begin to retire."

"Mr. Trump is also very concerned about those issues," Meredith said. "He wrote a great book about it."

"*The America We Deserve*," Kim said.

"Yes," replied Meredith. "He wrote about his concern with those issues as well as the threat of terrorist attacks even before the attack on September 11th."

"Before 9/11?" asked Kim.

Meredith nodded, "He has a whole section not only on terrorism, but he also talks about the out-of-control national debt. But he doesn't just identify problems; he also goes into his unique solutions."

Kim nodded. She had loved the book.

Meredith continued, "There is a lot more to Mr. Trump than simply television shows, beauty pageants, casinos and real estate. Anyone concerned with our current global problems and how to solve them should read his book."

"So we definitely have some issues in common. We have both been teachers and speakers. I find it interesting that such a rich and famous celebrity as Donald Trump would speak to the general public. In fact, I have been curious about why he teaches. But we're both always in such a hurry, I never get a chance to ask him."

"He's a natural teacher," Meredith said. "I've seen that over the years working for him. Just look at *The Apprentice*. When Mark Burnett proposed the idea for the show to him, Mr. Trump insisted the show have educational value or he wouldn't do it."

"Exactly," Kim said. "I watch for the lessons in business. And I like learning how he handles different situations. But the best part is how he shares the thought process behind his actions. I like knowing why he fires someone."

I said, "*The Apprentice* is entertaining as well as educational. I don't feel like I'm wasting my time. I always feel I've learned something practical, something I can use."

"Maybe the angle of this book is that you are both teachers," Kim chimed in. "After all, you both are entrepreneurs and real estate investors. You founded a gold-mining company in China and took it public, also a real estate investment company, a silver-mining company in South America, and an oil company. Lots of people know that, just like they know about Trump Tower and Trump Place. But they don't know the two of you are teachers."

"I failed to find oil," I said sarcastically.

Kim laughed. "Not every business succeeds," she said.

"And Mr. Trump has not always succeeded," added Meredith. "He's had his challenges, too."

"He was very public about his financial challenges in *The Art of the Comeback*," Kim said. "That was a great book, too."

> Most rich people don't want others to know how they got rich, much less tell people about their failures...
>
> I want people to know because it's how I learned so much. I want people to know that, rich or poor, we all have financial problems.
>
> – *Robert T. Kiyosaki*

Meredith smiled and nodded, "In spite of your financial challenges, you have both been very public about your successes as well as your failures. Tell me, why have you been so open about your financial troubles?"

"Because I want people to know that it's how I learned so much. I want people to know that, rich or poor, we all have financial problems," I answered.

"Exactly! Mr. Trump is the same. He truly wants people to learn. That's why he shares his wins as well as his losses. How many other rich people will do that?"

"Not many," I said. "Most rich people don't want others to know how they got rich...much less tell people about their failures...and that includes my rich dad's family."

"How so?"

I looked to Kim, and she smiled reassuringly. "After I wrote *Rich Dad Poor Dad,*" I said, "I took the book to his family, and the family asked that their family name not be disclosed in the book…even though I said nothing bad about my rich dad. They simply didn't want anyone to know how they got rich. So to respect their wishes, I have not disclosed the name of my rich dad."

"And has that caused you problems?" asked Meredith.

"Yes," I replied. "Some people have even called me a liar, saying there never was a rich dad."

"It's ridiculous," Kim said. "All Robert was doing was respecting the wishes of the family." We respect their privacy. This was a sore subject for both of us. "Most rich people want to keep their success secrets to themselves."

"Which is where you and Mr. Trump are different from other rich people," smiled Meredith. "You are both teachers and are willing to share what you know, in spite of the criticism."

"Mr. Trump is criticized for teaching and sharing his knowledge, too?" asked Kim.

"Oh, yes. More than you know." said Meredith. "A lot of people think he talks and writes and creates educational products like his TV show and his board game because he wants more publicity or more money. While he does make more money and the publicity is good, his primary motive is to teach and educate people. He really wants others to become rich. He is very concerned about the financial situation our nation and people face. He is worried about how mismanaged our economy is and how it will affect the world. He wonders why there is no financial education in our schools. That's why he is very generous with his knowledge."

Suddenly, there was a knock on the door. It was Rhona, Donald's personal assistant. She said, "Mr. Trump will see you in five minutes, and he apologizes for the delay. He hates to keep people waiting, but he was tied up on a phone call."

"Not a problem," I said. "The extra time with Meredith has been useful."

After Rhona left, Meredith stood to lead us out of the boardroom. I looked around the plush interior and thought back to places I had worked. "You know," I said, "Donald and I both had rich dads who we learned from and often worked for. So, in many ways, we were both apprentices as youngsters."

"So maybe what you have in common is that you really are teachers, and you can become mentors to the world," Meredith said as we headed out of the boardroom and across the hall to Donald Trump's office.

A Meeting of Minds

"Welcome," Donald Trump said, standing up from behind his desk. "My apologies for keeping you waiting."

"Not a problem," I replied as I looked around his office, noticing all the awards and plaques and gifts from people all over the world. Beside his desk was the radio equipment he uses for his weekly radio show. It was all very impressive.

After the usual pleasantries, we got around to why we were meeting in the first place. "So what should our book be about?" asked Donald.

"I believe we've all had the same question," I replied. "Since there is such a wide gap between our respective real estate dealings as well as the size of our respective financial statements, I don't think we match when it comes to money. After all, you're a billionaire, and I'm a mere millionaire."

Donald chuckled. "Don't ever put down being a millionaire. Billions of people would love to trade places with you financially."

"I realize that, but there is a definite difference between millions and billions. After all, today, there are many millionaires who are actually broke."

"What do you mean, exactly?" asked Donald.

"Well, we all know people whose homes have increased in value but their incomes have not. For example, I have a classmate from Hawaii who inherited his parents' home after they died. Since the real estate prices have skyrocketed and the house has no debt on it, he is technically a net-worth millionaire, but he and his wife still struggle financially because they earn less than $90,000 a year. They have three kids in school and are wondering about how to afford their college educations."

"So they are asset-rich and cash-poor," said Donald.

"Yes. They are millionaires on paper, but very middle class in reality. If one of them or their children becomes ill, they could easily slip into poverty."

"That does happen to a lot of people, especially after they retire and stop working. They have to sell everything if they become ill, just to survive," added Donald with a somber tone.

"And the problem will grow as the baby-boom generation retires in a few years."

"Yes, I know," said Donald. "Even more than Social Security, Medicare is the biggest debt our nation bears. I don't know how we will afford to pay for 75 million new retirees, their health care, their medicine, and their long-term care once they grow really old. I worry about my kids' generation and how they will afford to pay for our generation's financial dependence upon our government."

"Maybe that is what we should write about," I said.

"Well, I did write about it in *The America We Deserve*. Though it never got the readership I would have liked. I think it was my best book because it was about the problems we face, not just about getting rich. But it didn't sell nearly as many copies as my other books."

"I had one of those books, too," I said. "It was *Rich Dad's Prophecy*, released in 2002. It's about the demise of the stock market when baby boomers retire and the inadequacies of our 401(k) plans. It's also about how a lot of workers will lose their pensions and retirement in the near future."

"And it didn't sell either?" asked Donald.

"No. Like your book, many people said it was my best book, yet it didn't sell like it. But even worse was the Wall Street publications that didn't appreciate my predictions."

"What happened?" asked Donald.

"It upset me for a while. And frustrated me. Then, just a few months ago, both the *New York Times Magazine* and *TIME* magazine ran cover stories saying almost the same things I was saying in 2002."

"And what did they say?" asked Donald.

Since I had both publications with me for my PBS show, I pulled them out of my briefcase. "This is the October 31, 2005 issue of *TIME* magazine. The cover headline is, 'The Great Retirement Ripoff.' The subtitle says, 'Millions of Americans who think they will retire with benefits are in for a nasty surprise. How corporations are picking people's pockets—with the help of Congress.'"

"Yes! I did read that," said Donald. "I remember that part about corporations picking pockets with the help of Congress. The article said the rich are stealing from the workers, legally, with the government's help."

"Isn't that disturbing?" I asked.

"And what did the *New York Times Magazine* say?" asked Donald.

Lifting up the publication, I said, "Well, the cover on October 30, 2005 reads, 'We Regret To Inform You That You No Longer Have A Pension.' The subtitle states, 'America's next financial debacle.'"

Donald nodded. "You and I have been concerned about many of the same things."

"It seems that way. That's why I teach, write, and create board games. It's not for the money, although the money is good. There are far easier ways to make money. I teach and create educational products out of a deep concern. I believe our country is in trouble and so are millions of our people."

"Me, too," said Donald. "When you and I do events and speaking engagements, we often travel for two days, just to deliver a talk. That's a lot of time and energy for a two-hour talk. As you say, there are much easier ways to make money."

Kim and I nodded in unison. Kim, who teaches as well, added, "We all make more money, much easier money, in real estate and other investments. Yet teaching is our passion. It is passion that gets us on those planes to fly all day, spend a night, deliver a short talk, and then fly back home. It's sure not the money."

Donald agreed. "When we speak to those large groups of people, don't you feel for those people? Here they are, spending time and money to listen to us. While some are already rich and some will become rich, many will face lives of constant financial struggle. That breaks my heart."

"Maybe this is what you need to write about," said Meredith. "Maybe people need to know why you want them to be rich. What your concerns are."

"Also," interjected Kim, "why you two keep working even though you don't have to. You both have enough money, but you're not planning to retire. Why not write about what keeps you going…what really drives you. Isn't motivation more important than money?"

"Well, I teach because I like to teach," said Donald. "But I am truly concerned. I hope I'm wrong, but I think America is in financial trouble. I believe our government has been grossly mismanaged. Now, I'm not saying it's because of the Democrats or Republicans. It's senseless to point the finger and blame one group or another. I'm afraid the middle class is in trouble and shrinking no matter which party is in charge. As I have often said, I'm afraid many of today's middle class will become the new poor, or worse, slip into poverty, even after years of hard work."

"Maybe we should write a book about ending poverty through financial education," I said. "After all, it is the lack of financial education that got us into this mess. Why not let financial education get us out?"

"Great idea, but we need to let people know how to save *themselves* before we attempt to end poverty on a global scale…which may take generations. We need to do that first—before we can hope to change the education system."

He continued: "In just a few years, millions of baby boomers will retire, the government will have to admit it is out of money, the price of oil is going through the roof, our dollar is dropping in value, inflation is out of control, and we are still at war in the Middle East. We need to have some answers for those who are searching for answers now We need to teach people to be rich, or at least how to survive the next few years *today*… not tomorrow."

At that moment, I knew why we were coming together to write a book.

Donald's View

The Beginning

The first time I met Robert Kiyosaki was one of those big surprises that life likes to give us now and then. I knew of Robert's credentials, namely having sold millions of books and remaining on *The New York Times* best seller list for five years. These are no simple accomplishments. I expected him to be a powerhouse, and an intimidating one at that.

I was right about the powerhouse prediction—Robert has positive energy that spills out and touches everyone around him. He doesn't seem to be making an effort to do this. It's just a natural occurrence. I was impressed by that. What I found disarming about Robert was that he was very humble, very modest, even self-effacing. This was the guy who has sold over 26 million books? Amazing. I was wondering to myself if that was an act, a facade, a role he played for some reason. I can be skeptical sometimes.

It didn't take me long to figure out that Robert was genuine. After we spoke a few times, I knew he was sincere and that he enjoyed teaching—probably as much as I do. When I told him the only reason I agreed to do *The Apprentice* was because it had an educational subtext, Robert told me, "Donald, you're a teacher, on top of everything else!" Guess it takes one to know one.

We got to talking about the importance of education and he mentioned the mentor aspect of *The Apprentice,* and that he and Kim learned something from it every week.

I asked him what he would do if he knew he couldn't fail, and he quickly said, "We'd find ways to reach and teach many more people."

It was like I told him when I saw him in Chicago: I was the top business author and he was the top personal-finance author. Together we had a great shot at reaching millions of people. But more than that, it would be fun.

Robert got what I meant immediately, but I appreciated that he wanted to think about the book before committing to me. I knew he was a thoughtful person, that he would do a lot of soul-searching in order to make the right decision. When he met with me at my office in New York a few weeks later, he said right off the bat, "I have to admit I was a little intimidated at first. It was like an inner fight going on. I didn't know if we had enough in common. But the best person won—the one who refuses complacency!" Robert was honest with himself and me, and it confirmed for me why his books have been such monster hits.

Writing books can be enjoyable but it's a lot of work, and my schedule doesn't allow for much extracurricular activity, which is what writing books can be for me. But I found myself looking forward to working hard on something new—especially with someone who shared my concerns and hopes.

Emerson said, "The man who can make hard things easy is the educator." He also said, "Knowledge exists to be imparted."

When I read *Rich Dad Poor Dad* years ago, before I ever met Robert, I remember thinking that Robert had a knack for making things easy to comprehend. He's a bit of a storyteller, and that is one of the keys to making things accessible to people. It's another reason he's a great public speaker, and people have often said the same thing about me. I don't know if we have that "raconteur" ability naturally, but it has helped us to help others—and to use stories to make seemingly complex things a bit simpler.

I know that often when people think of me, they think, "Oh, the billionaire…" and it's a bit like having the door shut in my face. My son, Don Jr., has said that I'm like a blue-collar guy with a big bankroll, if that's any insight into my persona. He's spent a lot of time with me, and he knows I'm pretty simple at my core. That doesn't mean I'm easy, but I do have a simple approach to things. And while what I do can be very complex, I also know how to break it down. You don't start with a finished skyscraper—you start with a blueprint and a foundation. I'm aware that things take time and patience, and that applies to education, too.

If you've watched *The Apprentice*, you know that we are tough on the apprentices because real life doesn't give a lot of room or sympathy for excuses. As the old saying goes, *Life is not a dress rehearsal*. It's the real thing. So there's a certain amount of living on the edge that's needed if one is to excel. Robert and I are hoping to make that edge a little less scary and a little more attainable at the same time.

I will admit that people I know were surprised to hear I was going to collaborate with another entrepreneur to write a book. Entrepreneurs very much like being in control, and sharing the control is not high on our list of desirable situations. But when you meet someone who is on the same wavelength in so many ways, it becomes a pleasure. Joining forces makes us stronger, not weaker.

In fact, one of the weaknesses of many visionaries and entrepreneurs is the inability to successfully share their visions and goals. It can be a lonely road. The old saying, *It's lonely at the top—but not crowded,* can sometimes be true.

Entrepreneurs are people who like to try something new. Collaborating in this way is something new for both Robert and me, and I think we've enhanced each other as educators, speakers and people by bringing our diverse personalities together to achieve a whole that is both comprehensive and comprehensible. What's the point of having great knowledge and keeping it to yourself?

Here's another amusing point: Entrepreneurs are often marked by avoiding group efforts. They want to be in charge. They want to do it themselves, have it for themselves, and so be it. At least that's what the experts have said when analyzing personality types suitable to entrepreneurship. I guess Robert and I just don't fit the mold. But I don't think that bothers either of us too much.

What has evolved in this process took on a life of its own, and it became more than just another book with a proper outline. It has become a living example of what we worked on and lived through together from our initial meeting to the day we finished our first draft. It quickly became a joint effort to provide financial education to anyone seeking a better life at a time when we all need to be financially equipped for the future we face.

> What's the point of having great knowledge and keeping it to yourself?
>
> *–Donald J. Trump*

This book is for anyone who wants to move forward and get out of their comfort zone. You may be a millionaire already, or maybe not yet, but the lessons here can apply to everyone, no matter what your current financial circumstances might be.

I hope you will see the process as one from which you can learn while being entertained. There is nothing boring about business, which you are soon to discover. Robert and I have another thing in common—neither of us likes to be bored. We like to get things done. So pay attention, keep your focus, and enjoy yourself. *Why We Want You to be Rich—Two Men • One Message* has a lot to offer. Tune in, and stay tuned!

CHAPTER TWO

OUR
SHARED CONCERNS

Robert's View

Dallas, Texas: February 19, 2006

Once again, on Sunday afternoon, the black limo pulls up to the backstage entrance of another huge convention center for another real estate expo. Once again, the excitement builds as word spreads, "The Donald is here." And once again, the police escort comes in first to clear the way, two lines form, and Mr. Trump walks the gauntlet of adoring fans.

After about an hour, after the press has left, Donald asks me, "How big is the audience, and how are they?"

"Tens of thousands in attendance, and they're a great group. People have come from all over the world to be here this weekend. They're very excited about learning and hungry for knowledge."

I was excited, too—but for different reasons.

Since our last meeting, I had read Donald's book, *The America We Deserve*. The book addresses many of the problems we face as a nation and as a world, such as terrorism, the national debt and healthcare. The following are excerpts from his chapter on the healthcare issue. "The U.S. government's General Accounting Office, an objective investigative arm of the Congress, paints an ugly picture:

"Unlike Social Security, Medicare's HI program has been experiencing a cashflow deficit since 1992—current payroll taxes and other revenues have been insufficient to cover benefit payments and program expenses...In essence, Medicare has already crossed the point where it

is a net claimant on the Treasury—a threshold that Social Security is not expected to reach until 2013…'

"The current Medicare program is both economically and fiscally unsustainable. This is not a new message—the Medicare trustees noted in the early 1990s that the program is unsustainable in its present form."

As to what politicians are doing about this healthcare monster, he writes:

"Clinton stared at the beast—and blinked. He chose to avoid the hard decisions that will have to be made down the road where, as the GAO points out, they will be much more painful.

"But let's face it, Clinton is hardly the only politician to duck a tough issue. It will take a new breed of politician to push meaningful reform. It requires a risk-taker with titanium nerves and vision."

About long-term healthcare, he says:

"There's one more aspect of the medical-insurance story that is almost totally off the typical radar screen. This one involves long-term care. With the baby-boom generation heading toward retirement and their parents already there, this is a huge issue.

"A few numbers tell the story: The number of elderly will double to seventy-five million by 2030 and the number of seniors living in nursing homes will increase fivefold.

"I know the response: Doesn't Medicaid pay for nursing homes? This question is often asked by Boomers who figure their parents will be covered, as they will when their time comes to book some long-term care.

"Here's the answer: Medicaid was never meant to be a long-term care provider. And as Senator John Breaux and Representative William Thomas have pointed out, 'The growing demand for long-term care is pushing Medicaid into bankruptcy.'

"Nearly one in two Americans will need some type of long-term care, but only one in four can afford long-term private nursing home care, which now averages $41,000 (in 1999 dollars) a year. Only 1 percent of Americans have bought long-term healthcare insurance. So most are hoping to rely on Medicaid. As things are right now, they're in for a major disappointment.

"After a short initial contribution, Medicaid will drop out of the picture until the patient's resources are spent down to the poverty level. If the patients are your parents, that means everything they've worked for in life will be gone. And that often means one parent is left destitute. It can also create a massive financial burden on families. The Boomer who planned to sail around the world on his own boat might find himself selling his car to keep mom or dad in a decent facility."

As I've said, after my first meeting with Donald, I knew why we had come together to write this book. But once I read *The America We Deserve*, I knew—without a doubt—what our shared concerns were, why we were teachers and why we wanted people to be rich.

In the green room, that day in Dallas, I drew the following diagram:

INCOME STATEMENT

Income
Expenses

BALANCE SHEET

Assets	Liabilities

Social Security $10 T
Medicare $62 T

"You're saying it's $72 trillion in off-balance sheet obligations?" Donald asked. "Says who?"

"Two economists," I replied. "In 2004, Kent Smetters and Jagadeesh Gokhale painstakingly spent the time to compute how much, as of 2004, our government's obligations to the American people were."

"That's a lot of money," said Donald.

"That's more money than all the money in all the bond and stock markets in the world," I said. "I believe the value of all stocks on the world stock markets as of 2000 was around $36 trillion and the value of all the bonds on the bond markets of the world was only about $31 trillion. We owe our people more than all the money in the stock and bond markets combined."

"I knew it was bad," said Donald, "but not this bad. We can't pay it."

"Only if we print more money, which would wipe out the savings of everyone. One possibility is hyperinflation, but that wouldn't really solve the problem. Not only would savings be wiped out, people on fixed incomes would also be wiped out."

"And this is not just an American problem," Donald said. "While we are discussing in terms of American people and American finances, this problem is being felt around the world. People are living longer, and countries from Europe to Asia are concerned about how they are going to be able to provide for the health and welfare of their people."

Back to History

In the 1930s, the German government had printed so much money that the money nearly lost its value. One story tells of a woman who pulled a wheelbarrow full of money to buy some bread. When she came out of the baker's to get her money to pay for the bread, someone had stolen her wheelbarrow and left the money.

Hyperinflation devalues money. And while the social, political and financial environments that enabled Adolf Hitler to be elected German Chancellor in 1933 were complex, his rise to power was in no small part due to the middle class having their savings wiped out.

Back home, the 1930s brought the Great Depression, leading to Franklin Delano Roosevelt being elected president. Roosevelt brought in Social Security in 1935, a solution to a problem we still have to solve today. In other words, a solution to a problem caused over 75 years ago is again a problem today—an even bigger problem, in fact. We are trying to solve a problem with government money, instead of solving the real problem. Other government programs that were meant to be solutions were Medicare (1955) and Medicaid (1966). Today, these problems are much bigger problems, again because we failed to address the real problem soon enough.

> We want people to let go of the entitlement mentality and become rich so they can solve the problem...their own problems.
>
> – Robert T. Kiyosaki

In 1971, President Nixon took us off the gold standard, which is exactly what the German government did, and today the U.S. dollar is falling and savers find their savings wiped out with very little left for retirement... except for Social Security and Medicare, which are also in trouble. History is repeating itself; only this time the problem is bigger.

What We Are Concerned About

Donald said it first: "I'm afraid we have developed an entitlement mentality as a nation. And I'm not talking about just poor people. Too many people, from the president and senators on down, expect a pension from the government. I really wish we could afford to solve their problems, but to do that would bankrupt our nation. We could ask the rich to pay for everyone, but would it solve the problem? And for how long would it even solve the problem?"

I agreed. Donald and I want people to let go of the entitlement mentality and become rich so they can solve the problem...their own problem.

Consider the following diagram:

The best way to solve the problem of bad financial results is to change our thoughts—to start thinking like rich people rather than poor and middle-class people. That means losing the entitlement mentality— whether you are a military officer, government worker, schoolteacher, employee or just poor. If we do not stop expecting the government to take care of us, we will continue to have the same results—a bankrupt nation filled with well-educated but financially needy people.

Albert Einstein defined insanity as "doing the same thing over and over again and expecting different results." In this case, it is my opinion that it is insanity to keep sending kids to school and not teaching them about money.

When you look at the CASHFLOW Quadrant pictured below,

E *stands for employee*

S *stands for small-business person, self-employed or specialist*

B *stands for big-business owners such as Donald Trump*

I *stands for investor*

I believe we need to train more kids to be Bs, entrepreneurs who create jobs, and all kids to be investors in the I quadrant. Today, our schools do a pretty good job educating people to be Es or Ss, but hardly any education is allocated to be Bs or Is.

Instead of walking away with a solid financial education, most kids leave school—some already deeply in debt—prepared only to work hard, save money, get out of debt, invest for the long term and diversify.

Warren Buffett says the following about diversification:

"Diversification is protection against ignorance.

(It) makes very little sense if you know what you are doing."

One of the keys to becoming rich is to know what you are doing.

Back Onstage

"Fifteen minutes," said the event manager to Donald.

"OK," he said. "I'm ready."

As we headed toward the stage, Donald said, "So the reason we want them to become rich is so they can solve their own financial problems. Too many people are betting on the stock market, the government or a pension to be the solution."

"That's a good place to start," I said.

"We'll tell people *why* we got rich, not *how*…and why we keep working even though we have enough money."

"We want them to find out their own *whys,* rather than expect a handout from the government. That's how we can help solve the problem. Obviously we can't help everyone, because not everyone has the talent to become rich, but we can help those who do and have the desire to be rich."

"This entitlement mentality is a monster problem," said Donald.

"Huge," I agreed.

"Bigger even than the national debt, the falling dollar, the oil crisis and retirement programs. And those are very big and very real problems," Donald added.

"Problems aren't the issue," I said. "We all have money problems… even you and I. It's how we *solve* the problem that's the issue."

"That's exactly right," said Donald. "We, as a nation, cannot solve our financial problems if we think with an entitlement mentality. It's this mentality that's really at the core of the problem. That's why we want people to become rich."

As I headed up the stage stairs to get ready to introduce Donald, I said, "Our financial problems are caused by the way we think. We have to change the way we think about money."

With that, I walked onstage to introduce Donald Trump to thousands of fans and students.

Donald's View

Groupthink

As Robert says, "We as a nation cannot solve a large financial crisis with the same old thinking." I couldn't agree more. This entitlement mentality is everywhere. In fact, it has become epidemic in our economy.

I guess we've all probably heard the term "groupthink" by now. It's that old herd mentality that seems to bring out the best and the worst in people. By the best, I mean that sometimes a shepherd will surface. But that's an unlikely scenario. It's usually the wolves that will surface first, and the herd will be primed and ready to follow. What we're trying to do here is break up the herd before we are incapable of seeing, hearing, thinking and doing for ourselves. People who are capable of thinking for themselves will rarely be part of any herd.

While we are focused on the groupthink that keeps people from thinking for themselves financially and has them blindly turning their money over to financial advisors, it reminds me of another story.

For my radio program on Clear Channel, I decided to speak about "Object Orange." This isn't about Jeanne-Claude and Christo's "Gates" project last year in Central Park, but about something happening in Detroit, Michigan.

Detroit has a problem with ramshackle, empty homes because the city has lost nearly a million people in the last 50 years. A group of artists in the city was tired of looking at vacant, dilapidated buildings around town. So they decided to do something about it.

To call attention to the abandoned buildings, the artists secretly painted the eyesores bright orange overnight. Because it's hard to miss a bright orange, rundown building, several of the houses have since been torn down—which was the goal in the first place.

The artists are remaining anonymous because obviously they could get in trouble for trespassing. They are also hoping other renegades with paintbrushes will join their project.

This is a great example of people taking action and accomplishing something. They took matters into their own hands instead of waiting for someone else to do something about it. It's unconventional, but it seems to be working.

> People who are capable of thinking for themselves will rarely be part of any herd.
>
> – *Donald J. Trump*

It's an overused term at this point, but "out-of-the-box" thinking is obviously alive and well—certainly in Detroit. Artists aren't the only people around who have the right to exercise that part of the brain—we all do. Let's try to start thinking like that no matter where we live or what we do. The worst thing for us, individually and as a nation, is to become passive observers—or to slowly sink into our comfort zones.

As I've said before, the best way to have an edge is to live on one. We are not in a position—even if we are the so-called superpower—to rest on our laurels. That is the first indication of impending decline. We've got some challenges ahead, and it's best to be aware of them. Let's not succumb to the Big Groupthink, which is really just a good way of sinking our own ship.

Today, more than ever, people must change the way they think about their finances and their financial futures.

Robert and I want you to expand your thinking. We can all benefit from the wisdom of Descartes: "I think; therefore I am."

Think bigger!

CHAPTER THREE

THE SHRINKING MIDDLE CLASS

Robert's View

Raising Your Financial IQ

There are many definitions of intelligence. One of the more practical ones I learned from my rich dad is, "Intelligence is the ability to solve problems." For example, in school, if you can solve math problems, you are considered intelligent. Out of school, if you can fix a car, you are deemed to have automotive intelligence. When it comes to money, the bigger financial problems you can solve, the higher your financial intelligence.

Today, our world faces some serious financial problems. Many are interrelated problems, one causing the other. Some of the more pressing ones are:

1. Value of the dollar falling
2. National debt increasing
3. Baby boomers starting to retire
4. Oil prices rising
5. Gap increasing between the rich and everyone else
6. Wages decreasing
7. Jobs being exported
8. Social Security and Medicare going bankrupt
9. Savings being wiped out
10. Lack of financial education being taught

The pressing questions are:

1. What can we do?

2. What are the solutions to these problems?

3. Is our financial IQ high enough to solve these problems?

4. How do we avoid becoming victims of these problems?

5. How do we protect our families from falling victim to these problems?

Many of today's financial problems exist because we did not solve the problems when they first arose. Rather than increasing the financial IQ of the population, we taught people to expect the government to solve their personal problems for them. This is why no politician dares touch Social Security and Medicare…even though most of us know these programs are doomed.

Now I can hear some of you readers saying, "We need to take care of those who cannot care for themselves." And I agree with that. We, as a civilized society, should take care of those who cannot take care of themselves. However, most of us *can* take care of ourselves if we *have* to and if we have been trained to.

It's time to raise our financial IQ.

Changing Demographic

Because of the low financial IQ solutions we used in the past, today our demographic population is changing from

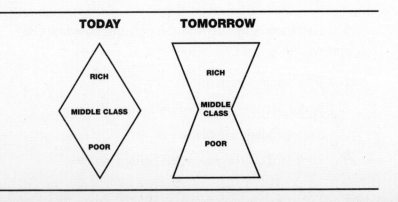

What the diagram shows is that the rich are getting richer, and everyone else is getting poorer, even though many people are making more money. Unfortunately, the United States is not the only country heading in this direction. Many world economies are becoming two-class societies: the rich and the poor...classes or masses.

The April 16, 2006, Sunday edition of *The New York Times* ran a front-page article with the headline:

"Revival in Japan Brings Widening of Economic Gap"

The second paragraph of the article states:

"Today, in a country whose view of itself was once captured in the slogan, '100 million, all-middle class society,' catchphrases harshly sort people into 'winners' and 'losers,' and describe Japan as a 'society of widening disparities.'"

In other words, the middle class is being wiped out. Today in Japan, you are either rich or poor, a financial winner or a financial loser. The same thing is happening in America and in many European countries.

The Price of a Low Financial IQ

In my conversations with Donald Trump, we agreed that we cannot solve today's complex financial challenges with yesterday's financial intelligence. If we as a nation attempt to solve Social Security and Medicare by giving people more entitlement payouts, the golden goose will be cooked and eaten, and there will be no more golden eggs.

The reason why we write, speak and create educational games and other products is because we want people to become rich and solve their own financial problems rather than expect others to solve their problems for them. We both agreed that by giving people money, we only made the problem bigger, harder to solve and more dangerous.

Simply said, America is on its way to becoming a well-educated nation of rich people and poor people. The middle class is becoming extinct. The problem is our nation is filled with people like my poor dad—a good man, well-educated, hard-working, yet expecting the government to take care of him when he retired.

> There are many definitions for intelligence. One of the more practical ones I learned from my rich dad is, "Intelligence is the ability to solve problems."
>
> – Robert T. Kiyosaki

We've mentioned that in a few years, the first of approximately 75 million baby boomers will begin to retire. This is the first generation that has contributed fully to Social Security and Medicare. The problem is, the money they contributed is gone, disappeared into a Ponzi scheme.

There are two more problems: Since we do not teach much about money in schools, many of those 75 million do not know what a Ponzi scheme it is. Secondly, since most did contribute fully, they deserve to be paid. But if each (of the 75 million baby boomers) begins to collect just $1,000 a month in Social Security and Medicare benefits, the total added to the U.S. government's payroll is $75 billion a month. This is similar to the cost of one Hurricane Katrina or one Iraq War—every month. The good news is you still have time to prepare and avoid becoming a victim of the coming financial hurricanes…but not much time.

In Sunday School, I was taught:

Give a person a fish and you feed him for a day. And that is what we as a nation have been doing. This is the entitlement mentality of Social Security and Medicare.

Teach a person to fish and you feed him for life. This is what Donald and I have been doing. We want people to learn to be rich and teach others to be rich.

In *Teach To Be Rich,* a product I created to assist our CASHFLOW Clubs in teaching others to be rich, I talk about how some people do not want to give people fish or teach others to fish…instead they sell people fish. Many of these people are stockbrokers, real estate brokers, financial

planners, bankers and insurance agents. They are in the business of selling…
not necessarily teaching or giving. When you put the two words, *sell* and
fish, together, you get the word *selfish.* And even though most people in the
business may not be selfish, enough are to make the word ring true. I use it
here to emphasize the importance of staying on your guard to be aware of
the differences between those who give—the teachers—and those who sell.

Donald and I are concerned that most people do not choose to learn
to manage their own money or learn to invest their own money. Instead of
learn, they simply *turn* their money over to experts and then hope and pray
their experts are truly experts.

In Donald's book, *How To Get Rich,* he has this to say about financial
advisors…people who sell fish. The chapter heading says it all:

Be Your Own Financial Advisor

The chapter begins with:

*"Many people go out and hire financial advisors, but I have also seen
a lot of these advisors destroy people.*

*"Athletes, in particular, make a great deal of money at a very young
age. Too often, some manager squanders the athlete's fortune and
they wind up in their thirties with nothing left but their past glory—
and are forced to get jobs just to survive."*

We Want to Teach You to Fish

Donald Trump and I do not sell fish. We do not sell investment advice
or tell people what to invest in. We are teachers. We want you to learn how
to become rich, invest your own money and become your own financial
expert. We want to teach you to fish for yourself.

Rich Dad's Secret

As I mentioned before, many rich people are secretive. I didn't realize
how much so until my rich dad's family asked me to keep their name out of
Rich Dad Poor Dad. Many rich people would rather be anonymous. They

either do not want to be known and/or they do not want to share their financial secrets. That is why I was pleasantly surprised to find Donald Trump to be so open about his wealth and willing to share his keys to financial success.

In her book *Buffettology*, Mary Buffett writes:

"F. Scott Fitzgerald wrote that the very rich are different from you and me. He was right. But they are different in the strangest of ways, the oddest being the code of silence that they demand of family and friends. While married to Peter (Warren Buffett's son), I was instructed more than once not to speak to anyone outside the family about Warren and his investment operations. Writing this book simply would have been out of the question."

After her divorce from Peter, Mary Buffett broke the code of silence and went on to explain in detail how Warren Buffett does it, spilling Buffett's secrets. It is a great book and well-written. And it does explain Warren Buffett's secrets. It's Warren Buffett's *how-to* book, even though he did not authorize it. However, it is how Warren Buffett does it. It does not mean you or I or even Donald Trump can do it the same way. Nor we would necessarily want to.

You need to find the style and method that is best suited for you. While it is important to learn from people like Warren and Donald, it is also important to find your own secret formula.

Dreams vs. Goals

Many people have dreams. Rich people have goals. So the question is, what is the difference between dreams and goals?

Several years ago, I attended a church service at the New Birth Church in Atlanta, Georgia. Giving the sermon that day was not Bishop Eddie Long. Instead, the sermon was delivered by Archbishop Vernon Ashe. The sermon had a powerful lesson on the power of process and goals.

Archbishop Ashe said, "Every goal has a process." As he spoke I began to realize why so many people who have dreams fail to have their dreams come true. The reason is most people have dreams but do not focus on the process necessary to achieve their dreams. For example, many people want to lose weight. But what gets in their way of achieving their goal is the process of change in diet and exercise. So instead of achieving their goal, their dream of a healthier, more attractive body remains a dream.

The other day, I drove up to my gym in my Bentley convertible. A young woman walked out and said, "That's the car of my dreams."

Thanking her for the compliment, I asked, "How do you plan on making your dream come true?"

Her reply was, "I don't know. I guess I'll just keep dreaming."

And this is what Archbishop Ashe was talking about. His point was the process is as important as the goal...so any goal without a process is just a dream.

Many people, especially people with money problems, think that more money will solve their money problems. Instead of setting a goal, finding their own process—their own secret formula—and becoming a rich person...they buy lottery tickets, hope for a raise, get into debt keeping up with the Jones who are also deeply in debt trying to look rich, all the while dreaming of someday becoming a rich person. The Archbishop's lesson was that the difference between dreams and goals was the *process*...and in many ways, the process is more important than the dream or the goal.

What if You Lost It All?

Years ago, when a reporter asked Henry Ford what he would do if he lost his billion dollar fortune, he replied, "I'd have it back in less than five years." One of important aspects of finding your own formula, your own process, is that when you reach your goal, it will be the process of gaining knowledge that will make you rich. As my rich dad often said, "Money does not make you rich. Knowledge makes you rich." And knowledge is derived from a process.

As you know, Donald and I have had our own financial challenges. We know those challenges have made us smarter and richer. Financial challenges, the wins and the losses are all part of the process of becoming rich. For Donald and me, our process or learning was via entrepreneurship and real estate. Warren Buffett's process was by buying companies. Mohammad Ali's was via boxing. So this book is not about you getting rich quick. This book is about you finding your own process to become rich. It is about the process that makes your dreams come true.

Donald's View

The Shrinking Middle Class

When Robert and I were talking about the shrinking middle class, it made me aware that some things *can* be explained. It's like an hourglass with the middle class the pinched part, or like someone with a very small waistline.

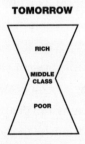

TOMORROW

RICH

MIDDLE CLASS

POOR

What happens when you flip the hourglass? Either way you flip it, you have the poor feeding the rich or the rich feeding the poor. It's either one or the other. I don't like that visual because it reminds me of the Old World and aristocratic ways that America revolted against. Are we headed back that way? Were the colonists just a bunch of misguided idealists to begin with?

I've been reading some newspapers while enjoying some travel time, but there were some stories in *The Wall Street Journal* that got me to thinking about risk. Just yesterday we heard about three climbers dying on their way down from Mt. Everest, evidently from exhaustion, after they had reached their goal. Today we have an article about the great racehorse, Barbaro, and his terrible injury, and we have the tragedy in the Volvo Ocean Race, where a young Dutchman was washed overboard from a yacht. Then, the crew of another yacht had to abandon ship in an incredible storm, and they were rescued by the yacht that had lost one of its crew. These are all experienced yachtsmen, and their seamanship was not in question. And with Barbaro, tens of thousands of people went to see horse-racing history being made and instead saw the horse break down during the race, an unbelievable tragedy that no one is likely to forget. Fans had reason to believe they would see a Triple Crown winner—a horse winning the Kentucky Derby, the Preakness and the Belmont Stakes—for the first time since 1978. *The Wall Street Journal* writer said the grief of the crowd was equal to their initial hope and expectation.

Expectations can lead to surprising outcomes. There is often a fine line between victory and defeat, and it makes me become philosophical in thinking about it. Sometimes the best-laid plans can just blow up in our faces due to uncontrollable events, such as weather conditions or an injury or maybe too much confidence (if there is such a thing). Philosophy is one way to try to comprehend the inexplicable things and events we all encounter at some point in our lives.

I've mentioned before that it's important for us to remain intact, otherwise we become a target. A small leak can sink a ship, or a huge wave can destroy it equally well, as the yachtsmen from the Volvo race can attest to. Either way, imbalance can create situations that can keep our equilibrium reeling and out of control.

Our country has been a superpower for a short amount of time, if you look at the history of the world. The biggest risk we have now is not being prepared for the future. As we have seen, there are no guarantees, but being ready sure beats being taken by surprise. During WWI, the battle of Gallipoli, no one expected a quarter of a million soldiers to be killed or for the combined British, Australian, New Zealand and French operations to be defeated and repelled by the Turks. It came as a big surprise to them—because they didn't know what they were getting into.

> There are no guarantees, but being ready sure beats being taken by surprise.
>
> – *Donald J. Trump*

China Today

Globalization is a fact of life in today's environment. As Robert described China and India as growing economies we must watch, I simply smiled—as once again we have been thinking alike. Many people think it will take years for China and/or India to approach America's position as the largest economic power. But this may be yet another example of groupthink in process. Both Robert and I have seen their global impact already.

Recently, I was talking to a friend who lives in Europe, and he mentioned the huge amount of coverage China gets over there, compared with what we have about it in the United States. It's a very big topic there. There are two facts alone about China that will indicate how that country is doing and where that country is going:

1. The first Starbucks opened in China two years ago. There are now more Starbucks in China than in the United States.

2. In the 1970s, Shanghai had exactly one skyscraper. It now has close to 800.

As a builder of skyscrapers and having a Starbucks in Trump Tower, I find those two facts staggering. Those are just two examples, yet easily visualized examples that should bring something home: China is a big force. Its population is such that one in every five people on the entire planet is Chinese. China has a vibrant economy and workforce and has adapted very well to the new technology. The Chinese are industrious and disciplined. What does this mean? We can either close our eyes and be blown aside, or we can study China and position ourselves to benefit from the changes.

India Today

My two eldest children, Don Jr. and Ivanka, who work at the Trump Organization, were in India recently, so I decided to do some research of my own. But first a story that happened recently at Trump Tower:

Last year, an employee of mine was taking a car service to the airport and was picked up at Trump Tower. The driver was a young man from India, and it was his first trip as a driver to the airport, but he was more interested in finding out if his passenger had ever seen Mr. Donald Trump. My employee replied, "Yes, about five minutes ago."

The driver was very impressed and said, "You saw Donald Trump five minutes ago? In Trump Tower?"

"Yes, his office is there, and we work there."

The young man was even more impressed. He said, "You mean Donald Trump *works?!*" He couldn't believe his ears. So my employee proceeded to explain the reality of my life, which is long hours in the office, and that we have Post-its, pencils, copy machines and everything else that any office has.

The driver remained impressed and then decided to explain some things about his country while he was navigating his way to the airport. He gave a history of India that was condensed to a few minutes. He also explained that there were hundreds of languages and dialects in his country, a different accent every 30 miles, but that no matter if you were in the provinces somewhere or in Punjab, there were two words everybody knew.

It was my employee's turn to be curious, and she asked, "What are they?"

The driver took his hands off the wheel to act out and say "You're fired!" with great glee.

My employee had a good laugh and then kindly asked him if he knew where the airport was, and he said not to worry, he would try to find it. Which, I'm happy to say, he did and with no problem. He obviously had a very good sense of direction, as well as a sense of sharing about his country.

Do we have any sense of the direction India is going? Do we know *anything* about India?

Here are a few facts to get us going:

- India is the world's largest, oldest continuous civilization.

- In the last 10,000 years, India has never invaded any country.

- India is the world's largest democracy.

- India is one of the few countries in the world that gained independence without violence.

- The art of navigation was born in the river Sindh 6,000 years ago. (Maybe that's where that young driver was from).

- Sanskrit is the mother of all the European languages.

- India was the richest country on earth until the 17th Century, when the British invaded.

- Chess was invented in India.

- India invented the number system. Albert Einstein said: "We owe a lot to the Indians, who taught us how to count, without which no worthwhile scientific discovery could have been made."

- Algebra, trigonometry and calculus originated in India.

- The value of "pi" was first calculated by the mathematician Budhayana, and he explained the concept of what is known as the Pythagorean Theorem. He discovered it in the 6th century, which was long before European mathematicians.

- India is the largest English-speaking nation in the world.

My point is that India is definitely worth looking into and knowing something about. Plus, 38 percent of doctors in the United States are of Indian descent, and 12 percent of scientists are as well. They represent the wealthiest of all ethnic groups in the United States as well as globally. Education is stressed and many Indians run large U.S. and global corporations.

India itself has become a major economic force on its own once again and deserves our attention, not just as a destination point or a piece of history. India is important to our future, and as globally aware citizens, we need to spend some time learning about this fascinating and dynamic country.

It definitely means the world has some very viable competition, specifically in China and India! Which is good—I've always believed that competition can get rid of complacency, and fast. Mark Twain said: "Don't go around saying the world owes you a living. The world owes you nothing. It was here first."

That can apply to a lot of things. Let's give that some thought. How can you use this information to your advantage? The rich will spot the opportunities, while the poor will hide their heads and pretend it isn't happening.

Can you spot opportunities that may arise from these economic changes?

Chapter Four

How To Make Yourself Rich

Robert's View

Solve Problems

Everyone has money problems. If you want to make yourself rich, solve problems. Identifying a problem creates the *opportunity* for creating a solution.

Every generation will have its own unique set of financial problems. For my parents' generation, their challenges included a Depression and a World War. Their solution to those problems was to go to school, get a safe and secure job with benefits, retire at 65, and play golf for the rest of their lives. Many of the World War II generation had a Defined Benefit Pension plan, savings, Social Security and Medicare. For many of my parents' generation, a good education and a good job were adequate for financial survival.

My generation, the baby-boom generation, faces a set of different financial problems. Today, a good college education and a good job are not enough. To make matters worse, jobs are being exported overseas. Today, because jobs are being exported overseas, employees in the richest nations become too expensive. One very expensive expense is the Define Benefit (DB) plan of my parents' generation. Companies are no longer willing to pay for employees for life so these DB plans are being cut and replaced with Defined Contribution plans.

In 1974, due to the changing global markets, many companies stopped offering Defined Benefit (DB) plans and began offering Defined Contribution (DC) plans, which later became known in the United States as 401(k), IRA and Keogh plans. My generation's problem is that a DB plan is a true pension plan and a DC plan is not a true pension plan; it is a savings plan. In fact, the 401(k) was never intended to be a pension plan. In other countries, the problem is the same; they just use different names for their Defined Benefit and Defined Contribution plans.

In very simple terms, a Defined Benefit plan will cover you for as long as you live. A Defined Contribution plan will cover you only as long as there is money in your account. In other words, a DB plan, in theory, will *not* run out of money while a DC plan *can* run out of money. That may be why *USA Today* found that the greatest fear in America today is running out of money during retirement. Most of us already know that up to 80 percent of the baby-boom generation does not have enough wealth to fall back on.

The generations following the baby-boom generation, often called Generation X and Generation Y, will have a different set of financial problems to handle. If the baby-boom generation does not do a good job cleaning up the mess left by its parents, there will be an even bigger mess for Generation X and Generation Y to handle. Generation X and Y will not only have to handle their own financial problems and the debts of our country (the biggest debt in the history of the world), they will also inherit their baby-boomer parents' financial problems, and maybe even their grandparents' problems, since we are all expected to live longer. By living longer, we may expect to extend our working years by retiring later, but what if we live longer and are not able to continue working?

The growing size of this problem, now in the trillions of dollars, is daunting. Merely pushing it forward, on to the next generation, just makes the problem bigger and more complex.

> Everyone has money problems. If you want to make yourself rich, solve problems. Identifying a problem creates the opportunity for creating a solution.
>
> – Robert T. Kiyosaki

The bigger and more complex the financial problems become, the higher the financial IQ is required to handle the problems. We're going to need all the brainpower we can get to solve this problem.

Worst of all, repeating the cover headline of *TIME* magazine, October 31, 2005:

"The Great Retirement Ripoff"

Millions of Americans who think they will retire with benefits are in for a NASTY SURPRISE.

How corporations are picking people's pockets with the help of Congress."

The lack of financial education in our schools makes it easy for unscrupulous people, even elected officials from both parties, to legally steal from the unsuspecting. So the problem compounds itself.

Tell Me About It

Donald and I hope we are wrong, but we sincerely believe America is in trouble...and if America is in trouble, the world is in trouble.

One of the bigger problems in the world today is the rising price of oil. Oil is the blood of the world's economy. If the price of oil gets too high, and we do not find a better alternative to oil soon, the world economy will begin to die. As Donald said to me one day, "If gasoline costs $5 a gallon at the pump, it does not affect you and me that much. But if you're earning $10 an hour, then $5 a gallon will take food from your family." He went on to say, "Oil affects *everything* in our economy, and the problem is, we're running low. Prices will only go higher. You and I will be OK, but millions of people will be hurt by it."

If oil goes to over $100 a barrel, and I believe it will sometime in the near future, the economy will suffer—but *you* do not have to. You can face the problem *now* and be part of the solution.

When I talk to people about some of the financial challenges ahead, I get different responses. One common response is, "Don't tell me about it."

Another response I get is, "We need to think positively. All this negativity is bad," or "God will solve the problem."

These responses are from people with low financial IQs. Rather than facing the problems head-on and asking, "How can I profit from these problems?" they would rather stick their head in the sand. And this is why millions, possibly billions, of people will be hurt in the coming years. Instead of looking at the problem as an opportunity, they choose to put their blinders on.

WEALTH = ENERGY

My rich dad taught me, soon after the first oil crisis in 1973-74 that oil and wealth were directly related. He would often say, "Wealth = Energy." Since I was an apprentice at Standard Oil, on their tankers, beginning in 1966, I had an interest in oil. Rich dad's explanation was a simple one. He said, "When the price of energy goes down, our wealth goes up." The equation looks like this:

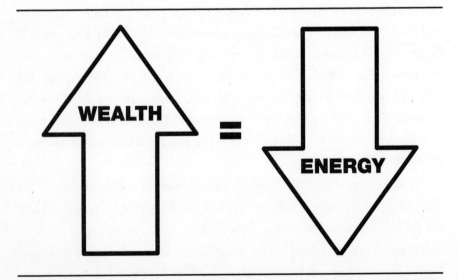

And for most people, when the price of energy goes up, our wealth goes down.

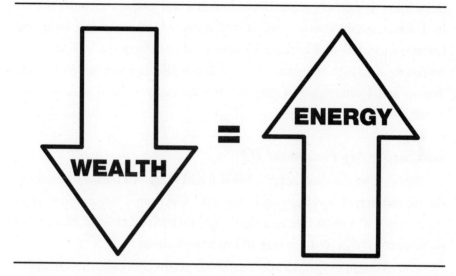

The year 1974, the same year I started my business career as a brand new Xerox sales rep, proved my rich dad's theory correct. In 1974, high oil prices had caused the economy to contract. People were not renting Xerox copiers. Instead, they were canceling their rental contracts. My first sale as a new rep found me on my knees in front of the customer— begging, not selling. I was begging the customer not to cancel his rental agreement. I remember one customer saying to me, "Why should I keep the copier? My business is gone." This is just a small example of what happens when the price of energy goes up.

Instead of making money the first two years, I owed Xerox money. I owed the company money because every time a customer cancelled a machine, the commission that was paid to the sales rep who sold the machine was charged back to the sales rep who lost the machine. I was not selling, I was starving, and I was nearly fired several times during those two years.

Bad Times Can Make You Rich

The good news was, the challenge of a contracting economy actually made me a better salesman. Even though I did not make much money back then, my sales training still pays off today. My businesses are successful because I can sell–and because I understand the importance of sales and marketing. In tough economic times, that can give you an edge. As Donald Trump and I often say, "If you are in business, you need to learn how to sell."

Increasing My Financial IQ

Since oil was in short supply, my rich dad suggested I learn more about the oil industry. I had been with Standard Oil from 1966 to 1969 as an apprentice and a ship's officer, a third mate on their oil tankers. Since I had an interest in oil, I found it easy to learn more about it.

Once I began to win as a sales rep for Xerox, in order to learn more about oil, I took a part-time position with an oil company out of Oklahoma that was selling oil and gas tax shelters. Back in those days, an investor could invest $100,000 and receive a 4-to-1 tax break on his or her investment. In this example, a $100,000 investment was worth $400,000 in tax write-offs. So the investor made more money from the oil production and paid much less in taxes—one reason why the rich got richer.

Selling these leveraged oil and gas tax shelters during this period of high oil prices taught me some important lessons. Lesson number one was that not all businesses were hurting because of the oil crisis. My eyes were opened to the reality that many people were getting richer and richer while others were getting poorer. With that realization, my financial IQ went up—I saw another world. After my experience selling Xerox copiers to businesses and then selling tax shelters to the rich in my spare time, I decided I wanted to be rich.

The Lesson

Take a look at the equation…

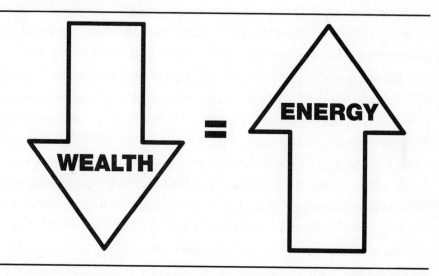

The harsh reality is, as energy prices go up, the wealth of the nation goes down, except for those with the financial IQ to invest wisely. Yet, if you are rich, your equation can look like this:

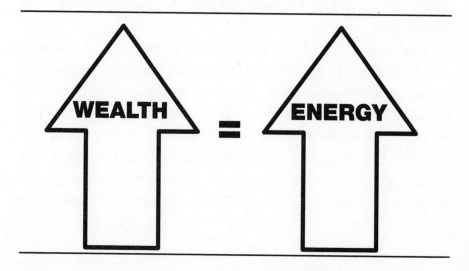

The choice is yours. You can choose which "wealth = energy" equation you want.

I became a partner in oil exploration ventures because I wanted to be on the side of the rich. Today, I continue to invest in oil and gas partnerships...just as I was doing back in the 1970s and 1980s.

Today, the tax breaks (while not as good as they were in the past) are still enticing. For the $100,000 I invest today, while not receiving a 4-to-1 write-off like I did in the past, can still receive a 70 percent write-off plus a 15 percent depletion allowance. That means I receive a $70,000 tax break when I invest, and for every dollar of income, I also get a 15 percent tax break, which means I earn more and pay less in taxes. Try getting that with savings, stocks, bonds or mutual funds. Knowing how to earn money and pay less in taxes is financial intelligence.

The trick for me was to find an honest oil company. As my rich dad said to me years ago, "The definition of an oil man is a liar standing next to a hole in the ground." You can also substitute *gold miner* for *oil man*.

Today, although I make a lot of money from my books and games, most of my wealth comes from my gold mine in China, my silver mine in South America, and my real estate companies and oil partnerships in the United States.

Every time a reporter asks me, "Isn't the best way to get rich to write a book about getting rich?" I chuckle. In reply, I simply say, "If you think writing an internationally best-selling book and creating an educational board game is easy, why don't you do it?" In my opinion, it is much easier to find oil or gold than to write a best-selling book.

Donald Trump and I write books because we are very concerned. Our message is, with the proper financial education and preparation, you can increase your financial IQ and ride the rough waters to become richer rather than poorer.

Donald's View

Education Replaces Fear

Robert's and my message is, with the proper financial education and planning you can ride out the turbulence of what is happening in our financial world today and through this education you can become richer by finding ways to solve the problems.

I am reminded of a simple example of problem solving. When Robert came to my office recently to talk about the book, I had a red chair in the middle of my office. I asked him how he liked the new chair and how much he thought it cost.

He was standing there looking at this elegant, fabric-covered dining-room chair and finally said, "I have no idea." I loved it.

"Mike, my golf course manager in California called and said he needed 150 chairs for the restaurant, and that he had been quoted $1,500 for each chair. That sounded very expensive to me, so instead of simply agreeing, I made a few calls.

"It cost me $90," I said quite proudly. "It's a fabulous chair. It's the best. Here, sit on it. And it's a better chair than the $1,500 one. Do you know how much money I saved, just by making a few phone calls?"

It's a matter of leadership and the ability to solve problems. If my staff thinks I spend money carelessly, then they will spend money carelessly. So I do this not only to preserve capital, but also to set an example for my team. You see, I am not afraid of spending money. I like buying the best. But I do not like wasting money. So many people struggle financially because they think cheap and buy cheap. You can get rich by being cheap, but who wants to be a rich cheap person?

Even when I was having financial difficulties, I was never cheap. When my company was struggling, I still paid my employees well. And that is why I buy the best chair at the best price. I don't like being ripped off, especially when I can get the best for less. I expect my staff to do the same.

One thing we all need to remember is that a little effort is the best replacement for excuses. If we were all to make an effort to understand what's going on around us, to make that quantum leap to using our higher, non-complacent minds, some lucid thinking might result. Problem solving is education at its best. Just as understanding can replace hatred, education can replace fear.

Ignorance can be easier, but it is often the result of fear. As Robert Frost said, "There's nothing I'm afraid of like scared people." Reduce your fear and fuel your courage.

I like Robert's diagrams and when I look at his wealth and energy arrows, I think of how our individual energy can create wealth. If you have the perseverance to move forward with momentum, that is a great force of energy in itself. And with the right focus, it's likely you will succeed. I always liked Alexander Graham Bell's statement: *Concentrate all your thoughts upon the work at hand. The sun's rays do not burn until brought to a focus.* If you can control your energy then you stand a good chance of creating and controlling your own wealth. Your arrows will both be pointing in the right direction.

I have learned that what is essential can sometimes be invisible to the eye. That's where discernment comes in. Leaders are those people who have replaced fear with discernment, which means they can predict the inevitable. Their education has resulted in an insight that can effectively replace fear, and which greatly enhances their chances of success.

Problem solving is made much easier if you think of problems as challenges. You might as well view them that way, since problems are a part of life. Taking a positive spin on problems will inevitably give you more energy. I say 'inevitably' with confidence because I know that's a fact and I know it from experience. Confidence is a big step toward courage, and fear will evaporate when confronted with it.

Robert has said that a problem can create an opportunity. Well said, and I agree. If you will begin to view your problems in that light, I can guarantee you will be on the road to solving them. I've had some big problems, to the tune of billions of dollars of debt, but I never went bankrupt and I'm more successful today than ever before, so I am speaking from experience.

Trump Tower has been on the map as a destination site for so long now that people forget that it didn't just appear one day on the skyline of Manhattan. I had a lot of obstacles to consider and overcome when I decided I wanted 'the Tiffany location' for my new building. I had to solve a lot of problems. First, I wanted to buy the Bonwit Teller store and building, but they thought I was crazy. I didn't give up, but it was three years before I got anywhere with them. Then, I wanted to buy the air rights above Tiffany's. Purchasing those rights would give me the ability to build a much bigger building. Once I got those rights, I still needed a tiny parcel of land that was critical because of zoning laws that required a minimum of thirty feet of open space behind any building. That took more investigating and negotiating. In addition, my architect, Der Scutt, and I went over at least four dozen designs, finding the best elements of each and incorporating them into the final design. Then we had to have the final design approved by the city and get zoning variances.

> I have learned that what is essential can sometimes be invisible to the eye. That's where discernment comes in.
>
> – *Donald J. Trump*

That's just part of the story of Trump Tower. None of those steps were easy, but I saw each step as a challenge and enjoyed working out the details. If I didn't see it that way, it could have been very easy to become discouraged. But instead I have a beautiful building that has become world famous. Was it worth it? Yes! And it's a great example of problem solving.

Another interesting story about Trump Tower is the name itself. I was initially going to name it Tiffany Tower because of the location. A friend asked me why I would use another famous name to describe a building that I had envisioned and built, and his question hit home. Trump Tower it became.

Robert and I realize that problems can be complex and, at times, seemingly endless but we want to encourage you to see them as *challenges* that will give you a chance for great achievement. Remember, nothing is easy. But who wants nothing? Your financial intelligence is greater than that!

Robert and Donald checking out the course at
Trump National Golf Club/Los Angeles

CHAPTER FIVE

WHY WE WANT YOU TO BE RICH

Robert's View

When Charles Wilson, then-president of General Motors, was appointed secretary of defense in 1953, he was asked if he could make decisions that would adversely impact GM. He said he could, but that he couldn't conceive of a situation where that would happen "because for years I thought what was good for the country was good for General Motors and vice versa." The then-president of GM has since often been quoted as saying, "What is good for General Motors is good for America: though his message was certainly more complex. What he meant was that the two giants—GM and the United States—were intertwined. That is true today as well, though not in the same way it was back then.

General Motors is in trouble, and so is the United States. GM's problems stem from the fact that its cars are not as good as they need to be and the company has had management problems for years and, like the United States, has lived on its past successes, pushing problems forward rather than solving them.

An example of how poorly managed GM was comes from the book *Buffettology*. According to Mary Buffett:

"The same phenomenon can be seen in the financial records of the General Motors Company, which indicate that between the beginning of 1985 and the end of 1994 it earned in total approximately $17.92 a share and paid out in dividends approximately $20.62 a share. During this same period of time the company spent approximately

$102.34 on capital improvements. The question that should be running through your mind is, if General Motors' earnings during this time period time totaled $17.92 and it paid out as dividends $20.62, where did the extra $2.68 that is paid out in dividends and the $102.34 that it spent on capital improvements come from?"

This little example does not take into account GM's loss of market share, the number of employees who are not working (yet are being paid), an under-funded pension plan and medical liabilities. In other words, just like the United States, the biggest carmaker in the world is teetering on the edge of bankruptcy. What is obviously good for GM is also good for America, but can we afford the price?

When you look at GM's numbers, you do not have to have an MBA to understand them…sixth-grade math will do. Ask yourself this, "How can a company that earns $17.92 a share pay out a dividend of $20.62 a share and stay in business?" Any child can tell you that if you have $17.92 in your hand, you cannot find $20.62 in that amount. The next question is, "How can a company spend $102.34 a share when it only earns $17.92 a share?" Once again, a 12 year old can tell you that spending $102.34 when you only earned $17.92 is not good money management. It just does not make sense.

Yet, even though it does not make sense, millions of people are investing in GM, betting their retirement on GM's future, and listening to stockbrokers and financial planners who advise them to invest in blue-chip companies like GM. How can people be so naive? My answer: "No financial education."

Warren Buffett may have another answer to that question. A quote:

"It has been helpful to me to have tens of thousands (of students) turned out of business schools taught that it didn't do any good to think."

This quote may explain why a company such as GM, with thousands of smart people working for it, can make such foolish financial decisions.

Mr. Buffett has also said:

"If calculus were required, I'd have to go back to delivering papers. I've never seen any need for algebra."

I believe he is saying, in other words, that getting rich is common sense, requiring only simple math.

And that raises the obvious question: "How can so many educated people be persuaded to invest in a company that uses fuzzy math instead of logical math?" A quote from Mr. Buffett that seems appropriate:

"Wall Street is the only place that people ride to in a Rolls Royce to get advice from those who take the subway."

The Rich Are Getting Richer

Donald Trump and I are very concerned. We know something is wrong, just as we all know something more than the cars is wrong at GM. We are afraid this country and its wealth have been grossly mismanaged just as GM is mismanaged. While playing games with the numbers actually benefits the rich, making them richer, the price is paid by the poor and the middle class.

If you have been to Detroit recently, you know the place feels like a funeral home. Towns and businesses are dying. As businesses die, real estate prices drop and families are hurt in more ways than just financially. So is what is good for GM also good for America? Is Detroit an example of the future America?

The Perfect Storm

The financial problems we all face are now bigger than the U.S. government alone can handle. For example, our financial challenges cannot be solved simply by the Federal Reserve raising or lowering interest rates, yet millions of people all over the United States and the world worship the wisdom from the Federal Reserve. However, the problems have not been solved and now are becoming global problems, beyond the borders of our country and beyond the control of our political leaders.

Let's review some of the problems and how they are related:

1. A growing trade deficit: The U.S. trade deficit for 2006 is forecast to be $423 billion. This means we as a nation will consume $423 billion more than we produce. On a smaller scale, this would be the same as a family who earns $5,000 a month spending $6,000 a month. This $5,000-a-month family is only making their problem bigger. This problem leads to the next problem.

2. A growing U.S. national debt: According to the Treasury Department, 42 presidents, from Washington (1789) to Clinton (2000), borrowed a combined total of $1.01 trillion from foreign governments and financial institutions. Between 2000 and 2005, the Bush White House borrowed $1.05 trillion—more than all the previous administrations combined.

Many of these $5,000 a month families tried to solve their problem by taking out home equity loans. You have seen the ads on television telling you how smart it is to pay off all your credit card bills with a home equity loan. This is a smaller example of pushing the problem forward. The president and the government today are solving the problem in much the same way, taking out a home equity loan on our future. This problem leads to the next problem.

3. A falling dollar: In 1971 the dollar was converted from real *money* to a *currency*. In 1971, President Nixon was trying to solve a problem—too much of our gold was leaving the country. Why was gold leaving the country? Going back to problem number one—a growing trade deficit. Because we were buying too many Japanese and European goods, the difference between what we sold to them and what we purchased from them was collected in gold, because back then our dollar was backed by gold. To solve that problem, President Nixon simply changed our dollar from an asset to a liability—an IOU. Today, our trade deficit is higher than ever before and our IOU to the world is massive.

Instead of backing our dollar with gold, the United States can just print more money (just as we as individuals use credit cards or write checks without any money in the bank—the difference being that you and I can be arrested and thrown in jail for writing bad checks).

Printing as much fake money as we wanted was intended to temporarily solve the problem in 1971, but it did not solve the problem of overconsumption. A problem that we are paying for today.

> The financial problems we all face are now bigger than the U.S. government alone can handle…However, the problems have not been solved and now are becoming global problems, beyond the borders of our country and beyond the control of our political leaders.
>
> – *Robert T. Kiyosaki*

Between 1996 and 2006, in just 10 years, the U.S. dollar has lost half of its value, when compared to gold. In 1996, gold was selling for approximately $250 an ounce. By 2006, just 10 years later, gold was selling for over $600 an ounce. As an example, in 1996, if you had put $1,000 in the bank, today (2006) it would be worth less than $500 in gold. Instead, if you had purchased four ounces of gold for $1,000, today that gold would be worth $2,400.

This 1971 change in the rules meant that savers became losers. People who believed that their money was safe in the bank lost, simply because they did not really have money in the bank—they had a currency, an IOU from our government. People who live on fixed incomes will find life more expensive—their dollar will not go as far. What the government is telling these people is that the problem is *inflation.* What the government does not tell them is that the problem is really *devaluation.* Our dollar is dropping in value simply because our government is printing more money to solve their problems. By the year 2020, a loaf of bread may cost $12, but pension checks, for those who get them, will stay the same. This problem leads to the next problem.

4. Baby boomers without money: We've emphasized the fact that in the next few years, the first of 75 million baby boomers will begin to retire. Many have inadequate funds to retire on. This lack of savings is caused partly by a law known as Gresham's Law. Gresham's Law states that when bad money enters the system, good money goes into hiding. This has happened throughout history, as far back as the Roman Empire. In 1964, the United States took real silver coins and replaced them with fake silver coins. Immediately, real silver coins went into hiding.

I believe that people may not be saving because, either consciously or subconsciously, they know the money they receive is not real money, so they spend it as fast as they can. We are a nation of debtors today simply because many people know their money is worth less and less— so why save it, since savers are losers. Most middle-class Americans have more money in their home equity and retirement accounts than dollars saved in their banks. Americans have one of the lowest savings rates in the world. They are living longer with less money and less opportunity. This problem leads to the next problem.

5. An entitlement mentality: Since millions of people lack financial resources, they now expect the government to solve their financial problems or to take care of them. If the government does not take care of them, who will? With prices going up, who can afford to take care of them?

The problem cannot be pushed forward much longer. With Social Security in debt $10 trillion and Medicare in debt $62 trillion, it seems the only way to solve this problem is to keep doing what we have always done—spend more than we earn, borrow more than we can afford, and print more money. It is a death loop caused by the inability to solve the problem—a problem caused by a lack of financial education. This problem leads to the next problem.

6. Higher oil prices: Higher oil prices are not caused by a lack of financial education; they are caused by greedy self-interests and a lack of financial vision. Although we have the technology and alternative energy resources to replace oil, we have not done so. As a nation and a world, we will suffer financially because of this greed and lack of vision.

High oil prices create the domino effect on the previous problems. The United States was able to borrow as much as it wanted to solve our problems because our economy was growing. As long as we were growing, other nations and lenders were very willing to lend us money...as much as we wanted. The problem with higher energy prices is that the higher prices cause the economy to contract, not expand. If and when the economy begins to contract, the people we have been borrowing from may be hesitant to accept more of our debt. If this happens, the economic problems cannot be solved by bigger promises and more debt. The house of cards may come down.

7. Tax breaks for the rich: Most of us know about the Golden Rule that reminds us about doing unto others. The Golden Rule I am talking about is the one that goes, "The person who has the gold makes the rules." It is a tragedy that in America the poor and middle class have lost their representation in government. Today, the rich make the rules, which is why the rich are getting richer.

On May 11, 2006, *ABC News* ran the story about the latest tax cuts. Quoting from the story:

"The tax policy center, a Washington think tank, discovered that the top 0.1 percent of tax payers—the people who make more than 1.8 million—would get back $82,000. Middle-income Americans making between $27,000 and $47,000 would get $20."

Voodoo Economics or the Trickle-Down Effect

One monetary theory encourages tax laws that favor the rich—the idea being, if the rich had more money, they would invest it, thus creating more jobs. Money would trickle down to the poor and middle class. This theory is sometimes called "voodoo economics" or the "trickle-down effect." While it sounds good in theory, and while some money does trickle down, the net result is the money stays in the hands of the rich.

In many cases, asset prices increase because the rich have more money. Why do asset prices increase? Asset prices increase because that is what the rich buy with their money—assets, which is one of the reasons why they are rich. When asset prices increase, it makes assets (things of real and lasting value) more expensive, out of the reach of the poor and the middle class. Just look at the price of real estate and ask anyone who has not yet bought a house if they think it is easy to afford the house of their dreams today. It's tough to buy a house with money that is only trickling down.

In Summary

In his book, *The America We Deserve,* Donald Trump talks about what he would do if he were president of the United States. After reading his book, I found his ideas bold and imaginative. I think he would make an excellent president and would campaign vigorously for him, if he should ever decide to run.

Personally, I am less optimistic. My father ran for Lieutenant Governor of the State of Hawaii and was defeated. That experience left me with less faith in the political process. My plan is simply to be financially astute, personally responsible for my life, and not to allow myself to become a victim of our government's mismanagement.

My father believed he could change the government. After his bitter defeat, I decided it was best to change me. Instead of attempting to change the laws, such as trying to make the tax laws more fair, I simply decided to become rich and use the tax laws to my benefit. If you would rather join the rich than fight them, then read on. This book is for you. If you would rather change the government, then this may not be the book for you.

Donald and I believe that the best way to change the rules is to first get the gold. If you have the gold, then you have more power. When you have the power, you are better able to enforce the real Golden Rule, the rule that states, "Do unto others as you would have them do unto you."

Donald's View

You have to know what's going on first. Then you go from there. You go from learning to doing. The worst thing is to learn hard lessons by doing *before* learning. Learning in itself is an investment. Robert and I are trying to bring that home to you in an accessible way.

Rules aren't always pleasant, but unless you're in a position to change the rules, laws, and constraints, it's a good idea to know about them. For example, I've had people come to me with what they thought would be a tremendous development, the building to end all buildings. Then I find out they know nothing—*nothing*—about zoning! In New York City, zoning rules. It's like saying you're going to build a ship to end all ships but that you know nothing about shipyards. How do you sail out of the harbor if you don't know how to build a ship? Episodes like this, and believe me, there are more than you might imagine, really make me wonder about the way people think. Education is supposed to help us think. The thinking process seems to be lacking in a lot of people, even those with education.

There is an island mentality Robert and I share and that is: Taking care of your island. After 9/11, New Yorkers shared a common bond that few of us who were here will ever forget. Manhattan suddenly became "our" island, not just the big, famous city in which we happened to live. It also became the adopted island of many people who had never been here before. The 9/11 attack did not destroy this island; instead, it made it better and stronger. In that sense, I'm happy to say 9/11 was a failure for the terrorists.

We all know the old saying, "No man is an island." There are a lot of ways to interpret that, but I like to see it as saying, "We're all in this together." That was in evidence after 9/11, and I hope we will be able to retain some of that spirit. We need to be solid when facing the economic forces of today and the future.

This is serious business. But it doesn't mean we can't have some fun along the way. I have to tell you, Robert thinks big. He thinks *the world* is his island! When it comes to selling books, he could be right. And his determination to educate people financially has taken on global dimensions. Rightly so. It's a global problem. But the solutions can start with you, and with us.

We're a good team, Robert and I. I finally found someone who thinks as big as I do. And don't fall for Robert's "Donald Trump builds skyscrapers, and I have a duplex" or some nonsense like that. He's highly accomplished, very successful and he is most definitely a global thinker.

What Motivates You?

But let's focus on something more important—namely, what is the most important thing to you? Is it your family? Their well-being? Their future and yours? Then you're reading the right book. Robert and I both have things that are very important to us. We've been willing to go to great lengths for them. Therefore, we believe we have something in common with all of you.

Suppose your family and your well-being is threatened. What do you do? You prepare yourself, you equip yourself for what might happen.

I don't want to be a financial fearmonger, but I have to tell you that things aren't looking so great. Our financial security is shaky. Just because you can shop at Saks today or online tonight doesn't mean that everything is just fine and that there's nothing to worry about. Don't fall for that comfort-zone happy state. Don't be shortsighted.

Robert has spotlighted some very real problems that face us all today:

1) A growing trade deficit

2) A growing national debt

3) A falling dollar

4) Baby boomers without money

5) Entitlement mentality

6) Higher oil prices

7) Tax breaks for the rich

Any one of these problems could spell financial ruin for any country. It is more important than ever that you educate yourself and your family so that you can protect yourself financially in the future. Through education, you gain vision. Through vision, you gain the ability to spot economic problems and turn them into economic opportunities. However, you must be careful about what kind of education you receive.

I once heard someone say, "Before advertising entered in, I saw the world." Things were clearer to this person before he let advertising and the media and the politicians take him full sway. He admitted to foggier vision after the worldly experts came in to clear things up for him. The media is a powerful tool, for good and for bad. So the bottom line is you have to learn to think for yourself.

Robert and I are not here to do the thinking for you. But because we've both done a lot of thinking, and have been successful, we believe that what we have to say might be able to lift some of the fog from the horizon, and maybe even tune down the media blasts we are all subjected to.

What Are Your Natural Instincts?

Growing up in Hawaii, I'm sure Robert is an ace swimmer. He'd better be, considering he was a surfer. I never would've thought I'd be coauthoring a book with some surfer-dude type from Hawaii. I remember a statement from his book, *Rich Dad's Prophecy*: "You cannot learn to swim from a textbook." It was followed by: "You cannot learn business from a textbook or from business school." In other words, nothing compares with frontline experience.

Which brings me to something else I was thinking about that has to do with instincts. Robert spent a year at sea, going around the world as part of his training at the U.S. Merchant Marine Academy. He said it taught him vigilance in looking for signs of approaching changes in weather. After a while, you develop a sixth sense, an instinct about when patterns might change. I think he's applied that instinct to economic forecasts. He described the economic condition as resembling the components of "the perfect storm" we've all heard about. That isn't exactly a comforting thought or image.

My experience with instinct started with baseball. Baseball players need to have a sixth sense or they won't make it into or past Little League. Not many people know this, but I was a good baseball player, good enough to be offered college scholarships on merit of my ability. I just knew how the game worked, and I had the athletic skills to correspond.

I've applied that same game knowledge to business. I will sometimes see a situation, wait for things to fall into line and be thinking, "OK, bases loaded? Good." Because that means grand slam to me. A grand slam is a great feeling.

On the other hand, Robert might be thinking "The perfect wave? OK, let's go!" But who knows how ex-surfers think? I certainly don't. In fact, someone once told me that there was no such thing as an ex-surfer. Surfers remain surfers for the rest of their lives.

If it weren't for his military training and experience at sea, I don't know if I'd be working with this guy. Except that he's got vision and tenacity, which are two very important things.

Financial IQ

Both Robert and I have used the term "financial IQ" in our writings. Not long ago, Kim, Robert's wife, came out with her first book, *Rich Woman*. She gave me an early copy to read, and it was so well-done that I wrote a jacket blurb for it. Her goal is for all women to increase their financial IQ and not depend on men to take care of them. I would recommend her book for both men and women.

We all have our definitions of financial IQ, but it's a living term, therefore it's always changing. To me, it means having the ability to chart the economic waters nationally and internationally, to be able to look beyond the present and into the future, and to make decisions based on those assessments and insights. That's not an easy endeavor, and it's a daily discipline, but it's a necessary discipline if one is to succeed in today's world.

I may have an advantage because I'm one of those people who don't require a lot of sleep—maybe three or four hours a night. So what do I do with those extra hours? I read. I keep up with world events and read about history.

You have to figure, if a person has an extra 28 hours a week to read, that can add up to a lot of reading. I'll let you do the math. I know that Robert likes to do group reading, where people get together to study a book. That's a good idea, but since I usually read in the early morning hours, I don't think I'd be too popular with any groups.

The Importance of History

I'd like to emphasize the importance of studying history. Knowledge is power. We can learn from history, from the civilizations and empires that have made up the history of the world thus far. Some very big things have disappeared in the course of history. Do you remember the Ottoman Empire? Do you know how long it ruled? Do you know how and why it disappeared as an empire? Maybe you should find out. It could be pertinent to world events and your understanding of them. In other words, the things you don't know about just might possibly affect you someday in some way. When they do, who will you have to blame if you are surprised?

> This is serious business. But it doesn't mean we can't have some fun along the way.
>
> – Donald J. Trump

Robert and I are both history buffs, and one reason we connect is that we both use history as a guidebook. It's better to learn from history than to repeat the same blunders. As the old saying goes, "Those who haven't learned from history are destined to repeat it."

If today were suddenly to become a memory, what would you like to remember about it?

Two quotes come to mind, one from Ralph Waldo Emerson and one from Albert Einstein:

"What lies behind us
And what lies before us
Are tiny matters
Compared to what lies within us."
— Emerson

"The mind that opens to a new idea
Never comes back to its original size."
— Einstein

Emerson's quote keeps me from being complacent, knowing I have a lot more to learn and accomplish, and Einstein's quote keeps me thinking big. I could be more erudite in my explanations, but these thoughts are so clear that it would be redundant to elaborate any further. I also believe that simple is better. Not that simple is so easy. Distilling something down to its essence can take time and a great deal of thought. That's a good reason to read great thinkers and writers—in many cases they've already done the distilling process for us.

But here's your assignment first: Give some thought to your roots and why you're doing whatever it is you're doing today. It's a good way to start thinking for yourself—and it's likely no one else but you will come up with the right answers.

Robert and I have told you why we want you to be rich, but what we want is not important. What is important is what *you* want for yourself and your family. Do you want to be rich?

Part Two

Three Kinds Of Investors

There are three types of investors in the world. They are:

1. People who do not invest at all

2. People who invest not to lose

3. People who invest to win

People who *do not invest at all* expect their family, the company they work for or their government to take care of them once their working days are over.

People who invest *not to lose* generally invest in what they think are safe investments. This is the vast majority of investors. These people have the saver's mentality when it comes to investing.

People who *invest to win* are willing to study more, want more control and invest for higher returns.

Interestingly, all three investor types have the potential to become very rich, even those who expect someone else to take care of them. For example, when the CEO of Exxon retired he was paid nearly half a billion dollars as a going-away present.

Donald and Robert both invest to win. This book is for you if you want to invest to win.

CHAPTER SIX

INVESTING
TO WIN

Robert's View

Donald and I share the same concerns, and we want you to be rich, so what are our solutions?

One day, during a brief meeting in his office, Donald simply said, "I invest to win. Don't you?" With that statement, the defining difference appeared. He and I *invest to win,* while others *invest not to lose.*

We've talked here about the advice, "Save money, get out of debt, invest for the long term (generally in mutual funds) and diversify." Late that afternoon, Donald and I discussed how we did not focus on saving money. In fact, we are both millions of dollars in debt—but good debt. We do not diversify…at least not in the context that most people use the word diversify. And while we are definitely long-term investors, we do not invest in mutual funds, at least as a primary investment vehicle. Why? Because we invest to win.

Donald and I started talking about how our books were different and more popular than those of other financial authors. Again, the obvious became more obvious. "Most financial authors tell their readers to *live below their means,*" I said. "One author recommends not having that daily cappuccino and saving the cappuccino money in mutual funds instead—so that later in life you will become rich. You and I do not live below our means. We like being rich. We expand our means. When we write or teach, we encourage others to be rich and enjoy the good life."

Pausing for a moment, Donald smiled and said, "You know, you're right.

I don't know anyone who likes to live below their means, at least not amongst my friends. The people I know want to enjoy life, and we do enjoy life. We play to win and we *do* win. You win, and you enjoy life. That's why you and I sell more books and draw bigger crowds when we teach. People like winners."

"Most other financial experts are telling people to play it safe, to live below their means. They're telling people that investing is risky and that they need to save and avoid losing. These experts aren't focusing on winning. They're focusing on *not* losing," I added.

"There's a very big difference," said Donald.

All I did was nod. For years, ever since *Rich Dad Poor Dad* came out, many people, including journalists, often said that what I talked about was too risky. Yet to me, what most people were doing was far riskier. In a world of less and less job security, it seemed foolish to count on job security. With the stock market booming and busting, taking trillions of dollars from unsuspecting investors, it seemed foolish to count on the stock market for financial security. And with our school systems teaching students little to nothing about money, it seemed risky to simply count on a good education as being adequate.

It made me reflect back upon my life, to the defining moments in my life when I decided that I would play the game of money to win, rather than play the game not to lose.

"You know, we don't invest in the same investments most people invest in," said Donald. "Isn't it ironic that the investments most people think are safe are really risky?"

I simply nodded.

"There's something else," said Donald. "You and I look at making money as a game. We have fun. We enjoy the game. Sometimes we lose, but mainly we win. We have fun."

"It *is* fun," I said. "I love the game."

"But most people don't see making money as a game," said Donald. "They think of it as life and death, winners and losers."

"Survival," I said. "A struggle for life itself, which is why they are terrified of losing money. That's why they look at investing as risky."

"And wind up in risky investments," Donald added, gently slapping his desk. "It's a financial tragedy."

"Their loss of money?" I asked.

"No, the fun they miss out on. Making money is fun. Life is supposed to be fun. And millions of people are living in fear instead of having fun. That's the tragedy."

"That's why they play it safe, invest in 'safe' investments, cling to job security and live below their means." I added. "On top of that, millions are deeply in debt, bad debt, because they want to have fun but haven't learned how to invest to win. They really do want to live the good life but are punished by excessive bad debt."

"And that's no fun," said Donald. "You and I love the game. We created educational games. Games are fun. If you have fun, you learn more, you want to win, even though sometimes you lose. I haven't seen a popular game called *Save Money* or *Live Below Your Means*. Have you? There may be such games, but I don't think they're as popular as our games. We play hard. We play to win. We have fun. That's what life's about."

The meeting was over. There was a lot to think about. As I got into the elevator and pressed the button for the lobby of Trump Tower, my mind was racing. Why do most investors play it safe or invest not to lose? And why do others invest to win? As the elevator door opened to the lobby, a question came to mind, "What is the difference between a person who plays to win and a gambler? And what about risk?"

As I reached the sidewalk on Fifth Avenue and hailed a cab, I realized the questions in my head were some of the questions that needed to be answered in this book. I realized the reason most people invest not to lose is because most people think investing is risky or that investing is gambling. Many also believe that to get higher returns you have to take on more risk. Nothing could be further from the truth.

The 90/10 Rule of Money

Sitting in the cab, I recalled the 90/10 rule of money my rich dad taught me years ago (and about which I have written in my other books). While most of us have heard of the 80/20 rule, the 90/10 rule applies more

> I realized the reason most people invest not to lose is because most people think investing is risky or that investing is gambling. Many also believe that to get higher returns you have to take on more risk. Nothing could be further from the truth.
>
> – Robert T. Kiyosaki

specifically to money. Simply put, in the game of money, 10 percent of the players win 90 percent of the money. For example, in the game of golf, 10 percent of all professional players win 90 percent of the money, and 90 percent of the professional players split the remaining 10 percent.

The 90/10 rule has served as a trusty rule of thumb in my life (though I know of no scientific studies that prove it). We've all heard how 10 percent of all Americans own 90 percent of the available wealth. When you look at real estate investors, it is safe to say that 10 percent again own or control 90 percent of the wealth, with the greatest amount going to the top 1 percent of that 10 percent.

One of the ways this 90/10 rule has been useful for me is in choosing my endeavors. For example, one of the reasons I have not taken up the game of golf as a profession is simply because I do not think I could be in the top 10 percent. Not only do I believe I don't have the talent, I do not have the desire. If you ever heard me sing, you would also know why I did not choose singing as a career. When I decided to write *Rich Dad Poor Dad* and create my board game *CASHFLOW®*, I was not only pretty certain my book and game could do well, I also *wanted* to do well, even though I had never been a good writer or ever developed a board game. I wanted to do well, I wanted to teach, and I wanted to win.

I believe the reason Donald Trump and I got together is simply because my book, *Rich Dad Poor Dad,* and my board game *CASHFLOW* are international winners. We are not doing this book together because I am an international winner in real estate as he is, although I do own millions of dollars of property and businesses around the world. In business and real estate investing, I have won, I am a winner, I am a professional, but I am not in the top 10 percent as he is. As an author, I *am* in the top 10 percent; in fact, *Rich Dad Poor Dad* has been touted as the third longest-running best seller on the *New York Times* best seller list and the #1 Personal Finance book of all time. Not bad for a guy who flunked out of English twice in high school.

Donald Trump Plays to Win

In Phoenix, Arizona, where I live, Donald came to town and stirred up quite a controversy. He and his team wanted to put up a high-rise on Camelback Road, between 24th and 32nd streets. This is the prime of prime locations in Phoenix. The locations between 24th and 32nd streets are like Boardwalk and Park Place in the game of *Monopoly.* He wanted to put up the tallest building on Camelback Road, but there were height restrictions where he wanted to build.

For a number of years, the debate went on. The question in town was, should Donald Trump be allowed to build the tallest building in the best location? My wife and I wanted Donald to win. Why? Because we also own residential and commercial properties on, near, or between 24th and 32nd streets. If Donald Trump won, we won.

In the fall of 2005, the residents of the area voted not to allow Mr. Trump to build the tallest building. After the vote was counted, the residents were willing to allow him to build a high-rise, but not the height he wanted. With that, Donald Trump simply pulled out.

During one of our meetings in New York about the book, I asked him about the vote in Phoenix. He seemed unphased. All he said was, "If I can't build the tallest and best building, I don't want to build." He then showed me a spectacular building in Dubai he was building. Pointing with pride to this futuristic building, he said, "Why should I be upset with Phoenix when I'm busy working on this?"

As my taxi headed down Fifth Avenue toward my hotel, I got clearer about this book. This book was going to be about living life to enjoy life. It was going to be about playing the game of life to win rather than living a life of avoiding loss. Instead of living life below one's means, not enjoying the cappuccino, this book was to be about living life beyond one's wildest dreams.

As the cab approached my hotel, I reflected back to a question a reporter had asked me at the start of the year: "Have you set your goals for this year?"

My reply was, "No, I haven't."

"Why not?" he asked. "You talk about the importance of setting goals in your books."

I replied, "Yes, setting goals is important. My problem is, at this stage of my life, I do not know what else to strive for. I have more than enough money, I have a great marriage, I love my work, I have my health and I am far more successful than I ever thought I would be. Today, I am living life beyond my wildest dreams. I have best-selling books, I have been on *Oprah,* I am doing a book with Donald Trump, and I love the people I work with. I do not know what else to go for."

"So what are you doing about it?" asked the reporter.

"I think I need to dream wilder dreams," I replied.

The cab pulled up to my hotel. As I paid the cabby, I knew this book was to be about living life beyond one's wildest dreams…but only if you dare live such a life.

Donald's View

Winners

I've known about the 90/10 ratio for a long time, but Robert gives us all a good reminder. Pretty soon, if we don't start paying attention, it could reach the 95/05 ratio or even 99/01 with 1 percent of the people owning 99 percent of the nation's assets.

Winners wouldn't let that happen, and I hope that includes you.

It's important to have dreams. "A man's reach should exceed his grasp," as Robert Browning said. That's what keeps us going. I like to say, "If your reality begins with your dreams, your dreams will become your reality."

Why is that? Because to think otherwise leaves us at the level of mere survival, which I believe is not the ultimate aim of most people. Ever hear a young person say they hope they become a burn someday? Usually they say things like, "I want to become the president." "I'd like to be an astronaut." "I'd like to be a fireman." "I want to become a doctor." These are demanding and sometimes heroic professions, and young people have the dreams and aspirations to match them.

Winners remain young at heart—they aim high and have the enthusiasm and the plans to achieve what they are aiming for. They may have wild dreams, but it's better than having no dreams. Then they pay attention and focus on what it's going to take to achieve them.

Being stubborn is a big part of being a winner. Some people have failed because they have given up too soon. If you are reading this book, that group probably does not include you. My father used to tell us this story about a guy who loved soda, so he went into the soda business, with a product he called 3UP. It failed. So he started again with a soda called 4UP. It failed, too. So he decided to name his product 5UP and worked just as hard to make it work, but sure enough, it failed again. He realized that he still loved soda, so he tried again with a product named 6UP. It failed, and he gave up completely.

Then, a few years later, someone else came up with a soda product and named it 7UP, which became a huge success. When I was young, I couldn't understand why my father kept telling us this story. He told it many times. Later, I realized he was telling us to never give up. Well, I never forgot that story, and I've never given up either. So his lesson was well-placed. Tell yourself that story if you need to, and the winner part of you will take over.

The other component of winning is, simply, a winning attitude. I tell people to see themselves as victorious. Positive thinking works. It has a lot of power. Winning requires that kind of power, whether you're a quiet person or a gregarious one. Power is strength, and being positive can work you through some pretty difficult situations.

When I was deeply in debt at one time, I became stubborn and refused to let it get me down. I simply refused to become negative. I focused on the solution, and I assured myself that I would work through the situation and come back to be more successful. That's exactly what happened. My demise was written about in major publications, and even then I refused to agree with them. My reality was about my dreams, not about numbers. I won.

Are you stubborn enough to be a winner? Then you are capable of investing to win! It's not a foreign territory and you don't need a passport or a visa to join the ranks of winning investors. I've heard a lot of people say about themselves, "I have a stubborn streak" and then they act like they don't have what it takes or even the right to learn about investing! As Robert pointed out, they will be missing out on a lot of fun and a better financial future at the same time an unnecessary misfortune.

Ignorance can be more expensive than education, and that certainly includes your financial education. Do not let the fear of the unknown hinder your aspirations and your financial well-being. There are people who will want you to feel inept so they can take advantage of you. I've seen that happen to very successful athletes, as one example. Don't let it happen to you—learn about money and make it work for you. That's the key to successful investing.

> Being stubborn is a big part of being a winner.
>
> – Donald J. Trump

CHAPTER SEVEN

CHOOSE YOUR BATTLE— AND BATTLEFIELD

Robert's View

I learned the importance of choosing your battle and your battlefield in military school, and it was reinforced in the Marine Corps. For example, the troops that had the high ground, such as a hill, often had the advantage over the opposing troops below them. The troops on the low ground had the option to fight or not to fight. That may be where the sayings, "Sometimes it's best to walk away and live to fight another day," and "Choose your battles carefully," have come from. The same ideas hold true in business.

In *Rich Dad's CASHFLOW Quadrant,* the second book in the Rich Dad series of books, I go into why some people find getting rich easier than others. *Rich Dad's CASHFLOW Quadrant* is the most important of my books for people who want to make changes in their life. If you are not looking to change your life, then it could be the worst book for you. Let's take a look at the CASHFLOW Quadrant again:

As stated earlier:

E *stands for employee*

S *stands for small-business person, self-employed or specialist*

B *stands for big-business owners such as Donald Trump*

I *stands for investor*

More than simply titles, the person in each of the quadrants is very different from the people in the other three quadrants. When it comes to attitude, most people in the E quadrant seek security. They say, "I'm looking for a safe, secure job with benefits." A small-business person in the S quadrant may say, "If you want it done right, do it by yourself." A person in the B quadrant is often looking for a president, CEO or other talented person to run his or her operations. One of the defining differences between S quadrant business owners and B quadrant business owners is the number of employees. *Forbes* magazine once defined a "big business" as a business with more than 500 employees. And I stands for investor. As you already know from the introduction to Part Two, there are three different types of investors.

The tax laws are also different for the different quadrants. The worst quadrant to be in for tax purposes is the E quadrant, simply because there is very little you can do to protect yourself from taxes—hence you really do not need an accountant to advise you. The quadrants with the best tax breaks are the B and I quadrants. Why? Most governments give tax breaks to those in the B quadrant because they provide jobs. And governments offer tax breaks to the I quadrant because they invest their money back into the economy. Special tax breaks are usually given to people who invest in real estate and oil because every country needs housing and energy.

In Which Quadrant Can You Win?

As stated at the start of this chapter, it is important to choose your battle and battlefield carefully. When it comes to getting rich, choosing the quadrant that is best for you holds a similar importance.

The CASHFLOW Quadrant is important because it can help you decide which quadrant you have the best chance of winning in. As you may have guessed, both Donald Trump and I chose the B and I quadrants to operate in.

Years ago, when I was in high school and having trouble with English, it was my rich dad who pointed out to me that I would probably never do well in school or in the corporate world. He said, "You're too much of a rebel to follow orders from people you do not respect. You will probably do better in business as an entrepreneur and an investor."

Although I did not like what he said, it helped me learn where I did not fit. It also warned me that I had to study subjects, develop skills, and gain experiences that most of my peers would not have to gain. To learn more about my experiences in the B and I quadrants, I suggest reading *Rich Dad's Guide to Investing* and *Rich Dad's Before You Quit Your Job*.

Some of you may be thinking, "But I don't want to be an entrepreneur." Or you may be feeling your heart pound at the thought of taking risks and not having a steady paycheck. Don't worry. This book is more about winning than it is about being an entrepreneur or professional investor. Even though there are three different types of investors, and we prefer investors who invest to win, people can become very rich as any one of the three. The same is true with the quadrants; people can and have gotten very rich from each of the quadrants. For example, the founder of General Electric was Thomas Edison. Edison was in the B quadrant. Jack Welch, a former CEO of General Electric, was in the E quadrant. Both men became very rich from the same business, yet from different quadrants.

> Most financial authors write about living below your means and saving money. When Donald and I write, we write about expanding your means, enjoying life and investing your money.
>
> – *Robert T. Kiyosaki*

I mention the CASHFLOW Quadrant to help you become clearer about which quadrant you might think you have the most chance of winning in. Although the tax laws favor the B and I quadrants, tax laws are not as important as which quadrant you think you have the best chance of winning in.

Our school systems are designed to train people for the E and S quadrants. That is why so many people say, "Go to school to get a job," which is programming for the E quadrant. Or they say, "Go to school so you can learn a trade or profession. Then you'll always have something to fall back on." That mind-set is perfect for the S quadrant. (Again, if you want to learn more about the B or I quadrants, there are also books written by Donald Trump. My personal favorites are *The Art of the Deal, The Art of the Comeback,* and *How to Get Rich,* which encapsulate his thinking as both a B and an I.)

Donald and I make more money than most schoolteachers and other authors simply because most schoolteachers operate from the values of the E quadrant and most authors write from the values found in the S quadrant.

Most financial authors write about living below your means and saving money. When Donald and I write, we write about expanding your means, enjoying life and investing your money. Again, the difference in financial advice can be identified by the different quadrants and the different values each quadrant represents.

So take a moment and ask yourself which quadrant is best for you. You may want to close your eyes and sit quietly to listen for your answer. This quiet process is important because it is crucial to be true to yourself—to be true to your own answer.

Donald was fortunate in that he had his father as a role model for the B and I quadrants. I had a father in the E quadrant. For me to announce that I was going to be a businessman went against all the values of my poor dad, a man who believed in job security and government entitlement. It was like I was joining the enemy…becoming a traitor. My dad sincerely believed the rich were greedy and exploited the poor…and some do. Yet, I did not share his values. I wanted to be an entrepreneur and an investor. Although I loved and respected my dad with all my heart, we did not share the same values when it came to careers and money.

Returning from Vietnam in 1973, I had to make up my mind about which quadrant I was going to make my stand in. My poor dad wanted me to stay in the Marine Corps because of job security. When I told him I was getting out, he advised me to get a job as a pilot with the airlines. When I told him I did not want to fly anymore, he advised me to go back to school, to get my master's degree and my Ph.D. so I could get a job with the government. Since he did not understand the CASHFLOW Quadrant, he did not understand that it was not the job I was turning down, it was the quadrant...or I should say the different values of each quadrant.

Once my real dad, my poor dad, realized that I preferred the professional and financial values of my rich dad, the B and I quadrants, the gap between the two of us increased and our relationship became strained. My poor dad valued *security*, and my rich dad valued *freedom*. And as many of you know, security and freedom are not the same thing. In fact, they are opposite values. That is why the people with the most security have the least freedom. The people with the most security are locked up in jail, in maximum security.

When asked, "Why is money so important to you?" I often answer, "Because money buys me freedom. Money buys me more choices in life." For example, when traveling, I don't like spending excessive time standing in lines at airports. By having more money, I have the choice of standing in line or renting a private jet. Today, I fly by private jet more than I fly by commercial airlines. Of course, Donald has his own private jet, which validates my point. One night, leaving Dallas, my tiny private-chartered jet taxied past Donald's private jet. It was humbling to realize that my jet was almost small enough to taxi under his jet.

And that is why I strongly suggest you sit quietly and decide which quadrant is best for you. Ask yourself, "What are my values? Do I need job security? Am I happy with security? Are my skills being tested in this quadrant? Or do I value freedom more?" Also, you may want to ask yourself what your parents' values are, as well as those of your friends. There is some truth to the saying, "Birds of a feather flock together."

So the lesson is, if you are going to choose to be rich, remember to choose your battle and battlefield carefully—or should I say your values and quadrants.

Donald's View

Choosing Your Battle and Battlefield

Robert's CASHFLOW quadrant is an effective tool, and that's one reason I chose his book, *Rich Dad's CASHFLOW Quadrant,* to be on my list of recommended books for Amazon. If you will take a little time and spend it thinking about what he's saying, you'll save a lot of time in the long run. It's important to know about yourself and your inclinations before setting out on any path, new or otherwise.

I know that some people's eyes glaze over when they see a chart or a formula because it means they've got to give it some personal time and effort. But that glazed look could turn into something like delight or even excitement when you realize how much you will be able to improve your cash flow and bottom-line success. The choice is yours to make.

When I was starting out in real estate, I could have easily stayed within my father's business and been successful, but I would not have been fulfilled. I had definite plans of my own and had to strike out on my own to achieve them. If I hadn't done that, I would have led a comfortable life, but not an exciting one. I also would not have lived my *own* life.

Just as Robert had to realize that his father's goals were not his goals, we all have to do some soul-searching to find out what we are destined to do and to be. Imagine living your life and then finding out you'd missed your own destiny in the process. I've seen some examples of that, and I think it's a great way to eclipse yourself. If you're not living your life, then who is? If you're not going to think about your life, then who will? You're here now, so give it your full attention!

I often think of battles and battlefields in the sense of being arenas. We all choose, to a certain extent I would hope, what arena we are operating in, and what arena we'd *like* to be operating in. It's about having goals and visions for achievement and fulfillment. It's sometimes difficult to change circles, but it's sometimes for the best.

We can be very much influenced by the people with whom we keep company, and it's not easy to break with the pack or to do the unexpected.

It can be a solitary season or two before we get enough momentum to expand our own circle, but eventually that can lead to a very full arena of events and people you happen to enjoy. That"s very much like writing your own script and having it become one you wind up enjoying watching and participating in.

Choice is a freedom we can all exercise. When I meet people who live in certain ways because they like it, but which I know I wouldn't, it reminds me of a menu at a restaurant—there's something for everyone. And if there isn't, there's always another restaurant to go to. It's also a good way to keep from being judgmental—as in, to each his own.

Back to the script idea. I heard someone say once that we are all in charge of writing our own movie, and that movie is our life. Imagine yourself writing scenes what kind would you want to have? Somehow, I don't think we'd choose drudgery, boredom or poverty. It's not only no fun to write, it's boring and depressing to watch. Give yourself a little freedom to develop into something or someone you'd actually like to be.

Notice I said "give yourself" in the above paragraph. Very often, the only person who will give you a chance will be yourself. Too many people want the status quo to remain the same, and that status quo will include you. But you have the ability to change that. First of all, you're taking the time to read this book, so I already know you are capable of moving beyond mediocrity or whatever might be holding you back. None of us should willingly join the lowest common denominator, which in many cases turns out to be the easy road. Those with uncommon lives have moved beyond the common.

Life and business can be combative. It can be a battle. But make sure you choose to fight the *good* fight—and get away from futile battles and battlegrounds as quickly as possible. Do not live or use your energy in vain.

> Give yourself a little freedom to develop into something or someone you'd actually like to be.
>
> – Donald J. Trump

Remember: Write your own script. Then produce it yourself and find yourself living the way you want to. That's freedom, that's power and that's winning.

Your View

Review and think about the CASHFLOW Quadrant and how It applies to your own life.

From which quadrant do you derive the most income today?

_____

Now envision yourself as the successful person you have dreamed of becoming. Which quadrant will you be in at the point when you reach the pinnacle of success?

_____

Compare your two answers. Are you already in the correct quadrant?

_____

If yes, then sharpen the skills you already have and get going!

If not, then create a plan for how you can move to the quadrant where you see yourself as a great success. Only you can do this exercise for you!

You do not need to move overnight. But you do need to start the process! With the plan in mind, what are the steps necessary for you to make the move?

1 . _____

2 . _____

3 . _____

CHAPTER EIGHT

THERE IS A DIFFERENCE BETWEEN SAVERS AND INVESTORS

Robert's View

Many people invest in mutual funds. When I talk about not being a saver, many of them respond, "But I *am* investing. I have a portfolio of mutual funds. I have a 401(k). I also own stocks and bonds. Isn't that investing?"

I take a step back and explain myself a bit more, "Yes, saving is a form of investing. So when you buy mutual funds or stocks or bonds, you are sort of investing, but it is more from a saver's point of view and a saver's set of values."

Let's look at the passive investor philosophy. Once again, most financial planners will advise you to:

- Work hard
- Live below your means
- Save money
- Get out of debt
- Invest for the long term (primarily in mutual funds)
- Diversify

Putting this in financial planners' language, it often sounds like this. "Work hard. Make sure the company you work for has a matching 401(k) program. Be sure to maximize your contribution. After all, it's tax-free money. If you own a home, pay off that mortgage quickly. If you have credit cards, pay them off. Also, have a balanced portfolio of growth funds, a few small cap funds, some tech funds, a fund for foreign equities, and when you get older, shift into bond funds for steady income. Of course, diversify, diversify, and diversify. It's not smart to keep all of your eggs in one basket."

While not exact, I am sure this sales pitch, disguised as financial advice, has a familiar ring to you.

Donald Trump and I are not saying everyone should change and stop doing this. It is good advice for a certain group of people—people who have a saver's philosophy or are passive investors.

In today's environment, I believe it to be the riskiest of all financial advice. To the financially unsophisticated, it sounds like safe and intelligent advice.

Getting back to the difference between a saver and an investor, there is one word that separates them, and that word is *leverage*. One definition of leverage is *the ability to do more with less.*

Most savers do not use financial leverage. And you should not use leverage unless you have the financial education or financial training to apply it. But let me explain further. Let's look at this standard advice from the viewpoint of a saver and then an investor, or an E and S-quadrant person versus a B- and I-quadrant person.

Work Hard

Let's start with the advice "work hard."

When most people think about the words "work hard," they think only about *themselves* working hard. There is very little leverage in you working hard. When Donald and I think about working hard, while we both work hard individually, we mostly think about other people working hard for us to help make us rich. That's leverage. It's sometimes known as other people's time. As already discussed, the B-quadrant person receives more tax breaks than the E and S quadrants because the B-quadrant person creates jobs. In other words, our government wants us to create jobs...not look for a job. Our economy would collapse if everyone started looking for a job. For our economy to grow, we need people to create jobs.

Save Money

While I covered saving money in the last chapter, there are a few other points that are worth mentioning.

The problem with saving money is that the current economic system needs *debtors,* not *savers,* to expand.

Let me explain with the following diagram, as originally described in *Rich Dad Poor Dad:*

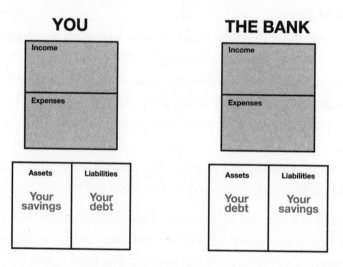

Take a moment to study this diagram. Your savings are a liability to the bank even though those same savings are an asset to you. On the other hand, your debt is an asset to the bank, but it is your liability.

For our current economic system to keep growing, it needs smart borrowers…people who can borrow money and get richer, not people who borrow money and get poorer. Once again, the 90/10 rule of money applies—10 percent of the borrowers in the world use debt to get richer—90 percent use debt to get poorer.

Donald Trump and I use debt to get richer. Our bankers love us. Our bankers want us to borrow as much money as we can because borrowers make them richer. This is called other people's money (OPM). Donald and I recommend more financial education for you because we want you to be smarter when it comes to the use of debt. If we have more debtors, our nation's economy will grow. If we have more savers, our economy will shrink.

If you can understand that debt can be good, and carefully learn to use debt as leverage, you will gain an advantage over most savers.

Get Out of Debt

Most savers think that debt is bad and that paying off the mortgage on their home is smart. And for many people, debt *is* bad and getting out of debt *is* smart. Yet, if you are willing to invest some time in your financial education, you can get ahead faster using debt as leverage. But again, I caution you to first invest in your financial education before you invest with debt.

There is good debt and bad debt. The purpose of getting financially smart is to know when to use debt and when not to.

Donald and I love real estate simply because our bankers love to lend us money to buy good real estate—real estate that is well-managed. Of course, there is also good real estate and bad real estate.

Savers who invest in mutual funds have a difficult time using leverage, simply because most bankers will not lend money on mutual funds. Why? Apparently bankers think mutual funds are too risky and consider real estate a safer investment.

Just as my poor dad fell behind financially in the early 1970s because he was a saver, millions of people today are falling behind financially for the same reason.

In this economic environment, savers are losers and debtors are winners. You should always be careful when using debt for any reason.

Invest for the Long Term

"Invest for the long term" has many meanings.

1. Look at this advice as a sales pitch: "Turn your money over to me for years, and I will charge you fees for the long term." I call it a sales pitch because "invest for the long term" is like the airlines offering you a frequent-flier program. They want to keep you as a lifetime, loyal, paying customer.

2. It also means they can charge you fees for the long term. This would be like paying your real estate broker a commission for selling you your house and then paying the broker a residual commission for as long as you occupy the house.

3. Mutual funds may not perform as well as other investments due to the fees paid for management of the fund. While I do not mind paying fees, I do not like paying fees for sub-par performance.

   Many people invest in mutual funds for the long term. However, mutual funds provide no leverage. As I said earlier, my banker will not lend me millions of dollars to invest in mutual funds, simply because they are too risky. There is also the lack of control (a subject that will be covered later).

One of the differences between mutual funds and hedge funds is leverage. Hedge funds often use borrowed money. Why do they use borrowed money? With borrowed money, you can increase your ROI, your return on investment, if you are a smart investor. In other words, the more of your own money you use, the lower your returns.

There is a time and place for mutual funds. I invest in them occasionally. But to me, mutual funds are like fast food; it's OK occasionally, but you do not want to make a habit of consuming it.

Diversify, Diversify, Diversify

Warren Buffett, reportedly the world's richest investor, has this to say about diversification: "Diversification is protection against ignorance. (It) makes very little sense if you know what you are doing."

So the question is, whose ignorance are you protecting yourself from? Your ignorance or your financial advisor's ignorance?

Again, there are multiple meanings for the world "diversify." Generally, it means not putting all of your eggs in one basket, which is what Warren Buffett does. To this, I once heard him say, "Keep all your eggs in one basket, but watch the basket closely."

Personally, I do not diversify, at least not in the way the financial planners recommend. I do not buy a lot of different assets. I would rather focus. In fact, the way I get ahead is by focusing, not diversifying.

One of the better definitions I have heard for the word "focus" is using the word as an acronym.

F = Follow

O = One

C = Course

U = Until

S = Successful

This is what I have done. Years ago, I invested in real estate until I was successful. Today, I still invest in real estate. When I wanted to learn about bonds, I invested in them until I was successful. Once I was successful, I decided I did not like bonds and so do not invest in them anymore. I have successfully taken two companies from startups through to IPOs (Initial Public Offerings). I made millions and was successful, but decided I did not want to go through that process anymore. Today, I still prefer real estate.

To me, diversification is a defensive posture, so I see very little offensive leverage in diversification.

For most people, diversification is a good strategy only because it protects investors from themselves and from incompetent or unscrupulous advisors.

This traditional financial planning advice of work hard, get out of debt, invest for the long term and diversify is *good* for the average investor—the passive investor who simply turns a little bit of money over each month for someone else to manage. It is *good* advice also for the person who is rich, but not interested in learning how to become an investor. Many movie stars, rich professionals, pro athletes and rich children with inheritances fall into this group. The key is to find a *good* financial advisor.

Know, however, that there is very little leverage in following this path—and leverage is the key to great wealth.

Leverage Is the Key

Ever since humans lived in caves, humans have sought leverage. Two of the first forms of leverage were fire and the spear. Fire and the spear gave humans leverage over their harsh environment. When a child was able, the parents would teach the child how to make his or her own fire and to use the spear as protection and for killing animals for food. Years later, the spear was reduced in size and the bow and arrow was developed, a higher form of leverage. Again, one of the definitions of leverage is *the ability to do more with less.* A bow and arrow is an example of doing more with less…over a spear.

As time went on, humans continued to use their brains to develop more leverage. Learning to ride a horse was a powerful form of leverage. Not only was the horse used for transportation and tilling the soil for planting crops, the horse also became a powerful force in warfare.

When gunpowder was developed, the ruler who had cannons conquered rulers who did not. Indigenous peoples such as the American Indians, Hawaiians, Maoris of New Zealand, the Aborigines of Australia and many other cultures were conquered by gunpowder.

> Getting back to the difference between a saver and an investor, there is one word that separates them and that word is leverage. One definition of leverage is the ability to do more with less.
>
> – Robert T. Kiyosaki

Only a hundred years ago, the automobile and the airplane replaced the horse. Again, both new forms of leverage were used for peacetime purposes and for warfare. Today, the countries that control the world's supplies of oil have leverage over much of the world.

Radio, television, telephone, this computer I am writing on and the World Wide Web are all forms of leverage. Each new breakthrough adds more wealth and power to those who have the access and the training to use these leveraged tools.

If you want to become rich and not be a victim of global changes, it is important that you develop the greatest lever of all: your mind. If you want to be rich and keep your wealth, your mind—your financial education—is your greatest lever of all.

Donald and I both had the advantage of having rich dads who introduced us to the world of money. But all our rich dads could do was introduce us. We still had to do our part. We still had to study, learn, practice, correct and grow. Just as the father and mother in the cave taught their children to start a fire and use a spear, we had rich dads who taught us how to use money and our minds to become rich.

I can hear some of you saying, "But I don't have a rich dad. I wasn't born into money. I don't have a good education." This type of thinking may be the reason why your chances for attaining and, more importantly, keeping great wealth are slim. Your chances may be slim because you are using your greatest asset, your mind, against yourself. You are using your mind to make excuses rather than to make money. Remember, your mind is your greatest lever. But all levers can work in two directions—for good or bad. Just as debt can be used to make you rich, debt can be used to make you poor.

I did not have a great education, nor was I born into a rich family. The one thing I did have was a rich dad who taught me to use my mind to make money...and not to make excuses. Rich dad hated excuses. He used to say, "Excuses are a dime a dozen. That's why unsuccessful people have so many excuses." He would also say, "If you cannot control your mind, you cannot control your life." Today, whenever I meet someone who is unhappy, unhealthy and unwealthy, I know it is simply because he or she has lost control of his or her mind, the greatest tool given to us by God.

Although Donald and I have money today, we have both experienced financial losses. If we had used our minds to blame others or to make excuses, we would both be poor today.

We Are All Born Rich

So our message to you is the same message we received from our rich dads: "We are all born rich. We all have been given the most powerful lever on earth, our minds...so use your mind for leverage to make you rich rather than to make excuses."

In Summary

The difference between cavemen and apes is leverage. The difference between the rich, poor and middle class is leverage. The difference between savers and investors is leverage. The difference between the E and S quadrants and the B and I quadrants is leverage. A well-trained and disciplined investor can gain much higher returns with much less risk and less money, but it takes leverage...and leverage requires you to educate yourself and to use your mind wisely.

Donald's View

What is the difference between a saver and investor? Years ago, a friend of mine who is Jewish told me the answer to this question: "Moses invests, Jesus saves." I don't know if that will be of any help to us, but it could be an answer to think about on many levels.

I see investors as being active savers. Investing is a way to make money, and it may not happen overnight, but saving *definitely* takes time to pay off. The returns are much higher if you invest your money rather than save it.

A lot of people are afraid of the risk or the study time involved in learning about investing. Robert does a good job explaining the different approaches one can take when thinking about how to handle money. *Rich Dad Poor Dad* hasn't been a fluke as a success. There's a reason it's been monumentally successful worldwide, and that's because he takes the time to explain these things.

An investor takes big steps into the bank and big steps out of the bank. A saver takes big steps in and small steps out. That's a visual I've always had about the difference between investing and saving. The power of the saver's saved money has been diminished.

Investors are visionaries in some respects—they look beyond the present. They look into the future. If they are clear-sighted in that way, those steps into and out of the bank aren't so scary—they're based on the confidence that the risk involved will be good for everyone. They will be seeing everyone coming out winners.

I rarely feel the need to convince people that my ideas are good, because I wouldn't be speaking with them to begin with if I felt I had to convince them. I let them know—versus convincing them—that what I am proposing will benefit everyone. I don't go into deals without having those basic bases covered. Even when I was first starting out, I could see the results so clearly that a "done deal" feeling would pervade my thoughts and actions.

Money is like talent. It doesn't do much good if you keep it to yourself. It has to be developed. It has to be nurtured. It has to be used properly. It takes time, work, and patience. There are many gifted people who will never be discovered because they've never been developed. It's also like a potentially great idea that is never given a chance because the owner of the idea chooses not to give it enough thought, or worse, any thought at all.

Investing requires responsibility, an ongoing responsibility. Saving doesn't. Investing isn't for everyone, but it's like any skill—once you try it and learn about the results, it can be surprisingly exciting. I can hear it now, "Investing is *exciting?*" When I hear that reaction, I know that person hasn't tried it yet.

Most of you know me well enough by now to know that I like adventures. But I'm not a thrill-seeker when it comes to finances. And it's best if you're not either. However, avoiding what could radically alter your life in a beneficial way is not the best choice.

We've already talked a bit about fear and how to reduce it. That's one of the differences between a saver and an investor: Savers are still living within the realm of fear. Investors have conquered that fear and are reaping the rewards. Focus on what fears you are dealing with and then...deal with them!

When I was starting out, and had just moved to Manhattan, the real estate market had cooled off to the extent that—for the first time—people were talking about the city going bankrupt. This fear led to more fear and citizens started to lose confidence in the city. It wasn't a great environment to be in if you were an up-and-coming real estate developer.

But I saw the problem as a great opportunity, because to me Manhattan was the center of the world and I was going to be a part of that world, no matter what the current (and, in my mind, temporary) financial crisis might be. So this particular fear really served to fuel my ambition and courage, not undermine it. That is the time I started to think about an enormous piece of property along the Hudson River—100 acres of riverfront property that was undeveloped. A financial crisis didn't interfere with my dreams—and I didn't shelve my ideas for a better time or a less-rainy day. I was determined to

> Investors are visionaries in some respects—they look beyond the present.
>
> – Donald J. Trump

be a real estate developer, no matter what the climate was. The point is, I invested time and developed my ideas, despite the situation. I didn't table my plan...or wait until conditions were perfect.

Savers wait for a long time, which often means they will miss out on opportunities. You may not have the money at the moment, and conditions may not be ideal, but that doesn't mean your mind can't be working on your ideas and paving the way to a better future. Things are rarely perfect and having an active-investor mind will keep you prepared and ready for the opportunities that will surface. Give investing a chance in the most comprehensive way you can: Look for opportunities in every climate. That's leverage.

Your View

Review how you benefit from leverage in your life today.

Other people's time being used for your benefit:

_____

Other people's money being used for your benefit:

_____

How might you increase the use of leverage in your life?

_____

How do you see others using leverage in their lives?

_____

Could you see yourself doing what they do?

_____

Keep reading to see other examples of leverage—the examples may help you in answering this question.

CHAPTER NINE

THE TWO THINGS YOU INVEST

Robert's View

My rich dad often said, "There are only two things you can invest: time and money." He also said, "Since most people do not invest much time, they lose their money."

Using the 90/10 rule of money as a rough guide, I would say that 90 percent of investors invest their money, but they do not invest much time. And the 10 percent that make 90 percent of the money invest more time than money. By the end of this book, you will know why Donald and I make so much money, gain much higher returns, and use less of our own money. We can do that because we invest more of our time than our money.

Look at the following diagram of three investors. I think you will understand the relationship between investing time versus investing money.

NON-INVESTOR	PASSIVE INVESTOR	ACTIVE INVESTOR
Invest no time	*Invest no time*	*Invest time*
Invests no money	*Invests money*	*Invests money*
No Financial Education	No Financial Education	Lots of Financial Education

When you look at this simple diagram, it is easy to see why the first two types of investors, the non-investor and the passive investor, would say, "Investing is risky." They have no (or very little) financial education, and they have very little financial experience; hence, they fall prey to any financial advisor promising safety and security.

Donald Trump invested a lot of time in his financial education. He went to Wharton, possibly the finest business school in America. In 1969, when I graduated from the Merchant Marine Academy in New York, I considered going to Wharton also. One of my classmates from the academy, Al Novack, was accepted and wanted me to go with him. I did not go because the Vietnam War was raging, and I decided to go to flight school instead.

I did not have the formal business school education Donald did, but I knew *not* having an education was a handicap. Instead, I focused a lot of time and money getting my financial education outside the traditional halls of learning. I attended many seminars, listened to many tapes and CDs, read business books, and made it a practice to teach what I learned… because teaching is one of the best ways to learn. I also learned by finding a mentor and becoming an apprentice, just as my rich dad was a mentor to me and I was an apprentice to him.

I took two companies public because I found two mentors who taught me the process. I invest heavily in oil and gas because I had training from Standard Oil of California and from a mentor who taught me about oil and gas syndications (how to raise money for oil and gas investments).

I continue my financial education via real-life experience and by having great mentors as well as great advisors.

Donald Trump and I would not be writing this book together if I had ever stopped my financial education. I love learning about money, business, finance, and wealth. I will probably be a student until the day I die. I do not think I will ever feel I know enough, or that my cup is full, or that I have all the answers. I can always learn more and love doing so.

Financial Experts

Many investors think investing is risky because they take financial advice from financial experts who have very little financial training or experience.

1. Do you realize that it takes more time to become a licensed massage therapist than it takes to become a financial advisor?

2. Do you know that less than 20 percent of all stockbrokers and real estate brokers invest in the product they recommend you invest in?

3. Do you know that most financial journalists have very little financial training or real-world investment experience?

4. Do you know how many people invest off of hot tips—hot tips from poor people, not rich people?

5. How many of our politicians and lawmakers have any real-world investment experience?

6. How many schoolteachers have any real-world financial training or experience?

Don't Be a Patsy

I once heard Warren Buffett say, "If you are sitting in a poker game and after 20 minutes you do not know who the patsy is…then you're the patsy."

My rich dad would say, "The reason why most E- and S-quadrant people suffer is because they take financial advice from other Es and Ss." Or, as Warren Buffett has said (and I've referenced earlier in this book), "Wall Street is the only place that people drive to in a Rolls Royce to take advice from people who ride the subway."

Choose Your Advice Carefully

Since your mind is your most valuable asset and your most valuable lever, you need to be careful about what you put in it. Sometimes it is even more difficult to get rid of thoughts and ideas that are already in your mind than it is to learn something new.

Many financial journalists disagree with my thought process—my ideas clash with their ideas. They ask, "You say you can invest without money.

Isn't that risky?"

"Well, duh! If I don't have any money in the project how can there be any risk?" is how I want to respond.

A few days ago, I was speaking about investing in silver coins on the radio. A caller got through and said, "I'm making 9 percent on my money in mutual funds. Why should I invest in silver?"

I wanted to say "Silver has gone up nearly a hundred percent in less than a year." But I didn't. Instead, I simply said, "I'm glad you're happy with a 9 percent return."

Many people think investing is risky because for people without financial education and experience, it really is risky…and it is even *riskier* when you turn your money over to a financial advisor who has only a little more education and experience than you have.

One of my pet peeves is when real estate salespeople say to buyers, "This property will appreciate in value." In other words, they mean, "Buy this now, even though it loses money, because in the future, it will make money. Real estate always goes up in value." I would want the buyer to ask, "Will you give me a money-back guarantee if I do not make money?" That usually dampens the sales pitch.

When it comes to investments, the questions you should ask are:

1. How do you minimize taxes?

2. How do you reduce risk and increase returns?

3. How do you find great investments?

4. How do you know a good deal from a bad deal?

5. How do you invest with less of your own money and more OPM (other people's money)?

6. How do you get the experience without risking money?

7. How do you handle losses?

8. How do you find good advisors?

I wish these questions could be answered easily. But they are questions without specific answers. They are questions that keep me studying, learning and searching. By continually asking myself these questions, I get better answers, but I have yet to find the one answer that makes me feel comfortable, safe and secure. These are questions true students know they will probably never find the *right* answer to—because there is always a better answer. We know we can always get better.

It is the search for the answer—the answer I may never find—that makes me rich. It is the search that keeps me going, getting richer and not retiring, even though I have the money to retire on. You see, it is not the quest for money that makes me rich. It is the quest for knowledge. It is the desire to learn more, do more, accomplish more and help those who want to learn that drives me…and money is just the score, a measure to tell me how we are doing. Money is the celebration of success, just as the lack of money is the reminder that we need to learn more. Just as a traveler watches for mile markers, I look at money simply as a marker—a marker that measures the journey and distance traveled.

Tiger Woods may appear to play for money because he has so much of it. Yet, if you ask him, he says he plays to master the game…and money is his measure of his mastery. I would guess that the Rolling Stones tour not because they love the money, but because they love to entertain. If they did not entertain, life for them might be over. Many an ex-football star would play the game for free, if he were young and healthy enough to just get back in the game.

A great book I read recently is *The War of Art* by Steven Pressfield. I recommend this book for anyone who knows that their life is a journey, not a destination. In *The War of Art*, Pressfield says, "Many people think amateurs do not play for money, but they play for the love of the game. In reality, the reason amateurs are amateurs is because they do not love the game enough." Pressfield's main point is that you must overcome resistance in order to achieve your "unlived life within." He discusses the types of *resistance* that confront us and reveals how often it is self-imposed. What is his advice?

He recommends:

1. Loving what you do

2. Having patience

3. Acting in the face of fear

I believe I win at the game of money because I love the game. When I was younger, I worked for free because I wanted to learn the game. Today, I go past golf courses and basketball courts and I see young and not-so-young people playing for free, often paying to play because they love the game so much.

I study and practice because I love the game and because I want to win. I have read and studied the history of the game, knowing I will never know as much as I need to know. I study the rules, and I study the players. I know my competition, and I study them because I respect them. Long before I met Donald Trump, I read his books and followed his successes as well as his failures. I also studied Steve Jobs, founder of Apple, and Richard Branson, founder of Virgin. As you can tell, I studied the rebel leaders of business, not the conformists. To me, conformists are boring.

> In *The War of Art,* Steven Pressfield says "Many people think amateurs do not play for money, but they play for the love of the game. In reality, the reason amateurs are amateurs is because they do not love the game enough."
>
> – *Robert T. Kiyosaki*

Like it or not, all of us are in this game of money. Regardless of whether you are rich or poor, living in the United States, Asia, Europe, Africa, South America, Canada or wherever, we are all in this game of money. The winners of the game are those who love the game the most. If you do not love the game, get out. There is probably something more useful for you to do, something more exciting for you.

Donald Trump and I win much more than we lose simply because we love the game. If you do not love the game and do not want to study and learn, Donald and I recommend you find someone who is as dedicated to winning (and dedicated to studying) and turn your money over to that person, once you have found him or her.

A Final Thought

PASSIVE INVESTORS	ACTIVE INVESTORS
Invest money	Invest time
Invest in: *A Job* *Savings* *Getting Out of Debt* *Mutual Funds* *Diversification*	Invest in: *Businesses* *Real Estate* *More Advanced Vehicles*
Lack of Money	Abundance of Money
Fear	Fun

This comparison shows that there are other differences that separate passive investors from active investors. Not only do they invest more time, they invest in different investment vehicles. I put businesses at the top of the list because building a business of more than 500 employees requires the most financial skill, education and experience.

Real estate is next, requiring more financial skill, education and experience than, let's say, stocks, bonds or mutual funds. Remember the big difference between investors in stocks, bonds and mutual funds and real estate investors is that real estate involves leverage. Therefore, you have to be more careful. And real estate also requires management skill, experience and expertise. It is the use of leverage and the requirement of extensive management that causes most investors in paper assets to fail when attempting to invest in real estate.

The more advanced investment vehicles are such things as hedge funds, which use leverage, as well as limited partnerships, private equity funding, syndications and others.

When you look at the picture of the game board of *CASHFLOW,* you can see the different investments for different people.

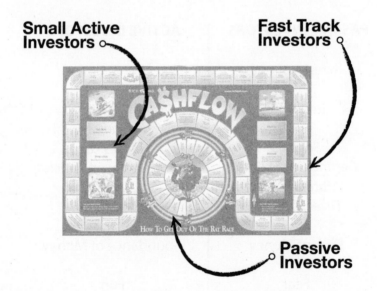

Small Active Investors

Fast Track Investors

Passive Investors

As you can tell, there are three levels of investors. Level one, the Rat Race, is for passive investors. They generally invest in paper assets such as stocks, bonds, and mutual funds. Why? Because paper assets, typically, require the least amount of financial education.

Level two is for small active investors. They invest in smaller investments, often in small businesses or real estate.

The fast track was created for the rich and financially educated investor. In 1933, Joseph Kennedy, father of President John Kennedy, created the Fast Track to protect the amateur investor from the rich and sophisticated investor.

Donald and I invest from the Fast Track. Why? Because that's where the fun is and that's where the high returns are. Is it riskier? The answer is "No," not if you have a strong financial education and experience. The answer is "Yes," if all you want to invest is money, but not time in your education.

The purpose of the *CASHFLOW* board game is to teach people about the three levels of investors and to inspire people to get out of the rat race and have more fun.

Are Games Good Teaching Tools?

In 1969, a study was completed within the education system that showed the effectiveness of different types of learning. The Cone of Learning was developed and is shown here. It reveals that the least effective way to learn is by reading and lecture, whereas the most effective way to learn is by actually doing. The next most effective method is through simulating the real experience.

Cone of Learning

After 2 weeks we tend to remember		Nature of Involvement
	Doing the Real Thing	
90% of what we say and do	Simulating the Real Experience	
	Doing a Dramatic Presentation	Active
70% of what we say	Giving a Talk	
	Participating in a Discussion	
	Seeing it Done on Location	
	Watching a Demonstration	
50% of what we hear and see	Looking at an Exhibit Watching a Demonstration	Passive
	Watching a Movie	
30% of what we see	Looking at Pictures	
20% of what we hear	Hearing Words (Lecture)	
10% of what we read	Reading	

Source: Cone of Learning adapted from Dale, (1969)

Isn't it interesting that the educational system still teaches primarily through reading and lecture? And it has been armed with The Cone of Learning since 1969!

Donald and I both believe in the power of games. In my game *CASHFLOW,* the players start with jobs and paychecks and have families. They learn investing skills by actually investing with play money, and they learn how each and every decision they make impacts their individual financial statements. It is learning through simulation that reduces the players' fear of investing.

Donald also has a board game called *TRUMP: The Game* that teaches negotiation skills related to real estate. Again, the players gain valuable experience and learn techniques that can help them in real-life or business applications.

Both games motivate the players and help them realize the importance of not letting emotion get in their way. Both games generate an adrenaline rush and excitement in the players.

Donald's View

I read Robert's chapter before I started mine, which is good because I had the same answers: time and money. He made such good points, and thoroughly explained points, that I'm wondering to myself, what can I add?

I'm not really into etymology, but recently it was discovered that the most used word in the English language is "time." "Money" may have been in the top 100, but it was nowhere near "time" in the ratings. Then I remembered how someone once explained life as a credit card that's given to us at birth—minus the expiration date. The time we have on that card becomes the big question, not the money.

The properties of time have always been of great interest to physicists and scientists. Time is measured by numbers. Which brings us to math. Which brings us to money. But if you've run out of time, all the money in the world won't change that situation.

My wife, Melania, and son Barron demonstrated perfect timing when it came to Barron's birth. I'd just returned to New York, we went to the hospital and he was born. Barron has displayed a very subdued temperament, which I think he got from his mother's side. But I still marvel at the timing of his birth.

> If something is going to affect your life, it's best to know as much as you can about it.
>
> – Donald J. Trump

We have no control over certain events, and yet sometimes they seem to be perfectly controlled.

I am never absolutely certain about anything—because I am not omniscient. I have instincts. And I have beliefs, but surprise is always a possibility. Because of that, I am far more humble than people might suspect. Oddly enough, I think I have been rewarded for that humility. It works that way sometimes.

Linda Kaplan Thaler is the CEO of the fastest growing advertising agency in the US, The Kaplan Thaler Group, and she appeared on *The Apprentice* to be a judge on one of the task assignments involving a car advertisement. Prior to that, Melania had been featured in a popular Aflac commercial and she mentioned how professional—and thoughtful—Linda and her team had been towards her and everyone on the set. In addition, the ad was very successful, and I was impressed enough to remember Linda when we had an opening for an advertising professional in one of our episodes. I am not surprised that her new book with Robin Koval, *The Power of Nice,* is becoming very successful. It is a powerful testament to the power of time invested wisely—by being courteous and thoughtful. Robert mentions that you should choose your advice carefully, and Linda's book would be a good choice for both time and money investment.

How does this apply to investing and finances? Actually, it applies to everything. What you do with your time is a very big subject, because lost time can never be recaptured. Very often, lost money can be regained. As Plutarch said, "Time is the wisest of all counselors." In short, be careful of your time and learn to invest it—thoughtfully.

This exercise will help to illustrate my point:

If you saw time as money, would you be more careful with it? For example, if wasting 15 minutes of your time meant you would lose $500, would you be more aware of how those 15 minutes were spent? I think so. And what would constitute "wasting" 15 minutes? If you were in the entertainment industry, watching a film would not be wasting your time. If you were in the hospitality industry, checking out a new restaurant would not be wasting your time or money. The answer would be different for each of us. I think we all know when we are squandering time.

The assignment for you is to see where you spend your time—and to assess how much money you've invested in doing so. All the money in the world cannot replace lost time, so proceed accordingly.

Another very good point of Robert's is that we are all affected by money, no matter who we are or where we live or what we do. Money, like time, is a common denominator we share. Most people need money to buy food, which is necessary to sustain life, so they are intertwined whether we choose to believe it or not.

Money will affect your life. My theory is that if something is going to affect your life, it's best to know as much as you can about it. Will you be able to find time to invest in your financial education?

Your View

Review how you spend your time.

There Are 168 Hours In A Week (7x24):

Hours spent working   _____

Hours spent commuting   _____

Hours spent getting ready   _____

Hours spent eating   _____

Hours spent sleeping   _____

Hours spent with family   _____

Hours spent on a hobby   _____

Hours spent exercising   _____

Hours spent getting educated   _____

Hours spent relaxing   _____

     Total   168 hours

Can you find 4 to 10 hours a week that you could spend on your financial education? Chances are you can. The question is: Will you?

Make a commitment to spend more time getting educated, and then do it! Reading this book is a good start. What else can you do?

CHAPTER TEN

WINNERS
TAKE CONTROL

Robert's View

Once you understand leverage, which is *the ability to do more with less,* you will probably begin to see leverage everywhere. For example, the chair I am sitting in is a form of leverage. It would be tough for me to sit on the ground and type with ease. Having partners is leverage. At The Rich Dad Company, I combine my talents with Kim's and the talents of our management team which gives me much more leverage than working on my own. Using strategic partners creates leverage and is often called OPR, other people's resources. We use a strategic partner to distribute our books so we do not have to build that capability inside Rich Dad. The important message is: Rich people use more leverage than poor people. If you want to be rich, you need leverage. If you want to be really rich, you need a lot of leverage.

In the CASHFLOW Quadrant, the E and S side of the quadrant usually has very little leverage. Both the E and the S quadrants involve you doing the work by yourself. The B and I side is nothing but leverage—other people's money and time.

Leverage can come in many forms. Leverage can be your thoughts. People who win are careful with their thoughts. They don't think to themselves, "I can't do that." Or, "It's too risky." Or, "I can't afford it." Instead, they think, "How can I do that?" Or, "How can I reduce my risk?" Or, "How can I afford it?" People who invest to win are also very careful about whom they take financial advice from. Just as Olympic athletes carefully choose which foods they put in their bodies, investors who invest to win need to carefully choose which advice they put in their heads. Sometimes, it may require clearing your mind of old thoughts. For much of my life, my mind staged a running battle between what my poor dad taught me about money and what my rich dad taught me about money.

The Power of Control

In addition to wanting leverage, investors who invest to win want *control*. People think investing is risky simply because they have no control.

I like business and real estate because I have control. I do not like paper assets such as stocks, bonds and mutual funds because I do not have control. Most people who think investing is risky invest in paper assets and have no control. Is that you?

Those of you who have seen my television show on PBS are familiar with the car metaphor I use. On the show, I have a mock-up of a car to demonstrate the importance of controls. On the car, I have:

1. Steering wheel
2. Brakes
3. Gas pedal
4. Gear shift
5. Driver's license
6. Insurance

Using the car as an example and a metaphor for investing, I ask the audience if they would drive a car without any one of these six factors. For example, if you got in a car and it did not have a steering wheel, would you drive the car?

Obviously, the answer is "No." Why? We all know: Because driving the car would be too risky without the control of a steering wheel.

Many people think investing is risky because they do not have control. And when you invest in mutual funds, stocks, bonds, or savings, you have almost zero control.

On top of that, most investors have no training, and to drive a car requires at least a license to prove the driver has had training and can drive.

What makes matters worse is that the investment advisors, financial planners and brokers have no control either, which may be why they recommend "diversify, diversify, diversify." Diversification is required when you do not have control. Warren Buffett does not diversify because he invests for control. He buys either all of the business or a controlling share of the business.

Donald and I love business and real estate because we have control. So what do we control? Most of the answer is found in the following diagram of a financial statement:

INCOME STATEMENT

Income
Expenses

BALANCE SHEET

Assets	Liabilities

As entrepreneurs and real estate investors, the six controls we want are:

1. Income
2. Expense
3. Asset
4. Liability
5. Management
6. Insurance

When we speak about financial education, we are speaking about education that gives you the knowledge about how to control these six factors. *Rich Dad Poor Dad* is about controlling these six items. For example, when it comes to insurance, I mention the importance of using corporate entities to protect personal assets from taxes and lawsuits.

It is control over these six factors that truly separates the rich from the poor.

Another example of control is the ability to increase sales and reduce expenses. Most people are pretty good at reducing expenses, but very few people are good at increasing sales. That is why, after returning from Vietnam in 1974, my rich dad recommended I get a job learning to sell. He said, "If you want to be an entrepreneur, you need to know how to sell." That's why I spent four years at the Xerox Corporation, learning to sell.

When people ask me what's the first thing they should do if they want to be an entrepreneur, I recommend they learn how to sell. Most do not take my recommendation. As Donald Trump says, some people are born natural salespeople and some aren't. Even if you aren't great in sales, you can learn…if you want to. I wasn't a natural salesperson, but I did learn. I am not a best-*writing* author, I am a best-*selling* author. It is my study of the subject of sales that allows me to have more control over the income from my investments and the number of books I sell. The world is filled with great authors with great messages; the problem is they don't know how to sell. The price of not being able to sell is a very high price to pay—a price greater than money.

Donald Trump and I recommend and support the network marketing or direct sales industry primarily because of the education aspect of the industry. Not only do most of these businesses focus on training people to be business owners, many of these businesses also have great personal development and sales-training programs. Select an organization for the education aspect more than for the compensation. This is another example of investing more in your education before investing your money.

If you cannot sell, you have very little control over your income, the income of your business or the income of your properties. Having the name "Trump" on a building not only increases sales, but also the price and value. That is sales power. That is control.

Teach To Be Rich

I created a product titled *Teach To Be Rich* for people who want more financial education in these six control areas. It is a product designed for CASHFLOW Clubs and it teaches the Rich Dad educational and philosophical content. *Teach To Be Rich* is comprised of two workbooks and three DVDs. The DVDs are included to reach people who prefer visual learning. The group leader can play the DVDs and lead a group discussion, supported by content from the two workbooks. In addition to going through the DVDs and workbooks, it is also recommended a person play the *CASHFLOW* games *101* and *202* to reinforce the lessons. This is the Cone of Learning in action. By having group discussions and playing the game, you increase your retention of the material—locking in the lesson. More importantly, it prepares you for the real world of investing, entering that world with more time invested in learning... before you invest your money.

> Leverage can come in many forms. Leverage can be your thoughts. People who win are careful with their thoughts, not saying "I can't do that." Or "It's too risky." Or "I can't afford it." Instead they say, "How can I do that?" Or "How can I reduce my risk?" or "How can I afford it?
>
> – *Robert T. Kiyosaki*

You can learn to control your investments through education. If you have control, your risk will go down and your returns on investments will go up.

No Control

Many people feel powerless because they do not have control over their jobs. I have met many people who lost their jobs—not because they were bad employees, but because their companies were sold and they were fired. With so many jobs going overseas today, more and more people are feeling out of control. It's tough to feel confident when you have very little control over both your job and your salary and you invest in assets such as savings, stocks, bonds, and mutual funds—assets you have no control over.

If our education system was doing its job, it would be teaching young people about the difference between learning to take control and learning to go through life without control.

In summary, there are three reasons why most people think investing is risky. They are:

1. They have very little financial education.

2. They invest in investments where they have no control—investments such as savings, stocks, bonds, and mutual funds.

3. They take investment advice from salespeople, who also have no control over the investment.

Step two is control. Once you understand what you are going to leverage, your next task is to make sure you have control.

Donald's View

Winners Take Control

I love real estate and businesses because I want control. Control is all about education. The more financially educated we become the more control we have.

I have a lot of interests as a businessman, and I retain control by keeping an active interest in *all* of them. I hire qualified people and trust they will do their best, but I make sure to keep in touch with them and keep my door open to them. I don't micromanage, but I know that, ultimately, the responsibility is mine. Knowing that the responsibility is mine means that I am in control—period.

The Trump Organization is the number-one privately held company in New York. I'm proud of that and of the work we have done. Notice I said "we"—because a lot of us work very hard, and I know that. But I make sure we remain winners by setting the standard myself.

Life is full of risk. We don't have total control—much as we'd like to think we do. But we can reduce the risk and increase our leverage by becoming educated, making moderate choices and keeping a positive attitude. A lot of people have been great successes when the supposed "odds" were entirely against them. They won because they decided to take control of their destiny and refused to give up.

One way to maintain control is to always keep the big picture in mind. When people talk about the big picture, I am often reminded of a tapestry. Someone once told me that if you look at the back of a beautiful and priceless tapestry, all you will see is a bunch of knots. Well, sometimes that's all people will see because they haven't seen the finished design on the other side yet. Destiny sometimes works that way, so don't give up control by leaving your own tapestry—the design of your life—unfinished.

Soon after I heard that analogy, someone said they were "in knots" about something, and I suddenly just saw that the guy wasn't visualizing his tapestry. He was losing sight of the big picture. When I told him the story, he became visibly more relaxed. Look at things from the other side sometimes. It will help you maintain control, giving you insight into how to deal with problems and people. You have to be able to control what is around you, at least to the extent that you aren't left in knots.

> Brainpower is the ultimate leverage.
>
> – Donald J. Trump

Some synonyms for control to think about are command, mastery, authority, dominion and determination. You may not have control over a lot of things, but you can start with yourself. Brainpower is the ultimate leverage. You've got a brain; use it. Call me a control freak, but I don't accept excuses. Winners take control by accepting responsibility.

Your View

Review your life today. Are you able to choose how you spend your day, or are you told how to spend your day? Do you direct how your money is invested, or do you leave it up to someone else?

What are you in control of?

_____

_____

What are you *not* in control of?

_____

_____

Just by becoming more active in your financial education and your investments, you will find yourself feeling more in control of your life.

If you are an employee and feel out of control, consider what you can do on a part-time basis (i.e. start a part-time business) to change that. You will be amazed at how quickly your confidence increases, just from feeling more in control of your life.

CHAPTER ELEVEN

RIGHT-BRAIN AND LEFT-BRAIN CREATIVITY

Robert's View

In an overly simplified explanation, the left-brain (the left hemisphere of the brain) is generally associated with linear thinking or logic. People who are good with reading and math are generally considered left-brain dominant. The right-brain (the right hemisphere of the brain) is more spatially oriented. People who are good with art, music and color are more right-brain dominant. In reality, it takes both sides to function, but you get the idea.

For many years, I have studied the subject of education and how we learn. Do you know that when we are born, we have an undivided brain? It is not until we are four or five years old that our brains have split into two hemispheres—a right side and a left side. Our current educational system caters to those that are more left-brain than right-brain dominant.

A Flash of Genius

Winston Churchill, as a child, would report a sudden flash in his brain that stunned him. He would sit quietly for a moment, and then he could explain what he had experienced. Researchers guess that the flash of intuition took place in the right-brain and then traveled across a part of the brain known as the corpus callosum into the left-brain. Since speech is associated with the left-brain, the theory was that the flash of genius went off in the right-brain and took time to travel to the left-brain, eventually allowing Churchill to speak about this bit of intuitive knowledge. Could this

> It requires both sides of your brain to be successful.
>
> Taking control and being creative requires both financial education and experience.
>
> – Robert T. Kiyosaki

be the way that God, or our maker, delivers new information to us as a species? Could this be the theory behind the term "brainstorm"?

As a society, we tend to think of left-brained people as smart and right-brained people as flakey. We tend to value people who are left-brained more than right-brained, typically by paying them more. That is why accountants, attorneys, doctors, dentists and MBAs are generally paid more in corporate America.

If, as a society, we have tended to assign more financial value to people who are left-brain dominant than those who are right-brain dominant, that trend may be changing. In his book, *A Whole New Mind*, Daniel Pink writes about the shift in value today away from left-brain people to right-brain people. He states:

> *"The future belongs to a very different kind of person with a very different kind of mind—creators and empathizers, pattern recognizers and meaning makers. These people…will now reap society's richest rewards and share its greatest joys."*

Creativity Makes You Rich

Understanding the functions of the left-brain and the right-brain is important because creativity has the power to make us very rich.

I find it interesting that the investments most people invest in—investments such as savings, stocks, bonds, and mutual funds—do not require creativity. In fact, as an ordinary investor, if you try to get creative with these investments, you might wind up in jail. The federal government, through agencies such as the Securities and Exchange Commission (SEC), becomes the watchdog against any kind of creativity. The SEC watches over the people selling these investments—people such as bankers, stockbrokers and financial planners—to make sure its rules are followed.

In many ways, investments such as savings, stocks, bonds, and mutual funds are perfect for left-brain people.

Real estate and businesses, on the other hand, are ideal for right-brain people. In fact, the more creative you are, the better your chances of becoming rich. Let me give you a few examples of creativity.

1. If I were to save money or invest in bonds, it would be the bank that sets the interest rate. In real estate, there are many times I determine the amount of interest I can collect.

2. When it comes to income, I can increase or decrease my income with real estate or business as I see fit. With stocks, bonds, and mutual funds, other people determine how much income I earn.

3. When it comes to taxes, if I were to sell paper assets, I would have very little control over taxes. With real estate and business, I can control when I pay my taxes, if ever, and how much I pay. The tax laws are written to support re-investment into one's business or real estate.

4. I can change the use of a property asset. For example, if I look at 10 acres of land as a farmer, I might be willing to pay $1,000 per acre. If I look at the same 10 acres of land as a developer, I can change the zoning, which would make that same piece of land worth $10,000 per acre.

5. I can use my connections and "inside information" to trade a piece of property or a small business. If I use such "inside information" to trade a security, it may be illegal.

6. I can take a bad piece of property, add some decorative touches, such as paint, and increase the value of the property.

And the list goes on and on. How much you make and how you do it is only limited by your creativity when you have control over your business or your real estate.

In business, I can hire and fire the management. If a stock or mutual fund has a bad management team, all I would be able to do is sell the stock or fund and look for one with better management.

1. In business, I can change my business model.

2. In business, we can create new brands.

As I said, the list goes on and on.

In reality, it requires both sides of your brain to be successful. It takes the combination of the left-brain (for the words and math skills) and the right-brain (for the creativity) to succeed.

Taking control and being creative requires financial education and experience. You may notice that Donald Trump is very creative and he has control—both of which contribute to his success. Once you have control, get creative.

Donald's View

Flashes

Robert's comments about control and creativity reminded me of something that may seem like one of those flashes he was talking about. In this case it's a memory flash, but I think it's worth mentioning. Earlier in this book Robert described his visits to my offices in Trump Tower, and one thing I haven't mentioned is how *his* offices are set up: They epitomize control and creativity. I'm not talking about his home office, which has a pool nearby and a well-stocked private library off to his left elbow, but his business offices in Scottsdale, Arizona.

When I think about the design of the Rich Dad offices, it's very clear to me why Robert's books and his many other endeavors have been so vastly successful—he has creative control. His offices in Scottsdale are completely functional, contain an audio and visual studio, and are very compact in comparison to the scope of business generated from them. I immediately knew that Robert and his team knew what they were doing. In short, if you know what you're doing, you don't need a lot of space to do it in.

Likewise, when people visit my core office at The Trump Organization, they are always surprised by how small it actually is. We generate a lot of activity from here because we don't have unnecessary energy sappers like overstaffing, overstuffing or unused space. Everyone knows what they're doing, and they do it. I know my name is synonymous with luxury, but that's because we know how to work to achieve it to begin with. It's hard to be creative when things are too big to control, and it's hard to control that which gets out of hand.

Robert also mentions that creativity makes you rich. Absolutely right! And here's another reason for that: Creative people don't need to be motivated by anyone else. They motivate themselves. They listen to and use both sides of their brains for maximum potential. They *find* inspiration instead of waiting for it. And they use their brains in the biggest way possible.

A few years ago there was an article about the most desired recruits for medical school: music majors. The reason is that their left and right brains are equally developed because music is mathematical and creative at the same time. It also requires discipline and long hours of practice—a great combination of attributes for med school students.

Creativity is also related to intuition, something I believe in. Some things are just inexplicable, but the creative mind can grasp them and put them into tangible form. When I'm working on a project, I am very focused, but I am also open to new ideas and inspiration that might come along. Sometimes I'm not exactly sure why something isn't right, but I'll know something isn't right. For example, when I was building Trump Tower, I had people telling me that the lobby should have paintings on the walls. I love paintings, but to me that seemed old fashioned. I wanted something more original. I had a dramatic atrium space and I wanted a waterfall. It's nearly 80 feet tall and cost $2 million to build, but it's fantastic. It suits the space.

Innovative thinking can have superb results. When I bought Mar-a-Lago in Palm Beach, it was a private residence. It had belonged to Marjorie Merriweather Post, and it was more like a Venetian palazzo than anything else. It was a masterpiece. It was also huge, having 118 rooms and set on twenty acres facing the Atlantic Ocean and Lake Worth. I restored it to its original grandeur and realized it would serve a greater public purpose as a

> Creativity and control
> can go hand in hand.
>
> – *Donald J. Trump*

club, and now The Mar-a-Lago Club is a thriving addition to the living history of Palm Beach. Those of you who have homes will know how expensive the upkeep of a 118-room home would be, so you can see the financial advantages of turning this into a membership club. But it has remained my second home and I treat it that way—and that's another reason for its huge success. It has to be perfectly maintained and every detail remains important to me.

Creativity and control can go hand in hand, and for the best results, that's how it should be. So start listening to both sides of your brain and you'll start seeing some results.

Your View

Are you creative? Earlier in the book, we talked about problem-solving. When you solve a problem, you are being creative—you are creating the solution.

Have you ever had a great idea? Of course you have!

Have you ever made money from your great idea?

If so, congratulations! Keep it up.

If not, think of how you can take your great idea and *leverage* it while you keep *control* over it!

How have you used creativity to solve a problem or challenge?

CHAPTER TWELVE

THINK BIG— THINK EXPANSION

Robert's View

One of Donald Trump's signature trademarks is the talk he gives on "Thinking Big." He definitely practices what he preaches. If you have any doubt about his ability to think big, all you need to do is go to New York City and count the number of skyscrapers with his name on them.

I have had the privilege of listening to his talk on thinking big, and each time he throws in something new and expands my own thinking. If you ever have the chance to hear his "Think Big" talk, grab the opportunity. If you can hear it more than once, keep taking the opportunity.

Even though my rich dad did not talk about "thinking big," he taught us the same concept. Instead, the words he often used were "leverage" and "expansion." When he taught his son and me to think about the differences between leverage and expansion, he used the McDonald's franchise as a teaching example. He would say, "When Ray Kroc bought McDonald's from the McDonald brothers, he leveraged himself. When he franchised McDonald's, he expanded his leverage."

When Ray Kroc purchased the hamburger stand, he leveraged himself because the burger business could make money with or without him. And this is where most S-quadrant business owners stop, keeping their businesses small. When Ray Kroc developed a franchise system for the small business, he expanded the hamburger business into the B quadrant.

You may notice I used the words "franchise system," the key word being *system*. In *Before You Quit Your Job*, written for entrepreneurs, I write extensively about the B-I Triangle. The B-I Triangle is the diagram my rich dad used to focus my thinking and to teach me about the eight parts, or 8 Integrities, that make up a business:

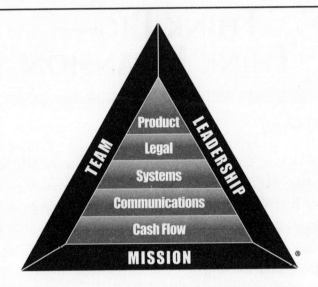

Statistics show that 9 out of 10 startup businesses fail in the first five years. And of the one that survives, again 9 out of 10 of the survivors fail by the tenth year. (Again, notice the 90/10 rule.)

Many entrepreneurs fail simply because one or more of the eight pieces of the B-I Triangle is weak or nonexistent. Whenever I look at a struggling business, I use the B-I Triangle as an analytical reference.

Notice that the word *product* is used to label the smallest section and the word *mission* is one of the largest sections—and the foundation for the Triangle. This is because the product is the least important item of the B-I Triangle and the mission is the most important. Too many times, I meet a wanna-be entrepreneur who says to me, "I have an idea for a great new product."

I often respond by asking, "So, what is your mission?"

More often than not, the reply is, "Well, to make money." In most instances, the business has little chance of survival.

The mission is the most important part of the business. It is the spirit of the business. It is the heart of the business. Without spirit and heart, most entrepreneurs will not make it, simply because the road ahead is a hard one.

The world is filled with great products that fail. The products fail simply because they do not have the power of the B-I Triangle behind them.

When you study most successful businesses, you will most likely find a complete and vibrant B-I Triangle in action. A great business will have a strong mission, great leadership, a competent team of managers who work well together, excellent cash flow and financing, clear and effective sales and marketing communications, systems that work efficiently, clear and tight legal documents and agreements, and, of course, a great product.

Most of us can cook a better hamburger than McDonald's. But few of us can build a better business system than McDonald's. Which brings us to the word *systems* again. One of the biggest differences between an S-quadrant business owner and a B-quadrant business owner is systems. Typically, the S-quadrant business owner is the system, which is why he or she cannot expand.

Too many businesses are *people-dependent*. McDonald's is *system-dependent*. It has well-designed systems. Regardless of where you go in the world, the McDonald's business is pretty uniform. Most importantly, their business systems are often run primarily by people with just a high school education. That is how good, how sound, their systems are.

> The mission is the most important part of the business. It is the spirit of the business. It is the heart of the business. Without spirit and heart, most entrepreneurs will not make it, simply because the road ahead is a hard one.
>
> – Robert T. Kiyosaki

I have looked at so many businesses that are top-heavy, staffed by highly educated and highly paid people who are working hard and accomplishing little. In most cases, these types of businesses focus primarily on people and not on developing great systems. A great team of highly paid people will fail without great systems.

What is the difference between an entrepreneur and a CEO? Making it as simple as possible, an entrepreneur is like a person who builds great race cars. A CEO is like the driver of the race car. If you have a great race-car driver, but a poorly built race car, the great CEO will lose every race. Rarely, you will find entrepreneurs who are great CEOs. Donald Trump is one of those people. So are Bill Gates, Michael Dell, and Steve Jobs. These men can build great race cars and drive them.

In Summary

I have met many people who have become very rich in the S quadrant. Many are small-business owners who are excellent builders and drivers of small businesses. There are also Es and Ss who become very rich attaching themselves to B-quadrant businesses. For example, Tiger Woods is an S (and in his case, S stands for superstar as well as self-employed or specialist), but much of his wealth comes from his endorsements of B-quadrant businesses. The same is true with some movie stars. They are in the S quadrant, but associate with B-quadrant businesses such as Sony or Warner Bros.

Donald says, "think big," and he builds giant buildings and megahit television shows. My rich dad said to expand, and he meant expanding the way McDonald's did. Both are forms of thinking big and expanding.

Are you beginning to understand why the 90/10 rule of money works? The 10 percent who make 90 percent of the money do the things that 90 percent of the other people do not do.

Donald's View

Think Expansively

Robert's explanation of "Think Big, Think Expansion" is great and totally on point. But let's take it one step further. Let's not just think big, let's think expansively. To entrepreneurs, thinking expansively includes seeing what is possible and making it happen. Entrepreneurs see the vision and call it good sense and inevitable. The rest of the world calls it innovation.

Recently, I read with interest about an innovation that was attributed to me. I was surprised, because I had never thought of it as an innovation, just a way to combine two elements that might work well together. Years ago when I was doing the first Trump International Hotel a Tower at 1 Central Park West, which was the former Gulf Western Building that had run into some problems, I decided it might be a good idea to do a condominium and hotel together. It turned out to be an amazing success and has been duplicated since, by me and many others.

So many times, innovation really results from common sense put together with uncommon thinking. It's creative, but it's about innovative assembly more than anything else.

I was reading about the young American composer, Jonathan Dawe, who has attracted attention with his innovations. James Levine, the famed conductor of the Metropolitan Opera, discovered some of his work and premiered it this year. It turns out that Dawe likes early Renaissance music, and he found a way to combine it with fractal geometry, and he came up with something new out of something old. His ingenuity comes from a 'collision of influences,' the same thing to which I attribute my success with the hotel and tower concept I decided to try. It may seem like a stretch to compare classical composition with real estate development, but if you spend more time analyzing this, you'll find that there's more in common than you might think.

Someone once said that my life bordered on the operatic. I thought that was an unusual analogy so I decided to find out more about opera. As were many things, opera actually began in Greece and was then taken up much later in Florence, with the first opera being performed in Venice. Considering the sound level in my office sometimes—and since I don't use intercoms—I can relate to opera in that sense. And since I've studied the Greeks, I can get that part too. So I figure when the Greek influence intersected with the music being written in the 17th century in Italy, this art form was bound to happen. Some things take centuries to evolve. I'm still evolving, so I'm pleased to be considered operatic, although sitting through an opera is something I just can't do. It just can't compete with baseball in my book. But I've always believed that you can respect something without having to embrace it.

Beethoven was another groundbreaker. He blew people away when he decided to add voices to his massive 9th Symphony. We all know the "Ode to Joy" at this point, and can't imagine this work without it, but back then it was considered to be innovative. It was a sensation. And it didn't happen overnight—he made sketches for this symphony in 1811 and the work premiered in 1824. Those ideas were developing for 13 years. I would say Beethoven had been thinking big for awhile.

Thinking expansively is just another way to innovate. Sometimes I ask myself, what else can I include in my thought process to make it more comprehensive? Is there anything I can add that might enhance the project or idea I've got spinning around in my head? Many times I will tell myself that something isn't quite right yet—because that automatically opens the door for more ideas to surface and enter in. I ask myself, "What am I not seeing? What else is possible?" Sometimes the answers wind up being innovative ideas. It's not necessarily some secret process, but it is a process, and it requires concentration.

> Thinking expansively includes seeing what is possible and making it happen.
>
> – Donald J. Trump

Robert and Kim visited me at my golf course in California.

I shared another chair story with them. My club has a beautiful ballroom, overlooking the Pacific Ocean and the number-one golf course in California, but the club held less than 300 people. We were unable to accommodate many events (such as weddings) because our capacity was too small, so my management team's answer was to enlarge the building. They came to me with plans to remodel and expand the ballroom, which would take millions of dollars and lots of time. We would have had to go through the permitting process and close for many months during construction, thus losing millions of dollars in business revenue—on top of spending millions of dollars to remodel.

As we were standing together looking around the ballroom, I noticed a woman having trouble getting out of her chair. The chair was very large, and she had trouble moving it away from the table so she could stand up. In fact, the room was filled with these huge chairs. I had an immediate vision: We needed new chairs—smaller chairs!

This one idea not only saved me millions of dollars, it even made me money. We made more money on selling the old chairs than it cost me to buy the new gold Chivari chairs. We are now able to seat more than 440 people, comfortably, and have increased the number of larger events we host as well as the revenue we receive. No expansion of the building was necessary and we had no downtime. So I turned what could have cost me millions into a profit!

That's the first step to visionary status—seeing something and knowing it could be different or better.

As I've said before, learn your lessons from as many sources as you can. Think and learn expansively. It won't be expensive, but it can give you some big returns.

Your View

Think creatively—and then leverage that creativity.

Are you comfortable in the world you live in? Try imagining expanding your world to include new adventures, new friends and new places. As you expose yourself to new experiences, you will generate new ideas. You will see new problems that you can find solutions to. And you will see how to use those solutions in many ways to serve many other people.

This all comes from expanding your world and your vision.

Think and live bigger!

Putting aside any fear of risk, what do you envision?

_____

What is one area in your life where you could think bigger? Name that big thought:

_____

What is one area in your life where you could think expansively? Name that expansive thought:

_____

What are you going to do about it?

_____

Chapter Thirteen

Getting Very Rich Is Predictable…Not Risky

Robert's View

Before going further, let's quickly review the process:

1. Me/You

2. Leverage

3. Control

4. Creativity

5. Expansion

Many people today are in financial trouble or not getting ahead simply because they never get beyond the "Me/You." People, some highly educated, go through life working hard, but without much leverage. They never harness or implement any power beyond themselves.

These people have little or no control over their jobs, how much they earn or their investments. Many are not allowed to express their creativity in their work or in their investments. They simply do as they're told, professionally and financially. And when it comes to expanding, all they know how to do is get another job, look for a second job or hope for a promotion or a raise.

Many people get caught in this cycle because that is what they were taught to do in school. To do anything else would be risky. They are afraid of losing the little control they have. They work for less because they fear they may get fired if they ask for a raise. They conform rather than be creative because they fear making waves or trying something that might fail. When they invest, many simply turn their money over to someone they hope is an expert and learn little to nothing for themselves. They are trapped by their own doubts, fears and limited knowledge of business and money. They live in fear of taking risks and think much of life is risky.

Many investment advisors, financial journalists and salespeople prey on such individuals' fear of risk, selling them the riskiest investments of all. They actually believe that saving money is safe and investing for the long term in mutual funds is safe...not risky.

To make matters worse, many of these same people (as well as their "financial experts") think that what Donald Trump, Warren Buffett, and I do is risky. Nothing could be further from the truth. Donald Trump and Warren Buffett make a lot of money simply because they know that the end-result of their endeavor is *predictable*—the opposite of risky.

Getting Rich Is Predictable

Besides using McDonald's as an example, my rich dad used an apple grower to explain predictability. He told me the story of an apple grower who started with one acre of apple trees. "Planting that first acre," my rich dad said, "was hard. The farmer did not have much money, and the apple trees needed time to grow. After a few years, apples appeared, and the farmer sold them. With his profits, he bought two more acres and planted more trees. Soon he had over a hundred acres of apple trees, all producing apples. It started slowly, but he knew if he kept doing what he was doing, he would soon be a very rich man." Though this example was a very simple one, it served me well.

"Yes, but what about bugs or drought?" some might ask. It's a valid question...and successful business owners don't count on everything going perfectly. For example, all store owners know that there will be theft by both customers and employees. A successful business will factor in reserves for these losses in their projections and build systems to control and minimize those losses.

Now I hear some cynics saying, "Yes, but if you plant too many trees and produce too many apples, the price of apples will come down." Yes, this is true. Bringing prices down is the object of competitive capitalism. Without competitive capitalism, we would not enjoy a higher standard of living at an affordable price.

My point is, once you understand predictability, you will see it everywhere. You can see it every time you pass a McDonald's. You can see predictability every time you see a pair of Levi's jeans. When you drive up to a gas station to fill your car with gas, it is predictability in action. You see it even playing *Monopoly*®. If you recall, one house pays you so much. If you add two houses, you earn more, and if you convert four houses into a red hotel, you earn even more. Once you understand predictability, you will see it everywhere. And wherever you see predictability, you will understand why someone or some business is making a lot of money without much risk.

Now you may better understand why I become frustrated when I hear people say, "Investing is so risky." Or when I hear a financial planner tell someone that the safe thing to do is invest in savings and mutual funds. To me, it just shows a lack of financial training and a low financial IQ.

Donald Trump makes his billions not by building just one building; he builds many buildings or he builds a building with hundreds of condominiums in it and sells them. His formula for success fits the formula I just described. He leverages, controls, creates, expands, and predicts. While there is always some risk, he has confidence in his projects because he is in control of the process.

When I invest, I go through the same process. For example, when I buy a building, I am confident that I will receive the following four types of income:

1. Rental income

2. Depreciation income (aka phantom cash flow)

3. Amortization (my tenant pays off my loan)

4. Appreciation (the dollar is dropping in value)

> Many people are
> trapped by their own doubts,
> fears, and limited knowledge
> of business and money.
>
> – *Robert T. Kiyosaki*

I put appreciation last because it is the least important of all the incomes. Yet, for most investors, appreciation (capital gains) is the only income they are going after when they invest. For example, when someone buys a stock for $5 and holds it until it gets to $12 to sell it, he or she is selling for appreciation or capital gains. The same is true for people who flip real estate.

I put appreciation last also because it is taxed income, capital gains. The one blessing real estate has is the 1031 exchange, which lets the investor defer the tax on capital gains—sometimes forever, if you plan well. To me, this ability to avoid capital gains makes real estate a far superior investment compared to paper assets such as stocks, bonds, mutual funds and especially savings. If you would like to know more about why real estate is legally the best investment of all, you may want to get *Loopholes of Real Estate,* written by Garrett Sutton, an attorney and Rich Dad's Advisor.

Again, I stress that this example of real estate and paying less in taxes is completely predictable.

In 1996, the year I came out of retirement, I created my board game *CASHFLOW* and wrote *Rich Dad Poor Dad.* I had no idea how successful The Rich Dad Company would become. Having the right team is the best form of leverage. In the same year, I also started an oil company, a gold-mining company and a silver-mining company. While the oil company failed, the mining companies went on to become public companies via IPOs and a merger. The companies are listed on the Canadian Stock Exchanges. Both companies have made me millions of dollars.

Many people said starting oil, gold and silver-mining companies was risky. While there *was* some risk, to me it was very little. I could mitigate the risk simply because I know we all use—consume—oil and gas. That is predictable.

I also knew that gold and silver would go up in value. How did I know? Because I knew the politicians running our country would not stop spending, would not stop borrowing and would not stop printing money. So, in this case, it was not gold and silver that were predictable. It was the financial incompetence of our political leaders that was predictable. They do not solve problems. They simply push the problem forward and make the problem bigger. Their behavior is predictable. And that is regardless of whether they are republican or democrat.

In Conclusion

Improving your financial education allows you to get to the place where becoming rich is predictable. Once a person has the education and the experience and understands leverage, control, creativity, expandability, and predictability, life will look different—at least it did for me.

As a child, my rich dad had me play *Monopoly* over and over again. As I played, I was learning and understanding the power of leverage, control, creativity, expandability and predictability. Suddenly, one day, after playing the game at least a thousand times, my mind caught a glimpse of the future—a future of great wealth. I believe I was about 15 at the time, and that created a problem. Once I could see a different world, I could no longer buy into the idea of life being risky, the need for job security and a company or the government taking care of me. The moment I saw a different future, I no longer saw life as risky, but as exciting instead, and that has made a world of difference in my life.

Donald's View

The rich get richer, in most cases, because it's easier to invest when you have the money to invest to begin with. You can still make mistakes and lose money, but the odds are that if you are rich and are a serious investor, you will make money.

That's not a risky scenario. Being prepared for what you're doing brings the risk factor down in investing. But bringing down the fear factor should not be left to investment advisors—you should learn enough on your own first, so that you will not be at their mercy for "good advice." If you want to be foolproof, do the proofing yourself.

There are some great financial advisors who have made fortunes for themselves as well as other people because they know what they're doing. They have learned the world of finance well enough to excel and be on target when it comes to predicting trends. What they do will have a limited risk factor because of their experience and expertise.

The reason this chapter title says *getting very rich is predictable* is because the *very rich* part indicates that you already have money with which to work. The deciding factor is whether or not you're going to let your money work for you to become *very rich*. Those who know how to do that stand a very good chance of joining the leagues of the über-rich.

When I build a new building, I definitely look into the risk factor, which to me is whether or not it will be profitable. I don›t like taking huge risks, especially when I can do some of the predicting in my head first. When I first decided to try the hotel-condo mixed-use idea, I could already see how the combination could prove to have a comfort zone attached, as in, owners of the condos could also participate in the success of the hotel. I knew this would have a huge appeal to investors and owners because I did the math, and I knew that idea would appeal to me as a businessperson, whether I was the builder or the investor. My risk factor and their risk factor had been lowered. It became more predictable, but I will admit that I was surprised how successful the idea became.

My father always emphasized that certain things are predictable, namely that intelligent work will result in intelligent results. He was a hard worker and he always said it saved time to work intelligently from the beginning. I began, at an early age, to learn to assess things in my mind first, before going off to see if they might work. That took a lot of the guesswork out of the process, and therefore a lot of the risk. It also saved me a lot of time and money.

> The biggest risk we all face is not moving forward with what we've learned.
>
> – Donald J. Trump

The leverage I had was a knowledge of construction and the good fortune of good instincts. I'd also studied real estate for many years. Years ago, when I decided I was fed up with New York City wasting years and many millions of dollars trying to rebuild Wollman Rink in Central Park, I predicted how long it would take me to do it and how much it would cost. I turned out to be right: I had it done in a few months and at $750,000 under budget. To me, that was predictable, and doing it was not a risk. It was watching it never getting done that was a risk to my health.

Becoming *very* successful can also be predictable—especially if one will take the occasional risk. I had to be convinced to do *The Apprentice* by Mark Burnett. Having my own reality show was new territory for me, and the odds for new shows are not the kind I normally like too much: 95 percent of all new television shows fail. I was already successful, but after *The Apprentice* became a hit, I was even more successful. The goods were there, which stood in my favor. The same thing applies to money.

It's true what Robert says about leverage, control, creativity, expansion, and prediction. Being multidimensional and alert on all those levels can be exciting and will produce results. If people think that's risky, so be it. To me, it's a great and exciting challenge. You can change your world if you want to, and by doing so, you might be making a great contribution to the world at large. That's worth thinking about.

The biggest risk we all face is not moving forward with what we've learned. Expansion has many dimensions. I'll conclude with some advice from Abraham Lincoln: "I don't think much of a man who is not wiser today than he was yesterday."

That's a good incentive to pay attention and apply what you've learned on a daily basis. If you do, my prediction is that you will be meeting with success before too long.

Your View

Getting rich is predictable.

Remember how we said Einstein defined insanity as "doing the same thing over and over again and expecting different results." For you to become rich, or richer, you may need to change what you are doing. Make a commitment to yourself (you are the only one who matters in this exercise) to change three things that you are currently doing. Include an action as well as a time frame to hold yourself accountable:

_____

_____

_____

Example 1:

I am going to stop watching TV one night a week and start looking for seminars to attend instead.

Example 2:

I am going to stop being a couch potato and visit a business broker this week and research what businesses I might be interested in.

PART THREE

DEFINING MOMENTS:
GOING BEYOND WINNING AND LOSING

The formula:

Leverage

Control

Creativity

Expansion

Predictability

This step-by-step process is one of the basic formulas for attaining great wealth. If you have studied the stories of great entrepreneurs or investors, you will probably find a similar pattern or process. Even Warren Buffett uses a similar thought process when deciding which company he will or will not buy. In Mr. Buffett's case, instead of *creativity,* the word *analysis* should be put in its place. Warren Buffett's genius is in analyzing businesses and being able to see the current and future value of the business, which is why when he buys a business, he rarely sells it. Donald Trump is very creative. He can see a golden skyscraper where others will only see a piece of vacant land or a run-down old building.

Today, many investors buy an asset only to sell it. They want to buy low and sell high. They invest for capital gains. In the stock market, this type of investor is known as a trader. In real estate, when a person buys to sell, he or she is known as a flipper.

A true investor buys to own the investment and pass it on for generations. While both Donald Trump and Robert Kiyosaki occasionally buy to sell, as do many professional investors, they invest following the above formula. It is the formula that creates and allows the 10 percent of investors to make 90 percent of the money.

The formula may appear simple, but it is not easy to turn it into reality. Most people do not attempt the process dictated by the formula simply because they do not know this formula exists. Most people have no idea what makes some rich people richer than other rich people.

Some of the people who know of the formula have attempted to follow the formula and failed. Most of us know of a person who was riding high one day and flat broke the next. For some reason, the formula eludes them for the rest of their lives.

And for some people, this formula is their life. This formula is their game. It is always a challenge. It is their fun, their excitement. It can almost be their reason for living—to master the formula. It is generally these people who become the 10 percent that earn the 90 percent of the money.

In this section of the book, you will find insights into why Donald and Robert love this game and win at this game. These insights are important because, as we said, the step-by-step process is simple, but it is not easy.

This section is not about the *how-to* of making money. This section is about the *why*. After finishing this section, you will be clearer *why* 10 percent of the people make 90 percent of the money. More people fail than succeed. And, to repeat a basic but key factor: While the process is a simple one, it's not easy.

This section is about defining moments, the point in a person's life when he or she makes a life-changing decision. We all have such moments. It is in these moments that we find our true character. We become heroes or cowards; we become truth-tellers or liars; we go forward or we go backward.

Most of us have heard about the Three Ds:

1. Desire
2. Drive
3. Discipline

Weallknowpeoplewhohavedesire—forexampleadesiretoberich, but they lack either the drive or the discipline or both.

Most of us have heard about the Triple As:

1. Ambition
2. Ability
3. Attitude

We all know people who have ambition, but they never develop their abilities—often because they have a bad attitude.

Most of us have heard about the Triple Es:

1. Education
2. Experience
3. Execution

We all know people who have great educations but lack real-world experience. When they lack real-world experience, they often are unable to *execute*—perform, get things done in a timely manner, produce results—in the real world.

And most of us have heard of the Four Hs:

1. Honor
2. Humility
3. Humor
4. Happiness

We all know people who are successful, but attained success without honor. And we all know people who are successful, but lack humility. We also know people who do not have a sense of humor—

they have lost their ability to laugh at themselves. And we all know people who are successful, but not happy.

As you read about Donald's and Robert's defining moments, you may want to make a mental note of how many of the traits expressed in the Three Ds, Triple As, Triple Es and Four Hs they touch on. These defining moments made them the successful businessmen they are today and keep them going. And you will notice that the moments and experiences that have defined their lives revolve around *why*... as opposed to the *how*.

As you read their defining moments, think about your life. What have been your defining moments? Have they helped you be successful? Have they held you back? Be honest with yourself. With honesty comes clarity, and with clarity comes the opportunity to change. You may start to see your life more clearly and have another defining moment, the moment you take control over your own life!

CHAPTER FOURTEEN

WHAT DID YOU LEARN FROM YOUR FATHER?

Robert's Response

My dad was a great man. Even as a child, I looked up to him and respected him. I was proud to be his son, and I wanted him to be proud of me.

On the first day of school, teachers would read the class roster and every teacher would stop after calling out my name and say, "Is Ralph Kiyosaki your father?"

My dad was the head of education for the state of Hawaii. He was tall for being Japanese, about 6' 3", so he stood out in more ways than one. He was known as a brilliant man and an independent thinker. He had graduated at the top of his class as valedictorian and was respected as a great educator in the school system of Hawaii. Just before he passed away, he was recognized as one of the top two educators in Hawaii's history. I remember him showing me the newspaper article about the award and he was crying. As the article said, he had dedicated his life to education and Hawaii's children.

My dad had originally planned on going to medical school. Our family, for generations, had been medical doctors. But when he was in high school, on the island of Maui, he noticed that his classmates were rapidly disappearing from class. As student president of his class, he went to the principal to find out where the kids were going. At first, he got the runaround, but he finally learned the truth. He found out that the sugar plantation where most of the kids' parents worked had a standing order that 20 percent of the kids had to be failed, regardless of how they were doing in school. This was to ensure that the sugar plantation had enough uneducated laborers. My father learned that teachers, principals and people at all levels within the education system *went along with that*. It was then that my father decided against medical school and went to college to become a teacher to try to change the system. In addition, he fought to bring the best education possible to kids whose parents could not afford private schools—kids who had no choice but to depend on the public school system to work *for* them instead of against them. He fought that battle all his life.

However, our country's education system is just getting worse. America has one of the worst educational systems in the world, yet it spends more money on education than any other country does.

As hard as my dad fought, the state of Hawaii continues to have one of the worst education systems in America. The May 2006 issue of *Honolulu Magazine* ran a cover-page article grading public schools in Hawaii. The article stated that the National Education Association (NEA) rated Hawaii as number 43 out of the 50 states—in other words, the seventh lowest in the nation. It issued a D- in standards and accountability, an F for school climate, a D for improving teacher quality, and a C in adequacy of school resources.

This is not caused by a lack of money. In 2001, the budget for the educational system was $1.3 billion and in 2006 it is $2.1 billion. As the article stated:

> *"But while legislators are forking over more money today than they did five years ago, taxpayers aren't seeing any payoff. One thing that hasn't changed much about our government-run school system is its remarkable ability to resist change."*

My father ran for lieutenant governor of Hawaii because he realized he could not change the system as only the superintendent of education. He needed to go higher, so he ran for office as a Republican, in a very pro-labor Democratic state. He was crushed in more ways than one. Not only was he never allowed to hold a government job in Hawaii again (because he went against the political machine that grips Hawaii), but his very own people, the men he brought up with him over the years, turned against him because they were so afraid of losing their jobs. More than not working, it was the cowardice of his friends and their betrayal that destroyed his spirit. My dad was about 50 years old at the time of his political defeat, and he never recovered from the loss.

In 1974, I returned from Vietnam and found my dad sitting in his home, only in his fifties, a broken man. He had tried to make some money by purchasing a national ice cream franchise. He took an early retirement and withdrew most of his savings and lost it all on the franchise. If not for the small check he received from the State, and later from Social Security and Medicare, he would have been destitute.

That was a defining moment for me. Seeing my dad, a man I loved and looked up to, sitting in his living room and watching television all day shook me. Here he was in the prime of life, highly educated but with a broken spirit. As time went on, he got angrier at himself and at the one-time friends that he felt had betrayed him.

He was sitting there watching TV when he gave me the advice I talked about earlier: "Go back to school, get your master's degree, then your Ph.D. and get a job with the government." He was sincere in his recommendation. That was what he had done. After all, he believed in education. He had dedicated his life to it.

At that moment, I realized that education was missing something vital. Our traditional education did not prepare us for the real world. It prepared us to be employees. It was then that I knew I would follow in the footsteps of my rich dad (the father of my best friend) and not my real dad's. I decided to follow in my rich dad's footsteps because he did not let his lack of formal education crush his entrepreneurial spirit or his desire to teach and mentor his son

> We all have defining moments. It is in these moments that we find our true characters. We become heroes or cowards; truth-tellers or liars; we go forward or we go backward.
>
> – Robert T. Kiyosaki

and me. For those of you who don't already know, he ultimately became one of the richest men in Hawaii.

1974 was a defining year for me. First, because I knew I would not follow in my father's footsteps. Years later I realized that 1974 was also the year ERISA, which led to the 401(k), was enacted. By seeing the world through my father's eyes, I knew it would be my generation, the baby-boom generation, that would be facing the same plight my dad was facing. My generation would be facing the world as well-educated, hard-working, honest people—in need of government or family support, and not knowing how to survive financially on their own. In the coming years, there will be millions of people all over the world who, just like my dad, will be facing the world without much money after a life of hard work, living in fear of running out.

Out of respect, I waited five years after my father's death to publish *Rich Dad Poor Dad*. Some people think my book was disrespectful. Yet, I am sure my dad would have been big enough to handle the realities in the book. He was a big man in more ways than just height.

I wrote the book to pick up the torch my father carried and continue the fight to reform and change the current educational system that is obsolete, out of touch with the world, and in my opinion, not preparing many of our youth for the world ahead. As I have been saying for years, "Why doesn't our school system teach us about money? Regardless of whether we are rich or poor, smart or not smart, the one common denominator we all have is that we use money."

TIME Magazine ran a cover story with a blaring headline about the United States being a dropout nation. The article in the magazine was about how our school administrators disguise the actual number of kids dropping out, much in the same way Enron hid its losses. The article accurately states that the problem today is much worse than it's been in the past because dropouts today do not have the high-paying factory jobs to go to. Today, their only options are low-paying jobs working as clerks or counter help for fast-food restaurants because America has become a nation of consumers, not producers. We will be paying for this massive problem for years to come—the problem being an obsolete and out-of-touch educational system that remains resistant to change.

And that is what I got from my dad. I carry on his fight. The only difference is, I do it from outside the system. I do not attack the system directly. I do it as a rich man, rather than as an employee who needs a steady paycheck.

As some of you know, The Rich Dad Company has several education initiatives in place. We have developed www.RichKidSmartKid.com for children (K-12), parents and teachers. The Web site includes a series of mini-games, lesson plans and instructor guides…all free of charge and free of commercial messaging. The games are creative and engaging and make learning an interactive, fun experience.

At the college level, The Rich Dad Company has created curricula for two college courses: Rich Dad's CASHFLOW Personal Finance Course and Rich Dad's Real Estate Investing. These curricula—as well as all of the lesson plans, supplemental materials and video lessons—are also free of charge and available to colleges and universities around the world. Courses are offered in cities across the United States.

Robert's family. Robert, in middle, is the first of four children.

Donald's Response

My Father's Influence

My legacy from my father was embodied in the saying, *"To whom much is given, much is expected."* I drive myself because I must.

Today is a very beautiful day in May, and I'm in my jet on the way to Canouan Island in the Grenadines, not far from St. Barts. I have a resort development there that includes a golf course and villas, and this is one fantastic destination point, provided you like paradise. I'm going to visit to check it out for a couple of days, and this quiet time while flying is one part of traveling that I like to take advantage of. However, Robert called me just before I left and asked me this question:

"Donald, what would you do if everything was taken away from you?"

He mentioned that Henry Ford said he'd make it all back in five years, and that Picasso would keep on painting, and so on. I've already been through one reversal that could have been a total wipeout and difficult to recover from. But I came back to be far more successful than I was before, so I can safely say I'd just keep at it, which is what I did.

But then I got to thinking about my father, Fred Trump, who had a wipeout in his life at an early age: His father died when my father was 11 years old, which left him as the man of the house with a mother and two siblings to care for and watch out for. It was the defining moment in my father's life. He immediately began taking odd jobs—shining shoes, delivering for a fruit market, hauling lumber on a construction site. He graduated from high school, but couldn't even consider going to college. So he went to work as a carpenter's helper for a home builder in Queens, New York. One year later, he built his first home, and he called his company Elizabeth Trump & Son because he was too young to be in business for himself and had to have his mother sign all the legal documents and checks.

> Know everything you can about what you're doing.
>
> — *Fred Trump*

My father became so successful that he was able to send his younger brother to college at M.I.T. where he earned a Ph.D., and he was also able to marry my mother and start a family. Long story short, he was a self-made man starting at age 11 and he was a great example to learn from. He was someone who never took anything for granted and who maintained very high standards for himself in both good times and bad.

My father never had the time to complain. He just worked. And that is something to learn from. When I was going through difficult times, I would remember my father's ordeal and just keep on working through it. I can tell you from experience that perseverance is what is required. I think Henry Ford knew about work and so did Picasso. The work ethic applies to whatever industry you might be in or aspire to be in.

Robert mentions his two fathers—one rich, one poor. He had two examples to learn from, to observe and to choose from when it came to having a mentor. The one he learned the most from was his father without the advanced education. He had learned to figure things out for himself, which is very much what my father had to do. There's a lesson in there for all of us. As much as I value higher education, sometimes it seems the school of hard knocks produces people with above-average common sense. My father was naturally smart, and that, combined with his work ethic, produced an effective dynamo.

My father was a great inspiration to me as well as a great example. He never had to tell us that success meant diligent work and discipline. We could see that by watching him work, day in and day out, for many years. But it was never drudgery for him. He loved what he was doing. He had a passion for his business, and his exuberance was genuine. That kind of example left a lasting impression on me, and I'm very grateful.

To this day, I receive letters from people who knew my father and were touched by his generosity and work ethic. I received a letter recently from someone who remembers that my father used to go around picking up nails from the ground at construction sites. He hated waste, and to him this wasn't an annoyance, but part of being conscientious and doing a good job. My father was thorough, and he always told me, "Know everything you can about what you're doing."

I listened to him and took his advice. When people ask me why I think I'm successful, the first thing I think about is my upbringing and my father's influence. Yes, I went to Wharton, but before Wharton was my father. If he could achieve what he did without the benefit of family financial support and education, my expectations for myself would have to exceed those of my father—simply because I had so much more to start with than he did. We had the same standards for achievement and the same work ethic, but the conditions were different. I literally couldn't accept doing any less than I am doing now, because I wouldn't have one single excuse for doing otherwise. So if I am perceived to be a driven man, there's a very good reason behind it. Replace your excuses with reasons and everything will become clear.

Your Response

What did you learn from your father that has helped you become successful today? (If your father was not a positive role model in your life, describe the influence of another man who greatly influenced your life.)

_____

_____

_____

_____

_____

_____

_____

_____

_____

_____

CHAPTER FIFTEEN

WHAT DID YOU LEARN FROM YOUR MOTHER?

Robert's Response

My mom was the most loving person in my life. As a young boy, I used to get angry at her for hugging all of my friends. I would say, "Mom, stop hugging us." Today, I wish she was around so I could hug her once more.

My mom died at the young age of 48. She was born with a weak heart. On top of that, she had rheumatic fever as a child, which left her even weaker. Maybe that is why she was so very loving. She cherished every day she was alive because, as a registered nurse, she probably knew she did not have long to live.

My wife, Kim, is very much like my mom. While they do not look alike, they have the same spirit. When I first saw Kim, it was her stunning beauty that attracted me to her. She would not go out with me for six months. But, finally on our first date, I knew I had met the woman of my dreams because Kim had the same heartfelt warmth as my mom. We have been together almost every day since that day in 1984.

I was in the Marine Corps when my mom died. I was stationed at Pensacola, Florida, going through Navy Flight School when my dad called to tell me my mom had passed away. At the funeral, I experienced a grief I didn't know was possible. My dad (who, as I said, was a giant of a man) collapsed in tears. It took all three of us kids to hold him and us together.

A few years later, I was in Vietnam. I had flown a Marine Corps general into a remote village where the United States was planning what turned out to be a last-ditch effort, a defensive against North Vietnam. The enemy was staging a major offensive across the DMZ. We were supposed to stop them the moment they headed south. We knew the war was over. We had lost.

My crew had gone into the village to get some food and to shop for souvenirs. I stayed with the helicopter, parked on the edge of a grass field. Suddenly, a group of young Vietnamese boys showed up and began climbing in and out of the helicopter. I rose to my feet and in English attempted to tell them to stay away. Obviously, they did not understand my English and kept going through the aircraft, as 9- to 12-year-old boys would.

Fearing that the boys might be Viet Cong, which many in the area were, I physically started pulling the boys away from the aircraft. I was now concerned that one of them might be placing a grenade or some kind of explosive in the aircraft. My fear got to me and I began being more physical with my efforts to keep the boys away. One young lad would not listen. As soon as I threw him off, he was back inside the aircraft, playing with the machine guns and other weapons.

Finally, in a fit of rage, I grabbed the boy by the hair and pulled him out of the cabin. Responding to my anger, he kicked me and bit my arm. With that, I lost control and instantly my Marine Corps training took over. I pulled out my pistol, pulled the hammer back, put the barrel in his ear and started screaming at him. Suddenly, our eyes met and he started to cry. He was terrified. He could see I was angry and crazed. I wanted to shoot him. In my mind, I was justified; I knew he was the enemy.

As I stood there with my pistol to his head, I looked into his eyes and saw his soul. There is a saying among professional hit men that goes, "If you are going to kill someone, don't look in their eyes." Looking in this young boy's eyes, filled with tears, I suddenly began to cry. I paused. I didn't pull the trigger. As I paused, I suddenly heard my mom pleading with me. Even though she had passed on a few years earlier, I knew her voice, and it was crystal clear: "Stop," she said. "I have been pleading with you all my life to be kinder. Please stop. I did not give you life to take another mother's child."

With that, I put the hammer of the gun back, looked into the boy's eyes, and let him know I was not going to kill him. Instead, I picked up a soccer ball the boys had carried, put the pistol down and signaled to his friends that we should play soccer instead.

As I lifted off that evening, with the general on board, we came under intense enemy fire. I cannot prove it, but I am certain those boys did tip the enemy as to our presence. They were the enemy. That evening, I sat alone on the flight deck and reflected back on that day. "Did I really hear my mom?" I asked myself over and over. In the end, I realized that it did not make much difference. I had finally heard her. I got the message.

My mom's message to me was that I was a good kid but I had a mean streak. While I smiled at lot, beneath the surface I wanted to fight. I had a bad temper with a short fuse. When my parents joined the Peace Corps for two years, while I was in high school, I informed them I was going to join the Marine Corps, and I did. And they were against the Vietnam war.

> It is not that I will not fight; I will not fight with weapons or violence anymore. Instead, I will fight with the wisdom of my father and the compassion of my mother.
>
> – *Robert T. Kiyosaki*

That day on the grassy field, outside a small village in Vietnam, was a turning point in my life. It was a defining moment. As I flew back toward the aircraft carrier, even after being shot at, I knew my career as a Marine was over. As the great American Indian Chief Joseph once said, "I will fight no more forever." It is not that I will not fight; I will not fight with weapons or violence anymore. Instead, I will fight with the wisdom of my father and the compassion of my mother.

In business, both Donald and I find ourselves surrounded— by choice—with strong and successful women.

I acknowledge my partner, Kim, for her dedication to our mission. I know the future of the Rich Woman brand, as well as Rich Dad, are in Kim's capable and compassionate hands.

Today, The Rich Dad Company offers financial education, free of charge, to children all over the world.

Donald's Response

The Mother of All Advice

My mother was of Scottish heritage, and she gave me some sage advice that I have always tried to follow:

"Trust in God and be true to yourself."

That covers a lot of territory, and I think it can help give us a strong sense of identity while keeping the big picture in mind. It's also so brief that it was easy to remember. I must've been thinking of my mother when I first said to "think big." They say brevity is the soul of wit, but it's also the key to a good memory.

My mother enjoyed lavish spectacle, and she liked to watch the royal processions and ceremonies from Europe. Maybe my more flamboyant side comes from her, even if she was Scotch and very careful with money and time. She always had time to give to charity and needy causes, so her interests were diverse yet well-balanced.

I like to think mine are, too, and I'm a quiet giver in many cases. Also, if you are famous and you give a lot and noisily, I can tell you your volume of requests for help—from everything from hot air balloons to college educations to summer vacations—will escalate by the tens of thousands. There's a lot to be said for being low-key.

We lost a member of our family when my elder brother Fred died at the age of 42. That had a huge impact on me, and I saw the grief my parents endured. Losing a child is never easy, no matter what their age. It is always a shock, and it affects you every day for the rest of your life. I think I realized how valuable life truly is, and I determined to make mine the best I possibly could for myself and those around me. It was a defining moment in my life.

> Trust in God and be true to yourself.
>
> – Mary Trump

That is one of those quiet reasons for being the way I am. The end result may not always be so quiet, but the impetus is there big-time because of this loss. I felt closer to my parents than ever and felt responsible for their well-being and happiness after that terrible event in their lives. Yes, it was hard for me, but it was much harder for them.

My mother was a devout person, and she lived her faith. That was a great example to me as a child and as an adult. She was very strong and yet very gentle, and she was also very humble. She gave everything she had without reservation. So when I speak so highly of my parents, you can see that there is good reason to.

My mother's advice was simple but wise. It cuts to the core and keeps me focused and well-balanced. "Trust in God and be true to yourself." It doesn't get any better than that.

Donald with his parents, Mary and Fred Trump,
at the New York Military Academy, 1964.

Your Response

What did you learn from your mother that has helped you become successful today? *(If your mother was not a positive role model in your life, describe the influence of another woman who greatly influenced your life.)*

_____

_____

_____

_____

_____

_____

_____

_____

_____

_____

CHAPTER SIXTEEN

WHAT DID YOU LEARN FROM SCHOOL?

Robert's Response

There is a saying that goes, "The cobbler's children have no shoes." In my case, the saying should have been, "The superintendent of education's kid has no brains." Even though my dad was the head of education, I was flunking out of school—not once but twice. I flunked English both my sophomore year and my senior year because I could not write. It must have been pretty embarrassing for my dad to have a son who was the class dummy.

In spite of poor grades, I did graduate and received congressional nominations to the U.S. Naval Academy and the U.S. Merchant Marine Academy. Although my grades were low, I had fairly good SAT scores and I was good at football, which helped with the admissions process. I chose the US. Merchant Marine Academy at Kings Point, New York, because I wanted to be a merchant seaman and the pay was much higher than for Naval Academy graduates. Back in 1965, when I made my decision, an ensign in the Navy made about $200 a month and a graduate from Kings Point made about $2,000 a month. When I graduated from Kings Point, Navy ensigns were still making about $200 a month and Kings Pointers, if they sailed merchant ships into the war zone, were making about $100,000 a year. So, to be honest, even though the Naval Academy is a more famous school, Kings Pointers were, at the time, some of the highest paid college graduates in America. A yearly salary of $100,000 was very good money in 1969, especially if you were only 22 years old.

However, I did not take one of those jobs. Instead, upon graduation, I took a job with Standard Oil of California, and shipped out of

San Francisco. The reason I chose Standard Oil, even though the pay was a lot lower, only $47,000 for seven months work, was because I was interested in oil and because our tankers sailed to Hawaii and Tahiti. (Think about it!)

In 1966, the academy sent its entire sophomore class to sea as apprentices onboard ships for a whole year (known as a sea year). During that year, I sailed on freighters, tankers and passenger liners as a student officer. That year of traveling the world was a great mind-expanding time for me. It was also fun running into classmates in faraway and exotic ports. I grew up a lot and learned a lot about life and the real world that my parents had tried to protect me from.

During my four years at the academy, I had two defining moments. The first was freshman English. Having failed English twice, I was certain that college-level English would be the end of my career as a student. I had nightmares thinking about failing and being sent straight to Vietnam, as was the fate of students who flunked out during that era. Instead, freshman English was a joy. I had a great teacher, Dr. A.A. Norton, a West Point graduate and B-17 Bomber pilot in World War II. Instead of punishing me for my poor spelling and radical ideas, he encouraged me to write. I finished his class with a B. More important than the grade, Dr. Norton renewed my confidence in myself as a student. In a school where more than 50 percent of the class is failed and asked to leave before graduation, it was Dr. Norton's confidence in me as a student that got me through those tough academic years. Today, my books have been translated into more than 46 languages, have sold more than 26 million copies, and I am more known as a writer than a ship's officer. If not for Dr. Norton, I may never have graduated from the academy and definitely never would have written a book.

Another defining moment of my life was when I discovered the power of oil and its effect on the world economy. In 1966, as an apprentice officer onboard a Standard Oil tanker, I learned that oil is power. Today, I invest millions of dollars in oil. As an entrepreneur, I have helped start two oil companies. One failed at the start and one went public then failed. I learned a lot from those failures.

As a pilot in Vietnam in 1972, I realized we were not fighting to stop communism. I realized we were fighting for oil and for big oil corporations. Today, we are in the same war—different countries, same corporations.

In the 1980s, I became a founding board member of an organization known as GENI (Global Energy Network International). The purpose of GENI, a not-for-profit organization, is to bring to the world the ideas of Dr. R. Buckminster Fuller, known as one of the greatest geniuses of our time. According to Dr. Fuller, the world has the technology to be energy self-sufficient, which means non-polluting renewable energy. The problem is the oil companies would rather see the price of oil go up, and these companies yield a lot of power.

I supported Dr. Fuller's idea because if GENI were a reality, the wealth of our world would increase, poverty would decline, population growth would decline and there would be a greater possibility of world peace.

I resigned from the GENI board in 1994. The organization is alive and well today. If you would like more information about GENI and its initiatives, you can go to their Web site at GENI.org. The ideas are bold, worthy of consideration, and would mean a completely different world, if the world could see the benefit of cooperating, rather than fighting for resources.

While I may sound like a hypocrite or a flip-flopper, I am still a capitalist. I still make my money from oil, and I also support the eventual replacement of oil with a non-polluting, renewable energy resource that elevates the world's standard of living and reduces poverty and war. As a line from the song *Imagine* by John Lennon goes, "You may say I'm a dreamer, but I'm not the only one."

> Instead of punishing me for my poor spelling and radical ideas, Dr. Norton encouraged me to write. I finished his class with a *B*. More important than the grade, Dr. Norton renewed my confidence in myself as a student…and Dr. Norton's confidence in me as a student that got me through those tough academic years.
>
> – Robert T. Kiyosaki

Donald's Response

College Days

I know this surprises people, but I was a very good student. I was serious, attentive, and applied myself to every class. When Robert and I were discussing our college days and what might have caused us to become rich, I remembered that I spent my spare time studying real estate and foreclosures on my own time. I always did more than was required.

That, I think, is a key to success. Not just financial success, but in everything. If you do only what you need to do to get by, then get by you will. But the end results will not be outstanding or exceptional. You have to do what others don't want to do to have an edge.

Golf legend Gary Player's saying, "The harder I work, the luckier I get," is one that I've adopted. The worst disservice we can do to ourselves is to expect things to be easy. I knew that real estate wasn't a snap, and I prepared myself. Whatever your interests are, be sure to do the same.

There were other students in my class that were exceptional students, but they didn't do so well in real life. I sometimes think they were focusing so much on the academics required, and not keeping an eye on the outside world, that when they graduated, they were surprised by what they faced. I think I was aware of the dangers and difficulties of the world and kept myself aware of national and international events, those related to real estate and otherwise, so that I'd be on an even keel when I stepped out of the study halls into the streets of business.

It's called having an advantage. It's important in sports, and it's important in life. Sometimes we are required to be isolated in order to excel, which is fine, but at the same time we have to be aware. People can be over-trained to the extent that they are of no earthly good. Bookwise versus streetwise surfaces again.

It's possible to be both. In fact, it's mandatory at this point. My advantage is that I had seen the rough side of real estate from working with my father and watching him from an early age. It can be a tough world, and I knew it. I had learned to step to the side of doorways when collecting rent to avoid being shot. So I knew what I could be facing. My father was streetwise, and businesswise as well, and considering I went to Wharton, I had the best of both worlds to learn from.

> Don't depend on anyone but yourself for providing your financial security.
>
> – *Donald J. Trump*

Maybe we're not all that fortunate. That's OK, too. You can make the most of what you have and where you're at. Just expect to do more. What you're willing to do may determine where you're willing to go. I was willing to add extra hours of study to my college curriculum, without expecting extra credit or a pat on the back. I did it on my own, and I believe that's a big reason for my success.

Your Response

What did you learn from school that has helped you become successful?

Was there a certain teacher who impacted you positively?

_____

_____

_____

What lessons from school have you applied in your life?

_____

_____

_____

What were the results?

_____

_____

_____

CHAPTER SEVENTEEN

HOW DID MILITARY SCHOOL HELP DEFINE YOUR LIFE?

Robert's Response

There are three reasons I went to a military school.

When I was 10 years old, my fifth-grade teacher had us study the history of the great explorers—Columbus, Cortez, Magellan and Da Gama. Reading those books inspired me to want to go to sea and explore the world.

When I was 13, while other kids were carving salad bowls for their moms, I talked my shop teacher into letting me build a boat for my wood shop project. I sent away for the plans and for the next few months, I was happily building an 8-foot El Toro class sailboat. That class was one of the few classes I got an A in.

Some of the happiest days of my life were spent sailing my boat on Hilo Bay, named after the town I grew up in. As I sat in my boat, my mind would drift as I dreamed of faraway ports and exotic women.

When my high school guidance counselor asked me, "What do you want to do when you grow up?" I replied, "I want to go to sea, travel to exotic places such as Tahiti, drink beer and chase women."

Instead of getting upset with me, she said, "I have just the school for you." She then took out a brochure for the U.S. Merchant Marine Academy and said, "Look this over. It's a tough school. But if you really want to go to sea, then I'll help you get into the academy."

After winning a congressional appointment from U.S. Senator Daniel K. Inouye in 1965, I left the sleepy little town of Hilo and traveled to New York to begin my education to become a merchant marine officer. In 1968, as part of my apprenticeship at sea, I sailed

> ...I realized that combat was the ultimate test of will and training. There was no second place and the winner was the one who was the most prepared.
>
> I changed my thoughts to, "Combat is not risky. Being unprepared is risky." I've come to realize that entrepreneurship is not risky. Being unprepared is risky.
>
> – Robert T. Kiyosaki

into Papaete, Tahiti, drank beer, and went out with one of the most beautiful women I have ever met. She was the weather girl on television and a candidate for Miss Tahiti. My dreams had come true.

The second reason I went to the academy was because my dad did not have the money to send me to college. He said to me, "The day you graduate, you are on your own." And I was. Going to the academy meant I had a full scholarship, room, board and clothing allowance, and reimbursement for travel. On top of that, we were paid a small (and I do mean small) salary each month.

The third, and probably the most important reason, was for the discipline. As a kid in high school, I was often surfing more than attending class. Even after my dad, the head of education, caught me, I still found it impossible not to cut classes when the surf was big.

I knew I needed the discipline. If I had attended the University of Hawaii, I never would have finished school.

At the academy, I learned discipline...the hard way. Punishment came often, and it was severe. Academics were tougher than I had expected. Without a strict military system, I would never have graduated.

I also learned to follow and give orders. In other words, I learned leadership. When you look at the CASHFLOW Quadrant, you can see that leadership is essential for success in the B quadrant. After three years of hard discipline and leadership training, in my senior year, I was promoted to Battalion Officer. My job was then to teach leadership to underclassmen who were just like me when I entered the school—little con artists who thought they could beat the system.

The Biggest Lessons of All

After four years of the academy, I volunteered for the Marine Corps because the Vietnam War was still going. It was in Navy flight school that I had two life-defining lessons that have served me well. They are:

1. One of the most exciting parts of flight training was learning how to fight aircraft to aircraft, often called a dogfight. The aircraft we flew at the time was a T-28 Trojan, a single-engine World War II vintage aircraft. It was big, fast and unforgiving. Many a student died because the aircraft was designed to be agile and maneuverable. If you were not a good pilot, the aircraft could kill you.

   One day, I was flying solo, on the lookout for my instructor who was going to jump me. Suddenly, I heard screaming through my helmet's earpiece: "Bang, bang, bang, bang!" It was the instructor letting me know the fight was on. Immediately, I did as I was taught, shoving the fuel mixture to rich to protect the engine and pulling the aircraft up to the right and rolling it over, trying to shake my attacker.

   Instead of losing him, all I could hear was, "Bang, bang, bang, got you, sucker." I could not shake my instructor. I climbed, I turned, I dove, I tried to stall, but nothing could shake him. I could barely see because my face shield was covered in sweat. For a good 10 minutes, my instructor rode my tail, not fooled by any of my evasive maneuvers.

   Back on the ground, the debriefing began. As my instructor used his hands to describe my flying, I got sick to my stomach. My ill feeling was not just because of the violent maneuvers we had just been through. It was the realization of how bad a pilot I was and how much more I had to learn.

   At that moment, my instructor said something that has stayed with me ever since: "The trouble with this business is that there is no second place. Only one pilot comes home alive." That was a defining moment in my life. After that day, I practiced and practiced and practiced.

Later in Vietnam, I would hear those same words several times. Only this time, it was for real. There were real bullets. Not my instructor screaming "bang, bang, bang" over his radio.

I win in business today not because I am smart or never fail. I win because, in my world, there is no second place. I suspect Donald has the same personal rule.

2. The other defining moment pertains to risk.

Whenever I hear someone say, "Investing is risky," I know it really means the person is not prepared and is not up to the task.

After that day in the air with my flight instructor, I realized that combat was the ultimate test of will and training. There was no second place and the winner was the one who was the most prepared. I changed my thoughts to, "Combat is not risky. Being unprepared is risky."

In business and investing, I am a fanatic about practice and preparation. I practice to reduce risk. I improve my skills to reduce risk. I study to reduce risk. I play to win, and the prize goes to the one who plays the game with the least risk and the most confidence.

If I need to take a risk, I take a small one. Before I invested with real money in my first real estate deal, I attended a workshop for investors. Following that workshop, I looked at over a hundred deals. Everywhere I went in Hawaii, realtors kept saying, "What you're looking for doesn't exist." After months of looking, I finally found a small deal on the island of Maui. It was a one-bedroom condominium, near the beach, for only $18,000. It was my first investment. Since then, I have looked at tens of thousands of possible investments and purchased only a few of them.

After losing my nylon surfer-wallet business, I went back to the discipline of study, practice, study, practice. I realized that entrepreneurship is not risky. Being unprepared is risky.

Understanding that, in my world, there is no second place and realizing that the biggest risk is being unprepared have made the biggest differences in my quest for wealth.

Most people invest money and do not invest much time. Donald and I invest a lot of time before we invest much money. We prepare to invest. I realized that entrepreneurship is not risky. Being unprepared is risky.

Military School vs. Business School

When you look at the B-I Triangle, it is easy to see why military school and military service are great preparation for entrepreneurship and investing. Simply put, business schools focus on the inside of the B-I triangle…the content. Military schools focus on the outside…the context.

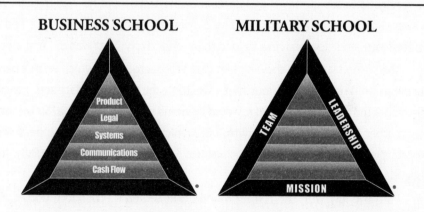

As you can tell from the diagram, four years of military school and nearly six years in military service prepared me for the real world of entrepreneurship and investing. It was a great education because the process taught me: 1. Discipline 2. Focus. 3. To serve a mission greater than my own self-interests. 4. To take orders, follow orders, and give orders. 5. To control my fears and my anger 6. To study and respect my enemy. 7. To trust my fellow soldiers and be willing to give my life for them as they were willing to give their lives for me. 8. To prepare before going into battle.

Donald's Response

Although I was sent to military school because I was a bit aggressive as a kid, what I learned there had less to do with discipline and channeling my energy more effectively than it had to do with learning about the art of negotiation. It was a great business lesson in disguise.

I was confronted with a former marine drill sergeant, and I realized I would never be able to match him or take him on physically, so I had to use my brain to handle the situation.

I had to get around the guy somehow, and I refused to back down, so I tried to figure out what might get him on my side. I saw my first opportunity: I was a very good baseball player and captain of the team, and he was the coach. I knew I could make him look good by playing my best, which I did. We had a great team, and I learned how to lead them effectively. That was the first step.

The second step was showing him that I respected him (which wasn't hard because I did respect him), but that I wouldn't let him intimidate me. I think he respected that and realized it would be pointless to go after me. So we met each other from a point of strength, not weakness, and a mutual respect was established. That's another great business lesson right there, especially for negotiation. We both won.

I am friendly with the former marine drill sergeant, Theodore Dobias, to this day, and meeting up with him at the New York Military Academy was a fortunate event for me. So was going to military school, although I wasn't that thrilled about it initially. I later realized that I enjoyed the challenges and the discipline, and I never lost the respect for time that I learned there. People who know me know that I hate being late, and I don't like other people being late either.

Military school underscored what my father had always taught us—that we should show respect. I respected Mr. Dobias and it served me well, and I learned to respect time, which has also served me well. My father was a real taskmaster as a businessman and I was ready to work with him after that training.

Another important lesson from military school was that excuses aren't acceptable. You learn not to whine, but instead to keep your equilibrium and persevere. When I faced difficulties and pressures later in life, I refused to cave in. I knew that the best way to deal with problems was to just keep going, to persist and continue working at solutions. That's a good lesson to learn.

While I was in military school, my father got into the habit of sending me inspirational quotes each week. I can remember a lot of them and they continue to inspire me today. A few of them are:

"He who has never learned to obey cannot be a good commander."

— Aristotle

"Never tell people how to do things. Tell them what to do and they will surprise you with their ingenuity."

— George S. Patton

"What you cannot enforce, do not command."

— Sophocles

"We are what we repeatedly do. Excellence then is not an act, but a habit."

— Aristotle

I realize my father was instilling leadership values in me by selecting certain bits of wisdom from many ages. These lessons went into my subconscious, surfacing to help me as I encounter situations that they might pertain to. That's why I'm still big on quotes; they can be a direct hit on negative or confused thinking. So when people hear me quoting or referring to a variety of great thinkers throughout history, they now know it's something that was started at a young age and that I have continued to do. And it started when I was in military school.

Another defining moment I had in military school had to do with history. There was a fellow student who was always studying WWII on his own. He was a history buff and a serious student. One day I said to him, "You must be an expert on WWII after all the time you've spent studying it." His reply is something I've never forgotten: "No, it has only made me realize how much I don't know." Then he explained that in order to understand WWII, he had to go back to WWI and study that, and then study the world situation before WWI, and he was beginning to see it would be a very long process. Then he said, "Studying history has made me very humble, because I know I'll never know it all." Coming from someone as well-read as he was, those comments left an impression on me.

As a result, I would study history in my spare time and try to read as much as I could. I started a habit that I've kept to this day, which is to ask myself, "What can I learn today that I didn't know before?" That's one way to keep my mind curious and alert. Aristotle was right: Excellence can become a habit.

When I entered Wharton years later, I found that my habits from military school helped me a great deal. As I mentioned earlier, I spent my spare time studying foreclosures and real estate and everything I could get my hands on —all in addition to the required curriculum. I didn't want to get by with just doing enough. I wanted to do more, and I found myself prepared when I left college for the real world where very often doing "enough" really isn't enough at all.

In the words of one of the Greek philosophers my father introduced me to, here's a final, defining lesson I learned at military school:

"The first and best victory is to conquer self."

— Plato

The more you learn, the more you realize how much you don't know.

— *Donald J. Trump*

I learned to be part of a whole. Military school provided the opportunity to understand how to be part of the big picture without losing my identity. It's been a great advantage in business, allowing me to diminish myself when necessary.

Sometimes the picture is clearer if you're not in the picture at all. A great lesson. Someone once said I was a bit like a chameleon when it came to negotiating, that I could blend myself out and then back in again. That ability came from my experiences at military school.

Most people see me as being mentally tough, and that's true. That's another advantage I've had from my time in military school. I don't like to complain, I can be tenacious, and sometimes I just won't budge. If I've done my homework, if I've worked hard and I've been diligent, then I know I have everything it takes to back myself up or defend myself. I can be a tough adversary.

As I said, I was sent to military school because I was a bit aggressive as a kid. In military school I learned to focus my aggressiveness for good instead of bad and became a leader as well as a member of a team with a common mission.

Robert at Camp Pendelton, California,
preparing to go to Vietnam, 1972.

Donald leading the New York Military
Academy contingent up Fifth Avenue
for the Columbus Day parade, 1963.

Your Response

What did you learn in military school that helped define your life?

You may not have attended military school, but did you belong to the Boy Scouts, Girl Scouts or other clubs where you learned the importance of discipline and leadership? How have you benefited from these experiences? Or, how could you have benefited from using self-discipline and leadership skills in your life?

_____

_____

_____

Where in your life could you benefit from more discipline (i.e., time management or financial management?) and/or more leadership skills?

_____

_____

_____

CHAPTER EIGHTEEN

WHAT WAS THE DEFINING LESSON YOU LEARNED FROM SPORTS?

Robert's Response

As a child, I played Little League baseball and Pop Warner football. At the age of 12, I began playing golf. At 15, I gave up golf to surf. And in high school I played football.

At the academy, I captained the rowing team and played football.

While at flight school, I was introduced to the game of rugby. Rugby is my game. It is the only game I have ever been passionate about. I have traveled the world playing the sport, and once I got too old to play, I traveled the world watching the great test matches. I have watched test matches in South Africa, Australia, New Zealand, Scotland, Ireland, and England.

I learned something different from each sport, something important that has influenced my life.

1. In Little League, I learned how to play hard even when losing. Our team was the early version of the "Bad News Bears." For most of the season, we never won…but we played hard and improved with each game. Finally, at the end of the season, we beat one of the best teams in the league. The reason we won was because they got cocky and we got better.

2. By playing golf, I learned to control my emotions, my thoughts and my body. The game of golf is simple in theory, but one of the toughest games played. In business, many times I use the same types of self-control I use in golf.

3. I loved surfing. By surfing, I learned to time the cycle of waves. Today, as an investor, I often use the intuitive senses I gained as a surfer to know when to enter a market and, more importantly, when to get out.

4. At the academy, I rowed because it was the most painful sport I could find. Since school was so challenging, I needed a sport that was painful enough to take my mind off the military and academic pressures I faced. From the sport of rowing, I learned the importance of precision teamwork. Rowing is a sport of precise synchronicity. The challenge of rowing is that during a race, most of our stored energy is burned up in the first few minutes. For the boat to win, it was important that each person gave his all, with precision, even though physically exhausted. If one person even thought about letting up, the chances were his oar would collide with another oar and the race would be lost.

5. In football, I learned the importance of each team member not only *knowing* his assignment, but more importantly, *carrying* out his assignment. I also learned the importance of getting along with people I did not like and respecting them for their abilities rather than their personalities.

6. Rugby is like basketball with tackling. It is a very fluid sport. Although rugby is the forefather of American football, size does not matter in rugby. You have big people playing with tiny people. In American football, it is estimated that players play at most a full 10 minutes per game. The rest of the time is spent in huddles or activities other than playing the game. In rugby, since the play rarely stops, players are running for most of the game. Regardless of how tired you are, you need to keep running in support of the play and the team.

7. I also have a black belt in Tae Kwon Do. In Tae Kwon Do, I learned the importance of chi—the inner power that flows through our body.

While I have learned many important lessons playing sports, the one that stands out is a lesson I learned while I was playing high school football. When I was a junior, our high school had a great football team. Because there were so many great players, that meant I sat on the bench for most games.

It was really embarrassing at the end of the game to come off the field with a perfectly clean uniform. My fellow benchwarmers and I would often accidentally-on-purpose trip and dig our knees into the mud just to get some dirt on our spotless uniforms. By mid-season, we had stopped tripping and were simply rubbing mud all over our uniforms.

As the season went on, with me still on the bench, I began to think that my coach had it out for me. I believed he didn't play me because he didn't like me. By mid-season I was planning on quitting. My feelings were hurt.

One evening, after a really tough practice, the assistant coach walked up to me, put his hands on my shoulder and said, "I want to talk to you."

This coach's name was Herman Clark. A former NFL player, he was a really big man. He volunteered his time because he loved the game so much. In his quiet and gentle way, he said, "Do you know why the coach isn't playing you?"

"No," I said. "I don't know. I do all the right things. I show up for practice. I run extra laps. I'm as good as Jesse." Jesse was the starter for my position.

"Yes. That's true," said Mr. Clark. "You also have more talent and speed than Jesse."

"So why does he play?" I asked. "Why not play me?"

"Because Jesse has more heart. Jesse wants the position more than you. In life, talent is not enough. If you want a starting position, you need to take yourself to a whole new level. You have the body, but you lack the spirit."

Although I still wanted to quit, I took Mr. Clark's words to heart. For the next two weeks, I practiced like I'd never practiced before. I was intense.

I was focused. I made more tackles and even intercepted two passes in practice, a tough job for a lineman. Although I still did not play and was still on the bench, I was feeling better about myself.

One day during an away game at another high school, Jesse broke his arm. The coach turned to the bench, looked over the candidates. Finally, he looked at me and said, "You're in."

That was a small but defining moment. Today, I realize that what I want in life is up to me. There is no one in my way. If I want something, I know that desire is not enough. I need to do what it takes to be a winner, before I can win. I often repeat to myself, "Life is a rip-off when you expect to get what you want." There is a world of difference between expecting to be a starting player and being a starting player.

At the start of this book, I wrote about the following process:

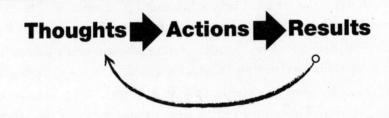

The lesson I learned from Mr. Clark was that for me to change my results, I had to redefine who I was and up my commitment to playing the game. Once my thoughts and attitude changed, my actions changed, and so did my results.

Today, whenever I feel wimpy and think the world is unfair or not recognizing my talents or that people are against me, I simply remember my talk with Mr. Clark. Then I work to upgrade my thoughts, my actions and my results.

Winning Principles

Joe Montana, one of the greatest football players in history, sent me an autographed copy of his book, *The Winning Spirit: 16 Timeless Principles That Drive Performance Excellence*. It is a great book for anyone who is committed to winning.

For those who may not know who Joe Montana is, he was the quarterback of the professional football team, the San Francisco 49ers. He led his team to four Super Bowl victories. He has been elected into the Pro Football Hall of Fame and was named by *Sports Illustrated* as the greatest football player of the past 50 years. The following are a few excerpts from his book:

> *"As I have watched my own children compete in youth sports over the years, I have noticed a growing tendency to deliver pats on the head, to say, 'Good job, everyone won today.' And hand out participation ribbons to all who got out of bed and made it to the game. That's not the way I was raised, and I don't dispense that message in my role as a parent. I think it's unfair for a parent to be an uncritical observer of a young person wanting to improve and play at a higher level. As a parent, you need to be not just a cheerleader but a coach. And I believe it is wrong to tell the next generation that they will be congratulated for simply showing up.*

> *"Competitive sports are one of the best preparations for life, reflecting as they do, the highly competitive nature of the world around us. I never wanted anyone on my team, in sports or business, who didn't passionately care about rising above the competition—and winning.*

> *"If winning wasn't important, people wouldn't keep score.*

> *"Like it or not, we live in a world that keeps score."*

This is what he says about winning Super Bowls:

> *"Recently, after I delivered a speech, someone in the audience asked me how old I was when I won my first Super Bowl.*

> *"'Twelve years old, and I've won a thousand of them since. All but four of them," I explained, 'took place in our backyard in my hometown of Monongahela, Pennsylvania, a few miles down the road from Pittsburg.'"*

In other words, in his backyard, he rehearsed winning the Super Bowl thousands of times.

This is what he says about individual preparation:

"Individuals prepare in different ways. What works for one person doesn't work for another. Some wait until the last minute. Some require a degree of fear as motivation. Others want to eliminate all distractions, have complete silence and shut themselves off from the world. Others prepare with music in the background or in the company of other people. Some need to rehearse over and over until they feel confident. Whatever the method, the goal of good preparation is the same: to ready ourselves for optimal performance, to play or work at our best."

And finally, this is what he says is the key to preparation:

"We do strongly believe and teach that repetition is king in the world of preparation. Whether in sports, running the same drills over and over, or in business practicing a sales pitch or refining a presentation we gain through preparation a sense of mastery and self-confidence that can be taken into the real game."

What Joe Montana says is one of the most valuable lessons I learned from sports. I meet people who say to me, "I played your *CASHFLOW* game once. What do you recommend I do next?"

Can you imagine that? They played once, and they think they know the game. When I recommend they play it at least 10 more times and teach it to 10 other people, they look at me strangely. Whenever I see that look, I know that person probably does not understand what it takes to win. As Joe Montana says, "Repetition is king."

That is why I do not diversify, diversify, diversify with my investments or my business. Instead, I FOCUS—Follow One Course Until Successful— and practice, practice, practice.

A final word from Joe Montana:

"Everyone who has been successful in his or her chosen field understands the importance of practice and preparation. To become outstanding in a particular area, we must learn to practice with concentration and focus. Practice is our chance to work on weaknesses and get better. When we're working to excel in something, it is not enough to do what is expected. We must constantly strive to exceed our own expectations. Nor should we keep starting and stopping a practice regimen. When we practice, we must be consistent."

And that is why my rich dad had me play *Monopoly* over and over again, until one day I saw a glimpse of my future. Today, all I do is play *Monopoly* for real. No matter how rich I become, I always know I can become better. And to me, becoming better at my game is far more important than money.

The Importance of the Game of Golf

While I am not a great golfer, I have learned much about business and human nature while on the golf course.

My golf career began when I was eight years old. My mom and dad would drive us out to a remote country town on the Big Island of Hawaii to visit an old friend of theirs. Like most kids, I found sitting around in the living room with a bunch of adults boring, so I went outside to find something to do. On the porch of their friend's home sat a set of golf clubs. Taking a wood driver out of the bag, I wandered down to his rocky driveway and began hitting rocks. After damaging his wooden driver, I got one of his irons and again began hitting rocks up and down his driveway.

Needless to say, my mom and dad's friend was not impressed with my introduction to the game of golf.

At the age of 12, I took up the game again. I was attending an elementary school filled with rich kids, so most of their fathers belonged to the country club. My dad and rich dad did not belong to the country club because, at the time, neither man was rich. The only way rich dad's son Mike and I could get on the course was to tag along with our rich friends whose fathers were members.

It was not long before the head professional at the country club began to let Mike and me know that we were overstaying our welcome. He let us know that if our fathers were not members, we could not play. At that moment, Mike and I began the first major negotiation of our lives. Somehow, we got the head professional to allow us to become members of the country club. In exchange for membership, we had to caddy for a set number of rounds of golf per month. Our dads were somewhat perplexed when we told them we had become members of the country club at the age of 12—a country club they could not afford.

From the age of 12 to 15, Mike and I golfed and caddied every chance we could. Many days after school, Mike and I would hitchhike our way to the country club. We caddied to keep our agreement and played every chance we got.

Eventually, caddying turned out to be a great source of income. We got paid $1 per bag per nine holes. Soon we were carrying two bags each for 18 holes, making $4 a day. That was a lot of money at the time. At 15, Mike and I had made enough money to afford surfboards, so we put our golf games on hold.

Two Reasons to Play Golf

Today, I play golf occasionally. I play primarily because my Kim is passionate about the game. In fact, she plays from the men's tees and out-drives me, which is not good for my male ego. I am a below-average golfer, scoring between 85 and 95 when I am on and worse when I am off I do not practice like I know I should.

Although I am not passionate about golf, there are two reasons that golf is essential for people who want to be rich.

The two reasons are:

1. **Games reflect behavior.** Most golfers would agree that the beauty of the game of golf is that it is a mirror, a reflection of a person's true core behavior patterns. Often, when I want to know who I am doing business with, I will play golf with them. As we are playing, I am not as concerned with the score as I am with how they play the game.

One of the things you notice is how they hit the ball. Do they swing hard to hit the ball long or do they swing for control? Do they cheat? Do they ever lie about their score or move the ball and not take a stroke?

A while ago, a friend of a friend wanted me to invest in his company. After looking over his financials, I asked if he would like to play golf. He eagerly accepted and soon we were at his country club. On that Saturday, I was not concerned about his score; I was there to watch how he played the game. He was a great golfer who hit the ball long and straight. He was doing fine until he hit the ball into the rough, alongside the green. Thinking I was not watching, I saw him move his ball. Because the grass was tall, it took him two strokes to clear the rough and get onto the green. When I asked him his score, he told me he was only one over par. I asked him if he counted his second stroke in the rough. Instead of coming clean, he denied taking the extra stroke. At that moment, I came to doubt the numbers on his financial statement.

> Once my thoughts and attitude changed, my actions changed, and so did my result.
>
> – Robert T. Kiyosaki

I've seen Donald Trump play golf. He plays golf like he does business. He hits the ball long and straight. He is also very accurate and precise in his shots.

I hit the ball erratically. That's why I believe I am better as a team player than as a golfer. I loved rowing, football and rugby because I am better on a team. I am the same way in business, which is why I am very careful about whom I have on my team.

2. **More business is done on golf courses.** Both my dads played golf. Both were pretty good. My poor dad played golf with his friends, his fellow teachers, for fun. My rich dad played golf to become rich. He said, "More business deals are done on the golf

course than in the boardroom." He went on to explain saying, "The tougher the negotiation, the more relaxed the environment needs to be."

It took me a number of years to grow and mature before I fully understood the wisdom in his words. Today, if a negotiation is involved and complicated, I will often ask the person to play golf with me so we can discuss the deal. With a relaxed golf course environment, the negotiation has more time to develop, and when the environment is relaxed, there is often more flexibility in thinking. It seems the open space of the golf course allows for more open thinking.

In Conclusion

Even though I am not a dedicated golfer, I am dedicated to winning at the game of business. Golf is the game of business. I still do not take the game of golf as seriously as many players do, but I take the game of business very seriously. That is why I am a member of three country clubs. A country club is often the best place to do business, as well as find out whom to do business with.

P.S. True to form of any great businessperson, when Donald and I became serious about doing this book together, he invited me to one of his golf courses, Trump National Golf Club in Los Angeles.

Donald's Response

The sports I have played the most over the years are baseball, tennis and golf. They are games that require finesse, a strong sense of timing and concentration. To this day I enjoy watching baseball and tennis, but I am a passionate golfer. I've developed fantastic golf courses because of that passion.

The lesson I learned from those sports is the importance of instincts. Stamina and technique are both necessary requirements, but being truly great usually means there is an "instinct" that can't really be explained. Think about Wayne Gretsky's famous explanation for his hockey success — he simply skated to where the puck was going. That's a great visual for understanding instinct.

Sounds so simple, doesn't it? Yes...until you think about it. How did he know where the puck was going? How come all the other guys didn't know where it was going? Well, because he had something special—instinct.

I've seen people who worked harder than anyone else and who still remained in the background as athletes. They were qualified, dedicated and competent, but that extra something just wasn't there. I was an excellent baseball player, and I realized that I had a natural sense of timing. Babe Ruth I would never be, but I had a sense of what it took to be great in that game.

Tennis, as a one-on-one game, made me realize that the idea was to obliterate your opponent. There's only one winner, not two. It's a fierce game. Have you ever watched the famed Swiss tennis player Roger Federer? He's got the instinct I'm talking about. As Andre Agassi once said of him:

"He's the best I've ever played against. There's nowhere to go. There's nothing to do except hit fairways, hit greens and make putts. Every shot has that sort of urgency on it. Anything you try to do, he potentially has an answer for and it's just a function of when he starts pulling the triggers necessary to get you to change to that decision."

It's interesting that Andre Agassi would use golf terms to explain Roger Federer because golf is famously a brain game. Golf requires technique, but more importantly, it requires extensive use of the mind. Roger Federer controls the game and knows instinctively how to handle his opponents. He's as fierce as he is graceful and good luck to anyone else on the court. Tennis is very much about knowing your opponent as well as yourself. That's another one of Federer's strengths.

Playing golf is a form of fun for me. Fun in the same way that making deals is fun for me. Golf champion Phil Michelson says the best golf advice he ever received was from his father, who told him to have fun. Even when he practices, he's having fun and enjoying it. I can relate to that, and it's solid advice for anything you're doing.

I have learned a lot about the integrity of people by playing golf with them. That's why so many business deals come about during and after golf games. A certain conduct is required in golf and people who keep to that form will usually be good business partners. Some people call it etiquette, I just call it honesty. A golf game can be a good indicator of that virtue.

Golf also requires flexibility. Keeping your equilibrium can make the difference between a great game and a bad one—and the same applies to business. Remain flexible. Don't stick to fixed patterns. Every game, every deal, will be different. Be in shape, be prepared, practice, and know there will be variables to deal with.

Nick Faldo, one of the all-time golf greats, says something that is absolutely right on: "Whether you hit the ball slowly, soft, or hard, everyone needs tempo...Tempo is the glue that sticks all elements of the golf swing together." I've always been big on tempo in business, in life, and in golf, and his advice on the importance of tempo should be noted by everyone, no matter what your industry or favorite sport might be.

Precision, instinct, and tempo are all necessary in order to become extraordinary.

– Donald J. Trump

These three sports have given me insights into business and life by both playing them and watching them. The number one lesson I learned from all of them is that precision, instinct and tempo are all necessary in order to become extraordinary.

Donald safe at first.

Donald's passion for golf.

Robert surfing.

Robert, far right playing rugby in New Zealand.

Your Response

What are the defining lessons you've learned from playing or watching sports?

———————————————————————

———————————————————————

———————————————————————

CHAPTER NINETEEN

WHAT DID YOU LEARN FROM BUSINESS?

Robert's Response

You cannot learn to ride a bicycle by reading a book. The same is true with business. Books and classes are good for new ideas, but like learning to ride a bicycle, learning about business is a hands-on process.

You have heard the saying, "The bigger they are, the harder they fall." Both Donald and I fell. His fall was much bigger and much more public. My fall was big, not as big as Donald's, and not as public...but it hurt nonetheless.

After receiving my sales training from Xerox, two friends and I started the nylon and Velcro surfer-wallet business. Unfortunately, the business was a screaming success. I say unfortunately because success went straight to our heads. We were three single guys in our 20s who hit it big. Our products were featured in *Runners World* magazine, *GQ*, and even *Playboy*.

One day, one of my partners drove up in a new Mercedes 450 SL. We asked him why he bought the car. "Because we're rich," he said. "Why don't you guys go and buy the cars of your dreams." So we did. Larry bought a 450 SL, like John, and I purchased a silver Porsche Targa with black trim.

You probably know the rest of the story. We were driving fast cars and dating even faster women. The business that went up fast came down even faster. In less than three years, we went from poor to rich to even poorer. We were successful, but deeply in debt from our losses. (If you would like to learn more about my many lessons learned about entrepreneurship, you can read about it in *Rich Dad's Before You Quit Your Job*. There is a lot of information for entrepreneurs in this book. It is informative as well as amusing.) As I say, as our income went up, we thought our financial IQ went up as well. The problem was, as our income went up, the only thing that went up with it was our stupidity.

That business failure was one of many defining moments I have had in business. The failure and the loss of nearly a million dollars was my wake-up call.

I had not been a strong advocate for education up to that point in my life. I did not think education was important. In school, I just got by. I was happy to be a C student. As my poor dad often said about me, "You're getting by on a shoeshine and a smile."

After that business failure in my early 30s, I realized I was way behind the learning curve. I saw people my age further ahead in life, simply because they had taken their education and their professional careers seriously. That business failure made me realize I needed to become a student, to study like I had never studied before.

> After a business failure in my early 30s, I realized I was way behind the learning curve. I saw people my age farther ahead in life, simply because they had taken their education and their professional careers seriously. This business failure was my realization that I needed to become a student, to study like I never studied before.
>
> – Robert T. Kiyosaki

For a number of years, instead of running from my failure, I worked to rebuild the business. I wanted to rebuild the business to find out what I did not know: What things had I overlooked? What had I not seen? They say that hindsight is 20/20. For me, hindsight was not only 20/20, it was painful. I had to face all the B.S. I had been telling myself. I had to face the lies I told myself and told others. After a few years of humility, the nylon wallet business was back on its feet. It was successful and profitable. It was the best education in business and the biggest dose of humility I have ever had.

In 1980, while going through that process, I attended a seminar that featured Dr. Buckminster Fuller. My life changed again. By 1984, even though my business was successful and profitable, I resigned and left Hawaii with Kim. I became a teacher, a profession I had not respected and swore I would never be a part of. From 1984 to 1994, Kim and I traveled the world teaching entrepreneurship and investing. In 1994, we retired financially free, putting into practice all we had been teaching. Kim was 37 and I was 47.

For two years, I went into hiding in the mountains of southern Arizona, near a little town known as Bisbee, where I spent my time developing the *CASHFLOW* board game and writing *Rich Dad Poor Dad*. In 1996, the first commercial game of *CASHFLOW* was played and on April 8, 1997, my 50th birthday, *Rich Dad Poor Dad* was launched at a small party. In mid-2000, a producer from Oprah Winfrey's show called. I walked onstage to greet Oprah, and the rest is history.

So losing that nylon and Velcro surfer-wallet business was a defining moment of my life. If not for that loss, I might never have become a student or a teacher.

Donald's Response

Being Visionaries

I'd like to share one of my business successes, but one that took 30 years to evolve.

Just as we are looking to the future financially, trying to keep our bases covered, *New York* magazine came out with their June 2006 issue called "2016 Tomorrowland," the projection of what NYC will be like in 10 years. I remember the uproar that I caused by wanting to build Trump Place on the Upper West Side of Manhattan, along the Hudson River, a few years back. It's a beautiful complex of 16 residential buildings including a park, and it should be done soon. Well, today they are projecting that the West Side below the Javits Center will be larger than the city of Minneapolis by 2016, so I guess I wasn't wrong in providing some housing on that side of town. Being a visionary can be worth it now and then, especially after encountering opposition, and this is one of those times.

One reason Robert and I point out certain things is because we can see them coming. As I've said before, we're not trying to be financial fearmongers. We're just hoping to be able to steer some of you in the right direction—before it's too late and you say, "Why didn't we see that coming?!" Fortunately, we're in a position, because of our individual success records, to give you some indications of what might be happening in the future.

I had to be very stubborn when it came to that development on the West Side that I just mentioned. In fact, I waited 30 years to see it happen. But I knew back then that it would be important to the future of New York City. I know this city. I was right.

Look at Mark Burnett. He saw a new direction for television and he too dealt with years of rejection. People just didn't get what he wanted to do. But he just kept at it, because he knew he was right. When the television executives finally did get what he was going after, who created a new genre and a new chapter of television history? Mark Burnett.

Sometimes it's hard to define what vision is. Usually, it's based on studying the history of something and surmising where it will be going in 10 or 20 or more years. Yes, there's a risk involved, but forward-thinking people are often on the mark. Another prime example is Leonardo da Vinci. He looked ahead by centuries in his inventions and ideas. The verification of his visionary gifts took centuries to clear, but verified they have been. Thoreau said, "If you have built castles in the air, your work need not be lost; that is where they should be. Now put the foundations under them." Vision remains vision until you focus, do the work, and bring it down to earth where it will do some good.

> Vision remains vision until you focus, do the work, and bring it down to earth where it will do some good.
>
> – Donald J. Trump

I remember Robert's frustration at seeing so many things that were clear to him and not at all clear to other people. He said the worst part was that people seemed to *not* want to hear about it! They preferred to remain ignorant—or at least unaware—rather than informed. We wondered—was it too much for people to handle?

We don't think so or we wouldn't be spending our time thinking about it and writing about it. We have reasons for what we're doing.

Have you thought about 2016 yet? We have. Stay tuned. As Henry Kissinger knowingly said, "History knows no resting places and no plateaus."

Donald giving Robert a tour of
Trump National Golf Club/Los Angeles.

Your Response

What have you learned from your own or someone else's business mistakes?

What have you learned from your own or someone else's business successes?

_____

_____

_____

Do you own your own business? If not, do you want to? What ingredients do you believe are most necessary for a business to succeed?

_____

_____

_____

What do you admire about successful business owners you know?

_____

_____

_____

Chapter Twenty

What Are Your Philosophies Concerning God, Religion and Money?

Robert's Response

While growing up, there were two points about God, church and religion that were confusing for me. The first was the idea that some people went to heaven and others did not, even if they believed in the same God. I remember asking my Sunday school teacher, "What is the difference between our church and the Catholic Church?" I was eight years old, attending the Protestant church my parents belonged to, and was curious about the differences. It shocked me when my teacher said, "Well, we both believe in Jesus Christ, but Catholics won't go to heaven."

That answer floored me. When I asked why this was, she simply said, "They don't belong to the right church."

Disturbed and even more curious, I asked my Catholic classmate if I could go to church with him. For the next few months, I went to a Catholic church and found that the congregation was made up of good people who believed in the same God as my family did. I stopped going to Sunday school at my parents' church and asked my mom and dad if, instead, I could find out about the different religions of my classmates. They agreed to it.

Over the next few years, I asked my classmates what religion or church they belonged to and then asked to go to their services with them. I attended Lutheran, Methodist, Evangelical, Buddhist, and Shinto churches or temples. In the small town where I grew up, I did not have any classmates who were Jewish or Muslim. I have since attended services in synagogues and mosques.

It continues to disturb me that there are so many people who believe they follow the "right" religion and others belong to the "wrong" religion. I strongly believe in the freedom of religious choice, so it disturbs me to hear people say that they are the only ones who will go to heaven or they are the only ones who follow the true God. This may be the reason we have so many wars over God and religion. In my opinion, the idea of a Holy War is an oxymoron.

A Trust in God

In Vietnam, I gained a very strong faith in a higher power. There were many times I should have died or saw a friend who should have died, yet we miraculously escaped harm.

In business, I have a strong faith that if I work with the highest good and fulfill a mission, a higher calling, I will enlist the powers of a supreme being. I believe that if I cheat, lie or am not forthright, I diminish the power of what Native Americans refer to as the Great Spirit. I also believe the more I strive to work at the highest legal, ethical and moral standards, the more the power of the Great Spirit enters my business.

The Golden Rule

I have tremendous respect for the real Golden Rule: "Do unto others as you would have them do unto you." Every time I am angry, upset or blame someone else, instead of retaliating with my hot temper, I ask myself, "How would I want this person to treat me now?" It's not that I always do what I know I should do, but at least I consider it. For example, I have an ex-friend whom I had a disagreement with. I wish he would call me first and apologize, which means I should call him first and apologize. But I remain stubborn and have not called him to clean up the upset.

Finding Your Path

Personally, I like what the Hindu religion calls *dharma,* which means following the path a supreme being has set for you by your own choice.

When I decided to teach and follow a profession my heart wanted to follow, my life changed dramatically. In *Before You Quit Your Job,* my book on entrepreneurship, I write about my decision to become a teacher and all the good fortune that came my way once I made that decision. One of the gifts from heaven was that my wife, Kim, came into my life the moment I made my decision to teach.

I have tremendous trust in God, a higher power. I just question some of the beliefs different religions have about God and who holds the key to heaven. In my opinion, our main job in life is to make life here on earth a little bit more like heaven.

The Second Bit of Confusion

The second bit confusion was about God and money. I still remember my friend's mom, who was very rich, always inferring that money was evil. I wondered why, if she thought money was evil, she simply didn't give all her money to the church she attended.

I did not know if it was anti-God to *want* to be rich. I even wondered if poor people were going to heaven and the rich were not. This confusion between God and money haunted me.

At a summer church camp, I found the answer. The church brought in a young youth minister, just for the summer. I still remember the day he walked into camp. All the older church leaders gasped as he walked in with a guitar slung on his back, wearing blue jeans, a T-shirt, and cowboy boots. Let me remind you that this was Hawaii in the early 1960s, and the only people we saw dressed like that were juvenile delinquents in the movies. Naturally, the kids liked him immediately.

Instead of preaching and telling us what to do and what not to do, he led us in song and dance. Instead of being taught to feel bad or guilty, we learned to feel good about ourselves.

The head minister of the church looked and dressed like a dried-up string bean. He often grumpily warned us of the potential evils of the flesh. So when this young, happy youth minister arrived, the tension between the two men was evident. During one of our evening bonfires, I asked my usual questions about money. The older minister started in about *the love of money being the root of all evil* and that *it was easier for a camel to pass through the eye of a needle than it was for a rich man to go to heaven.* I felt my spirit sink, as I felt guilty about wanting to be a rich man.

The youth minister had a different take on the subject of God and money. Instead of the rant about the love of money, he told us the story of the rich man and his three servants, known as the Parable of the Talents, which comes from the Book of Matthew. The story goes that before the rich master went on a journey, he gave his three servants some money (talents). To one he gave five talents, another two talents, and the third one talent.

The one who received five talents immediately traded and turned his five talents into 10 talents. The one with two talents, made two more talents. The servant who received only one talent dug a hole in the ground and buried it.

When the master returned, he said to the servants who doubled their money, "Well done, good and faithful servant. You have been faithful over a little; I will set you over much. Enter into the joy of your master."

At this point in the story, the youth minister said, "Notice the words, 'Enter into the joy of your master.' What do you think this means?"

A few of us fumbled around attempting to answer the question. Finally, a young girl said, "Our master wants us to be rich. Our master is happy when we are rich, when we share in his world of plenty?"

The youth minister smiled, but did not answer. Instead, he said, "Let me read to you what the servant who buried his talent said." With that, he put down his guitar, opened his Bible and read the servant's response:

"Master, I knew you to be a hard man, reaping where you did not sow, and gathering where you scattered no seed, so I was afraid, and I went and hid your talent in the ground. Here you have what is yours."

The youth minister looked up to see if we were still listening and said, "He claimed that his master was a hard man, so he did nothing."

"You mean he blamed his master?" asked the same young girl.

The youth minister again smiled and then read the master's reply to the servant, 'You wicked and slothful servant.'"

"The master called him wicked and slothful?" asked another person sitting around the bonfire. "Because he did not multiply his money? You mean he called him evil and lazy for not multiplying his money?"

The youth minister only smiled and read on, "'You knew that I reaped where I had not sowed and gather where I scattered no seed? Then you ought to have invested my money with bankers, and at my coming, I should have received what was my own with interest. So take the talent from him and give it to him who has the 10 talents."

"So the master rewarded the servant who made the most money?" I asked.

The youth minister said, "Is that what you understand?"

"Sounds like it to me," I said. "That means the more I make, more will be given to me?"

The youth minister just smiled and strummed his guitar softly.

"Is the master in this story God?" asked a young girl. "Are we the servants?"

"Does God reward rich people more than poor people?" asked someone else.

"If God is the master, does God reward the rich and punish the poor?" asked the person sitting next to me.

By this time, the older minister was shaking his head, wondering where this conversation was going. The youth minister just strummed his guitar, letting our thoughts swirl in our heads, allowing us to decide upon our own message from the parable. Finally, with the fire crackling and smoke drifting into the night air, he asked, "What does this say about people who have money and people who do not have money?"

"That people without money are lazy?" asked a boy across the fire from me. "Or that people without money are evil?"

"No, that's not what it means," said someone else. "That would be too cruel to even think. The world is filled with poor people."

"But what about the words 'enter into the joy of your master.' Doesn't that mean being rich makes you happy?"

"No, that's not what that means," shouted another young camper. "My mom and dad say that rich people aren't happy. They say that only poor and good people can go to heaven. They say that the love of money is the root of all evil."

"OK, OK," said the youth minister, quelling the brewing argument. "Let me finish the reading." Putting down his guitar, he finished reading, saying, "For to everyone who has, will *more be given,* and he will have an abundance. But *from the one who has not, even what he has will be taken away.*"

The fire crackled in the silence. No one talked. Both the older minister and the youth minister were quiet.

"Does that mean the rich will get richer and the poor poorer?" asked a young girl.

The youth minister and the older minister sat without speaking.

"That wouldn't be fair," said the young girl. "God should give to those who don't have anything. God should be generous to the poor."

"Yeah, that's not fair," said another person. "To say that 'to everyone who has, more will be given, and from those who have little, even what little they have will be taken away.' That sounds terrible."

> In my opinion, our main job in life is to make life here on earth a little bit more like heaven.
>
> – Robert T. Kiyosaki

"Does this mean people who are lazy are evil?" asked a quiet voice from a face I could not see in the darkness. "Is that why what little they have is taken away?"

The conversation around the campfire went on until the fire went out. Putting water on the coals, the youth minister said, "Time for bed. You can all find your own answers to the parable. Some of you will continue to think that money is not important, some of you will think that rich people are evil or that poor people have a better chance to get into heaven. Whatever answer you come up with will determine the rest of your life."

While I may not understand the full meaning of the parable, I did understand that the master gave the money to the person who multiplied the money. I also decided that the master could create where there was nothing. In other words, he was creative and creativity is infinite, therefore money was infinite—abundant. And to be creative and have abundance was the joy of the master. As to what happens to those who do not multiply their money and why the little they have is taken away, I am still not certain of the full meaning. I have my suspicions. Nonetheless, the youth minister's words that evening did ring true for me. The answer I came away with that night did affect the rest of my life.

The Difference Between God and Gold

My rich dad taught me the difference between God and gold. He said, "If you want to be more like God and turn anything into gold, you need to know the difference between God and gold." Explaining further, he said, "The difference between God and gold is the letter *L*. He then said "The letter *L* stands for loser, looter, lousy leader, and liar. If you do not get rid of those descriptions from your character, you will never develop your Midas touch—the ability to turn anything you touch into gold."

Donald's Response

I have noticed that people with deep faith of some sort often seem more grounded and more productive. They have a sense of purpose that can't be destroyed, and they are not easily discouraged. Whether they are Jewish, Christian, Buddhist, Muslim, or whatever religion they may follow, it gives them a direction and dedication that can defy business analysis.

I have some employees who observe the sanctity of sundown on Fridays, and they need to leave the office early. They are hardworking individuals, and I respect their devotion and faithful observance. When they are traveling with me, I have even scheduled my jet to arrive early enough on a Friday to accommodate their religious requirements. They have their priorities, and I can sacrifice a couple hours at the office to that end. I know they are devout and not just looking for an early-out or extra time off.

I was raised in a Christian family, and we were taught to respect the beliefs of other people. All of us had and still have friends of different faiths. I feel that has enhanced our understanding of the world and the people in it. Understanding can replace hatred, and that's an answer to some of the wars this planet has endured.

People send me Bibles quite often, sometimes because they think I'm a teacher and sometimes because they think I need them. I know I have gone against some of the teachings, namely because I've said to screw people back if they screw you. It's not exactly in keeping with the "turn the other cheek" lesson we've all heard, but that's the nature of the business I'm in.

In many cases, I follow one of the bits of wisdom I happen to like, which is "Be wise as a serpent and as gentle as a dove." That keeps my temper in check and adds to my intelligence quota.

> I have never believed that prosperity is bad or something to be shunned.
>
> – Donald J. Trump

I'm certainly no scholar on the subject, but I can see how people can spend decades studying the Bible. There's a lot of wisdom, lessons and tremendous history to be learned. My father was a friend of Dr. Norman Vincent Peale, so I knew him and am familiar with his famous book, *The Power of Positive Thinking*, which I still recommend today. (He is no longer with us, but his wife, Ruth, will turn 100 in September 2006.)

Having faith means believing in a power greater than yourself. I am certain there is a power greater than ourselves. That thought gives me strength to persevere in every circumstance. It's something that leaders have because they need to have it. They know they're not omniscient and omnipresent, but they do their best for the people around them, and they try as much as possible to have the big picture in mind in their decisions.

I have a picture of a galaxy that I often look at because it keeps me focused on how small my problems are in comparison to those of the universe. It gives me perspective, and then suddenly I don't seem pressured. I remain responsible to my family and to my employees and businesses, but I know that while I am famous and successful, there is a power that is far greater than I am. Faith keeps you going with confidence and keeps you humble at the same time.

Your Response

What are your philosophies concerning God and religion?

How do your religious beliefs impact your feelings about money?

_____

_____

_____

Do you believe we live in a world of abundance or scarcity?

_____

_____

_____

PART FOUR

IF YOU WERE IN MY SHOES, WHAT WOULD YOU DO?

One of the riskiest things a person can do is say, "I have $10,000. What should I do with it?" The problem with announcing that you do not know what to do with your money is that it attracts millions of people who do know what to *do* with your money—take it.

Most people want to be given a magic formula. People who want to be told what do with their money are often the ones who take the advice of the typical financial advisor who says to save, get out of debt, invest for the long term, and diversify. If you're looking for someone to tell you what to do with your money, most people will tell you the smart thing to do is to live below your means. If that appeals to you, then go for it.

People who look for a magic answer are usually people who invest not to lose. They are often terrified of making mistakes. If you are terrified of making mistakes, then find someone who has the magic answer for you and turn your money over to them.

Donald and Robert believe in financial education and preparation, not one-size-fits-all answers. They also would rather continually expand their means, not work to live below them.

In this part of the book, Donald and Robert offer their generic advice for specific groups of people on how they would get ahead by gaining greater financial education and preparation.

CHAPTER TWENTY-ONE

I AM STILL IN SCHOOL... WHAT SHOULD I DO?

Robert's Response

If you're in high school or younger, I suggest you focus on having fun. If you ever watch kittens or puppies playing, you'll notice they are actually learning many of the skills they will need for adult life by playing. Have fun, play and learn.

I feel for kids today whose parents are preparing them for Harvard in kindergarten. In Hawaii, well-to-do parents are paying over $1,000 a month for their six-month-old children to go to a college-prep day care. It's their choice, but I would not want to be their child.

The tough part for me, as a kid, was that I did not know I was poor until I went to school. What made it even worse was that it was not OK for me to tell my parents, adults or teachers that I wanted to be rich. In my family, to want to be rich, to actually desire money, was sacrilegious. I know in many families and groups, that is still true today.

If you are a child who is growing up in a family or in a circle of people who think wanting to be rich is bad, even evil, keep quiet. Don't antagonize adults. It's not worth it. Find friends in school or online who think like you, and be true to yourself without violating the values of your family. Your family is important.

If you have a family that is supportive of your desire to be rich, then take them along with you on your journey. At many of the seminars, like the ones Donald and I do together, it's often the kids who drag their parents along.

Many times, I have had fathers and mothers come up to me and say, pointing to their son or their daughter, "They read your book and insisted I bring them to this event. If not for them, I would not be here."

Remember this: Money by itself is not good or evil. Yet we all know many people do evil things for money. Many people are afraid that if you love money you will turn into a greedy person, which some people do. Always remember that if you decide to become a rich person, you can also choose to be a good person who is rich and generous, but not foolish with money.

One of the blessings I had in my life was that my rich friends were not snobs. They were nice to everyone. When we played baseball or football, we were all one team, rich or poor. Today, I know things are different. Many kids hang out in cliques, discriminating against less fortunate or less "cool" kids. If you should decide to become a rich kid, I ask you to remember to be kind and respectful to all kids and not to be a snob.

Two Challenges with School

There were two challenges I faced with school. The first was that it kept programming me to get a job. Teachers assumed I was going to be an employee in the E quadrant. I wanted to be an entrepreneur. Thank goodness schools today have business clubs and curriculums for students who want to be entrepreneurs. In my day, there were a few clubs, but they were taught by people who did not know anything about business.

> Most people struggle with money because in school they only learn how to work for money. Rarely do they learn to have money work for them.
>
> – Robert T. Kiyosaki

The second challenge was that schools punish people for making mistakes. Isn't that silly? The way we learn is by making mistakes. I learned to ride a bicycle, skateboard and surfboard by falling off time after time. If I had been punished for falling off, I might never have learned to ride. When you make a mistake, please do not lie about it or pretend you did not make one, as many adults do. Instead, take the time to learn from your mistakes, and you will learn faster than those who avoid making mistakes or pretend they do not make any.

Two Great Exercises

Exercise #1: When you are old enough and your parents are willing, an excellent real-world exercise is to budget and buy the food for your family for one week. Let's say your family's budget for food for one week is $100. Plan the menu and shop for the food, staying within your budget and keeping everyone happy with the menu. Do this several times until you become good at budgeting and your family is happy with your food selections. This is a great real-life exercise in budgeting money.

When I did this, I was 15 years old and all I heard were complaints. While I did stay within the budget, my family got sick and tired of hot dogs and beans. After that exercise, I felt a lot more compassion for my mom.

Exercise #2: Most people struggle with money because in school they only learn how to *work for money.* Rarely do they learn to have money work for them.

After you have mastered budgeting for food, you can learn how to make money with money. The exercise is simple if you are creative, but tough if you are not creative. All you have to do is take $10 and see how long it takes you to double it to $20. You might lend it to a friend and charge that friend $1 a month interest, taking you 10 months to double your money. Or you could buy something and sell it on the Internet. If you are good, you may double your money in one day. The challenge is to find out how many different ways you can take money and make more money with it.

Most adults struggle financially because they do not have a clue how to do this. They just know how to go to work, get paid, and spend what they earn. If you are going to be rich, you will need to know many different ways to make money with money.

Apprentice and Mentor

Donald and I both had rich dads as mentors. This may be why Donald has his hit television show, *The Apprentice*. Years ago, before there were government-controlled schools, young people learned by becoming apprentices to mentors. This mentor/apprentice system was the primary way we learned. All the way back to cave dwellers, children learned their craft by being apprentices to adults who were mentors.

Today, instead of mentors, we have teachers. While there are similarities between teachers and mentors, there are also differences. One difference is that a teacher teaches you a subject while a mentor is someone you want to grow up to be like—a role model.

One of the difficulties I had as a child was that my dad was a teacher, and although I loved him, I did not want to grow up to be like him. He taught me many things that are priceless—the importance of honor, the love of study, honesty and the courage to stand up to a corrupt government system, even if it meant losing his job. I have done my best to embody many of those traits in my life today. But I did not want to grow up to be a teacher in the government system as he was. I did not want to need a job or expect the government to take care of me when I retired. I wanted to be a rich entrepreneur who invested in real estate. That is why I sought out a mentor, my rich dad.

Today, I am a teacher. The difference is I am an entrepreneur who owns an education business. If not for my apprenticeship with my rich dad, I doubt if I would be an educational entrepreneur who invests in real estate, gold, silver, and oil. In other words, by seeking a mentor, I was able to become the best of both my dads.

Remember the difference between a teacher and a mentor. If you are lucky, and a mentor you like decides to make you his or her apprentice, honor that person with respect for his or her time and the wisdom he or she is willing to impart to you.

Life will introduce you to many different people. Some you will love and some you will wish you never met. You can learn something from all of them.

A Word About School

While I did not like school, did not do well in school and have not used much of what I studied in school, I still recommend all young people complete their education, at least through four years of college.

Why do I recommend this? For the following reasons:

1. High school and college are times to grow up. I believed I knew all the answers when I was in high school and college, and all I found out after I left school was how much I did not know.

2. A college degree is a ticket. It means you accomplished something. It means you focused for four years. If I did not have a college degree, I would never have been allowed into Navy flight school. As a helicopter pilot, I often let my enlisted crew chiefs fly the helicopter. Most of them were better pilots than me, but because they did not have a college degree, the ticket, the military would not let them fly.

3. College gives you the opportunity to explore many different subjects and interests. At the academy, I was surprised to find out how much I enjoyed the study of economics. If I had not gone to college, I would not know much about global economic trends and the language economists use. Just knowing a little about GNP versus GDP, and the differences between M1, M2 and M3, the measure of money supplies, has made a significant impact upon my finances.

What Should I Study?

Whenever I am asked by college students, "What do you recommend I study?" I recommend two things.

They are:

1. Accounting

2. Business law

I do not recommend these subjects because I think everyone should become accountants or attorneys. I recommend these two subjects because they give the student the ability to see into a business or investment. Understanding these two subjects is like putting on X-ray glasses and being able to see what most people cannot see.

Financial advisors are able to convince you to turn your money over to them because they know you believe they can see what you cannot see. They want you to think they have the inside track. Well, some do, but most don't. Most financial advisors are salespeople (which is why they are called brokers). As I've said, a majority of them do not invest in what they recommend.

One of the benefits of going to school and studying different subjects is that you learn the disciplines and the "languages" particular to different professions. For example, when I went to flight school, I learned the disciplines of pilots and the lingo they used. When I was at the academy, I learned the disciplines needed to live on a ship and become an officer. I learned that in the shipping industry, instead of using the words right or left, we use starboard or port.

When you study accounting, you will learn to read numbers and words particular to that field. For those of you who have read *Rich Dad Poor Dad,* you may remember that my rich dad had a different definition for the word *asset* than my poor dad. That is why my poor dad called his house an *asset* and my rich dad called his house a *liability.* My rich dad understood the definitions of that word, and my poor dad did not. That one distinction made a big difference over the lifetimes of both men. I still run into financial journalists and salespeople who want to argue with me over the definitions of assets and liabilities.

By the way, the reason most houses are a liability is because in accounting there are three basic reporting forms. They are:

1) the income statement, which is pictured here:

INCOME STATEMENT

Income
Expenses

2) a balance sheet, which is pictured here:

BALANCE SHEET

Assets	Liabilities

and 3) the statement of cash flow. It is this statement of cash flow that many people, even sometimes accountants, do not pay much attention to. If you are an investor, which many accountants are not, you will need to pay very close attention to the statement of cash flow. As any entrepreneur or investor knows, cash flow is king.

In the *CASHFLOW* game, the statement of cash flow is found here:

Recently, I was on the television show *20/20*. They did not paint a favorable picture of me or my books. On the program, they had a number of financial authors they liked. One financial expert, who prior to the year 2000, was recommending mutual funds in the technology arena, was in 2006, suddenly a real estate expert. On the *20/20* program, he was recommending people buy their dream home. This former mutual fund expert, now suddenly a real estate expert, was helping a cash-strapped couple buy their dream home. He told them the house was an asset—at the height of the real estate bubble, with rising interest rates and increasing foreclosures. Can you imagine that? According to him, the house was an asset because they were throwing the money they paid in rent down the drain. As a professional investor, I would have recommended the couple continue to rent until the market cooled down.

The other financial expert on *20/20* said that most millionaires drive Toyotas. As I said at the start of this book, today there are more millionaires than ever, simply because the dollar has dropped and values of homes went up. They are, indeed, millionaires—on paper.

Now there is nothing wrong with driving a Toyota. But I do not choose to live below my means as the other author suggests you should. I wanted to become rich because I want to live the good life…not live below my means. If you like living below your means as a millionaire, go ahead. It is up to you.

Study accounting and business law, and learn about market trends, so you will not be fooled by people who may position themselves as "experts" (or be anointed as such by the media) but are not really investors.

The show's host, a seasoned journalist, complained that in my books I do not give people specific answers. I do not give people answers like, "Turn your money over to me and diversify, diversify, diversify, so I can earn more commissions," or "Buy a home because you're wasting your rent money," because I would rather teach people to think for themselves. You see, there are times when it is better to rent than to own—and *you* need to be able to determine what is in your best interest. While I do agree owning a home is important, knowing when, where and at what interest rates to buy are also important. Just as every hard-core shopper knows when the sales are, a hard-core investor doesn't like to buy until there is a sale going on. To advise a couple to buy a home at the height of the real estate market and pay for it by not having a cappuccino sounds to me like a poor and foolish way of looking at home ownership.

People are better able to think for themselves by becoming financially literate…to be able to see with X-ray eyes rather than be led blindly by the nose. Take a course in accounting and business law, even if you have no plans on becoming an accountant or a lawyer.

A Word on Cash Flow

Cash flow is important because it is the primary control an entrepreneur or investor wants control over. As stated earlier, the reason I love real estate and buying or building businesses is because I have control. Most investors think investing is risky because they invest in investments they have no control over—investments such as savings, stocks, bonds, and mutual funds.

When you look at the diagram of a financial statement, you will see why control of cash flow is so important to professional investors and business owners.

INCOME STATEMENT

Income
Expenses

The sign of a high financial IQ is high cash flow flowing into the income column. The sign of a low financial intelligence is excessive cash flowing out through the expense column.

America as a country and many Americans are in financial trouble because they have not been able to increase the cash flowing into their income column and have lost control over the cash flowing out of their expense column. Also, rather than creating assets, they continually create more liabilities, which accelerates the cash flowing out through the expense column. Someone who has excessive credit card debt, takes out a home equity loan to pay off the credit cards, and then goes out and gets into more credit card debt is an example of someone who has lost control.

My rich dad recommended I spend a number of years learning to sell, knocking on doors, because he wanted me to learn how to have control over the cash from income flowing into my financial statement. Many people struggle financially simply because they are not good at sales or marketing. You may notice that Donald Trump is possibly the world's greatest marketer today. His brand means money, and it attracts money.

Interestingly enough, my rich dad said the expense column was the most important of the columns. He said, "Most people spend and make themselves poor. If you are going to be rich, you need to know how to spend to make yourself rich." The following diagram will explain why he said this:

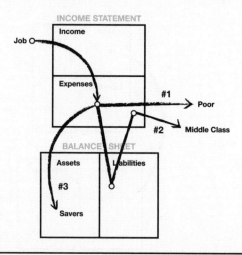

These are the three basic controls of the expense column. One of the reasons our country struggles and millions of people struggle is because all they have is cash flow #1 and cash flow #2. If you want to be rich, regardless of how much you make, you need to have cash flow #3.

As I said earlier, *USA Today* conducted a survey and found that the greatest fear in America was not terrorism but the fear of running out of money during retirement. Could it be because most financial advisors and people have a saver's mentality? Cash flow #3 is a diagram of a saver's mentality. To become very rich and not live below one's means, a person needs cash flow arrow #4. This is the arrow Donald and I have.

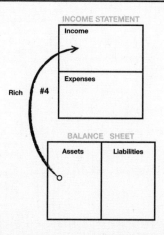

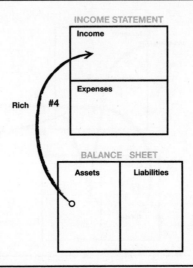

Whether or not we work, cash keeps flowing in from our assets. The harder we work at adding to this asset column, the more the money keeps pouring in. Both Donald and I have more than enough money flowing from cash flow #4. We do not have to work, but we choose to continue to work hard, adding more assets, which make us richer.

Let me give you an example of my wife's activities. In 1989, Kim's first investment was a $45,000 two-bedroom, one-bath home in Portland, Oregon. Her financial statement looked like this:

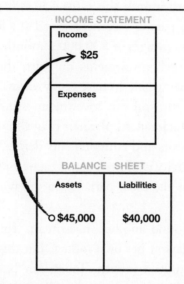

After looking at thousands of deals and actually buying maybe 25 of them, she made the following investment in 2004: She purchased a commercial property for approximately $8 million and put down $1 million, which she borrowed, so it was 100 percent financed by debt. Her net cash flow looked like this:

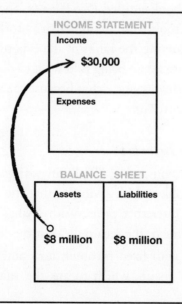

In other words, every month she earns $30,000 net income. Also, this income, because it is passive income, is taxed at a lower tax rate than that of someone who earns wages of $30,000 a month. This is an exceptional investment. While such investments do exist, they are rare. But being financially literate, being able to have X-ray vision, has its rewards. If you do the math, the return on this investment is infinite. It sure beats the 10 percent returns the financial planners brag about.

Real estate investors and entrepreneurs derive higher returns on their money because creativity is allowed in real estate and in business. Creativity and controls are, for the most part, taboo in savings, stocks, bonds and mutual funds.

In 2005, Kim found another investment. This time she had to put down a million dollars of her own money, but this 2005 investment also pays her a net $30,000 a month. Today, her passive income, which is income without working, is well over a million dollars a year.

This is why I recommend students take courses in accounting and business law in college. Once you graduate from college, begin practicing. You will need to convert your education into experience. The more you practice, the more you learn and the more experience you gain. You will find that your risk will go down and your returns will go up.

Kim has written a book entitled *Rich Woman*. She has earned the right to write this book. It took Kim about 10 years to become pretty good, and now I'd say she's joining the ranks of the experts. The subtitle of the book says it all: "Because I hate being told what to do." I can attest to that statement. The reason she became rich is because she wants the freedom to live life according to her terms.

My Bank Pays Me Interest

I can hear some of you saying, "Well, my savings pay me interest as a return." Again, the problem with savings is that the value of the dollar is falling faster than the interest it earns. With savings, you have very little control over your income or the return on your money.

People who retire with fixed incomes, now and into the future, will probably see inflation go up, which means the value of their dollar or savings will erode.

I would rather learn to control my income, returns on my money, instead of turn it over to a banker. I do keep some money in savings, as a reserve, but I am not counting on the dollar to keep me alive.

I encourage people to learn to develop an investor's mentality rather than a saver's mentality. You'll sleep better when you're older if you do.

In Conclusion

If you are in college, get a basic education in accounting and business law. Once you leave school, invest some time converting that education into experience. In theory, learning to have control over cash flowing from income, expenses, assets and liabilities sounds easy, but in reality, it is not. Converting educational theory to real-life experience is vital.

Business law is about the rules of the game. If you look at any game, there are always rules, and professional games always have a referee. Many times, I have gotten into trouble, not because I am a crook, but simply because I was not aware of the rules or had an advisor who was not aware of the rules. So rules are important, and the earlier you understand the basic rules, the better chance you have of winning the game.

If you can become good at budgeting, controlling the cash flowing to your asset column, you will have a better chance of becoming rich. If you are good at budgeting and understand control and leverage, you can become very rich without needing a high-paying job. There are many people who have high-paying jobs but are poor simply because they do not know how to budget or leverage and they have no control.

So take a course or courses in accounting and business law. Knowing a little about accounting and business law will probably make you better at choosing good accountants and attorneys. (By the way, adults can do the same thing in night school or at their local community colleges. And regardless of age, you can join or form a CASHFLOW Club and take control of your financial education.)

At The Rich Dad Company, we have our Web site www.RichKidSmartKid.com so we can make financial education available to schools free of charge. It is our way of helping to level the playing field for all children.

Donald's Response

Just this week, I received a letter from a professor at Georgetown University who had taught and known my son Eric during his college career there. Eric graduated last month from the business school, and while I knew he was a serious student who did well, I have to say I didn't know how diligent he was.

This professor mentioned that Eric was the only student in all his years of teaching who ever handed in his papers a week before they were due. Eric's work ethic became something all his other professors remarked about as well. He also received an award for excellence in negotiation and arbitration (among others). The teacher said he definitely stood out from the crowd, and not because he's 6'5" tall. Of course, I was very proud to hear of his over-the-top performance.

I've mentioned before that it's important to do more than is expected if you expect to excel. I studied in my spare time, and it's exactly what I'd do again today if I were back in college. It doesn't matter what you are studying; whatever it is, find out more. Read as much as you can, learn as much as you can, every day.

I knew someone who was a lit major, and he would read not only all the required books plus some, but then he'd go get the CliffsNotes and study those. I asked him why he did that if he'd already done the reading (and, knowing him, he read everything very thoroughly). He said, "That way, I can compare what they have to say versus what I think, and I can form a debate in my mind between the two sources. By the time I finish doing that, I will be very familiar with the work." Not surprisingly, he went on to become a lawyer—a brilliant and very erudite lawyer. He prepared himself for it by being thorough and doing more than was expected.

Raise the bar on yourself. Never settle for doing "enough." Today's world is competitive and moves so quickly that you will have to raise your stamina level if you expect to remain in the competition or to even get into the competition to begin with.

In addition, today is full of ever-changing and progressing technology, and keeping up with that is necessary. You have to know what's going on, and with so much going on, you have a big homework assignment.

The second big homework assignment is just keeping up with current events worldwide. Do not be negligent in this area. We've all heard of the global market. Well, it's here, so start plugging into it. Read about and keep up with international affairs.

In last season's *Apprentice*, we had a fellow named Lenny who was originally from Russia. For one task assignment, the apprentices were supposed to write a jingle. Well, he'd never heard of a jingle. He didn't know what it was. Some people didn't believe him, and they thought he was playing dumb. He wasn't playing dumb, because he started out by humming and then said to try adding some bells, so he was trying to figure out what a jingle was by thinking of "Jingle Bells," the Christmas song. I have to hand it to him for trying. But it proves that it helps to know what something is before trying to do it.

Let's face it, there's a lot to know in this world. If you are in college today, and you want to be a major player in the world arena, pay attention and go the extra mile—every single day. Don't wait for opportunity to come to you.

As Louis Pasteur said, "Chance favors the prepared mind."

Thirdly, do not neglect your life skills, which should include a healthy dose of financial education. Your financial intelligence can have a profound impact on your quality of life, no matter what your interests are. Do not allow blind spots to interfere with or ruin the blueprint of your life. It helps to think like a builder and know that every inch of a building, or every aspect of your life, has to be accounted for. In construction, we can't be haphazard, or hope that things might work out okay. That's setting the stage for a disaster. We have to know.

One reason I'm known as a great builder is because I am thorough. Thoroughness is not a choice, it is a prerequisite. Don't view your financial education as a choice unless you want to encounter big problems later on. Do a review of your financial status once a week to begin with. See it being as necessary as doing your laundry.

Lastly, spend some time on your focus. You should try to discover your ambitions and passions, if you haven't already. One good question to ask yourself is:

What would you do if you didn't need money?

Before I went to college, I had to make the choice of going into the film industry or going into real estate. I had an interest in both industries, and I seriously considered going to USC to study film before choosing Wharton. I love real estate and had no second thoughts after making my decision, but I've kept up my interest in the entertainment business, which better prepared me when I entered it, unexpectedly, later in life. Pay attention to what interests you, and your interest might be well rewarded later.

> Do not neglect your life skills, which should include a healthy dose of financial education.
>
> – *Donald J. Trump*

Another question to help you with your focus: What would you do if you knew you couldn't fail? Your answer might be outrageous, it might be sensible, or it might totally surprise even you. You might want to keep it to yourself. A hundred years ago if someone replied, "I want to walk on the moon" they might be considered a wacko. We know today that really was a possibility. In working on your focus, you might discover that you are a bit of a visionary.

Putting those ideas into action will require resources. So we're back to your financial intelligence, also known as your life skills. Learn about money and how it can work for you. Then get to work on making your dreams become your reality.

CHAPTER TWENTY-TWO

I AM AN ADULT WITHOUT MUCH MONEY, WHAT SHOULD I DO?

Robert's Response

For my parents' generation, the WWII generation, the rules for success were pretty simple: "Go to school, get a job, work hard, and the company and the government will take care of you once you are through working." They received regular pay raises and promotions because America's economy was growing, oil was cheap, and we were the leaders of the free world. Our dollar was strong, and after World War II, many nations owed us money. Today, almost everything has been reversed.

The rules of money have changed. As already stated, in 1971 our dollar changed from money to a currency, which means the government can print it faster than you can save it. The second change was in 1974, when big corporations let employees know they were not going to take care of them for life.

In 1996, there was another law change, known as the Telecom Reform Act. The reason this change is affecting the rules of money and employment today is because the Telecom Reform Act made it easy and inexpensive for businesses to hire workers in China, India, Ireland, and the rest of the world.

When I was a kid, the only people who were threatened by foreign competition were blue-collar workers. As you know, many factory jobs went overseas. After the 1996 Telecom Reform Act, white-collar, college-level jobs started going overseas as well.

Many call centers are no longer in the United States, but in countries such as India. This is because the Telecom Reform Act allowed companies such as Global Crossing, which no longer exists, to lay miles of fiber-optic cable all over the world. Now it may be far less expensive to call someone in Asia or Eastern Europe than it is to call someone in another U.S. city.

People primarily in the B and I quadrants benefit from this act, and many of those in the E and S quadrants suffer. People have been crying the blues about our jobs going overseas. While jobs have been going overseas for years, it was this 1996 act that accelerated the process. Today, even medical doctors, lawyers, and accountants have their income threatened by this change.

In 2001, something else happened—China was admitted into the World Trade Organization (WTO). Again, this is great for those in the B and I quadrants, but may be a threat to those in the E and S quadrants.

Asking for a Raise

The significance of the Telecom Reform Act and the admission of China into the WTO is that asking for a raise could now be a job-threatening move. Whether you're a blue-collar or white-collar worker, the person competing for your job may live thousands of miles away—this at a time when inflation is climbing, gas prices are climbing and housing prices are through the roof.

Some of you say, "Well, my job is safe. I'm a schoolteacher and someone has to actually be in the classroom to teach." Yes, there are many jobs like that—including the jobs held by police officers, desk clerks, firefighters, hotel maids, janitors, city workers, and more. Some jobs are protected from foreigners. But remember this: If blue-collar and white-collar workers are losing their jobs, they in turn will become local competition for your job.

Simplicity or Complexity

If you are an adult without much money, you have two basic choices:

1. Live below your means.

2. Expand your means.

Saying it another way:

1. Simplicity

2. Complexity

I have several friends who have simplified. They have simply downsized and decreased their living standards. A couple in southern Arizona built their own adobe home, so they had no mortgage. They are off the grid, which, for them, means they have their own solar power, their own well, raise cattle, and are heavily armed. The husband has a military pension and goes into town once a month for essentials. They are living the simple life and are very happy.

Many baby boomers are relocating to Mexico or Costa Rica for the same simpler life at a better price.

Donald and I have chosen a more complex life. We do business 24/7 because we have business interests all over the world. We have multiple homes, are in constant communication with our home base, and travel constantly.

Kim and I love our life. We have friends all over the world and our lifestyle affords long-distance relationships, both personal and business.

Most people fall somewhere between the two examples of the two lifestyles. Today, a person can easily buy their 100 acres, disconnect from the grid and still be in contact with the world and live the 24/7 lifestyle, if they choose.

The reason I say it is important to choose simplicity, complexity or both now is because all choices require time, money and planning. I know many people who would love to drop off the power grid and get out of the hustle and bustle of daily life today, but they cannot afford the time or the 100 acres of land.

As an adult, you should know what kind of lifestyle you want. There is no right or wrong. My point is: Start planning for it now—before it's too late, especially if you want to live on your 100 acres of land or on a tropical island. My suggestion is to start looking for your paradise now. Life is too short not to dream of paradise, whatever it looks like to you. There are things more important than money.

Donald and I do not recommend the hectic pace of our lifestyles. But we love it. We chose it. We want you to choose yours.

If you're not ready to retire to the ranch or the beach, and a more hectic, financially richer life is appealing to you, then you will probably need to increase your complexity. Increasing your complexity means increasing your financial awareness of the world around you as well as the world in front of you. For example, when I wake up, I need to know how the markets in Asia and Europe are doing. What is the relationship of the yen to the dollar? How is oil doing? How about natural gas, gold, silver and my companies in China and South America?

> In simple terms, competitive complexity means being a student of the world of money, people, and business 24/7/52.
>
> – Robert T. Kiyosaki

It also means reading business books and magazines such as *Forbes, Fortune, TIME* and *The Economist,* just to keep a pulse on the world. Kim and I are always attending investment and financial workshops, not only to meet new people, but to keep up on new ideas and find new investment trends. Complexity means meeting and doing business with many different types of people. In the world of entrepreneurship and highly leveraged investments, you meet many interesting characters and con artists.

Our lives also mean dealing with the press all the time. The press is good to us 90 percent of the time. But true to the 90/10 rule, it is the 10 percent who promise to do a fair article about us and then knife us in the back, often manipulating facts to support an agenda or position, distorting instead of informing. As my rich dad often said, "The freedom of speech does not mean you have to tell the truth."

In simple terms, competitive complexity means being a student of the world of money, people and business 24/7/52. Twenty-four hours a day, seven days a week, 52 weeks a year. I love this game. To me, it is like Super Bowl Sunday every day of the year. I do not know of a more exciting, frustrating, sometimes disappointing, and rewarding game. If you are foolish, the game takes back all your winnings. If you are smart, the game opens the gushers and money pours out to you.

Two Extremes

So those are your two extremes. It's a free country and your choice. I made my choice years ago when I was a kid in fifth grade, reading about the great explorers such as Columbus, Marco Polo, and Leif Erickson. I dreamed of following in their footsteps all over the world, and that's exactly what I've done. The difference is, I can now travel around the world and check on my holdings electronically, in less time than it took for Columbus to cast off the dock. The world today is a 24/7 market. Trillions of dollars are trading hands every day. That is why it amuses me when I meet people who are looking for a job or for a pay raise or wondering how they are going to make a few extra dollars. Obviously, they live in a different world than I do. Today, a person can live in the most remote parts of the world and still be doing business with the rest of the world.

Those who live in a free world have the option to choose the kind of world they want to live in. Instead of becoming angry with globalization, as many people are, I'd rather do my best to keep up with it. Recently, most of us heard of the riots in France. The riots were about demanding job security. The students wanted the government to write rules that make it impossible for businesses to fire people. While I understand their concerns and desire for job security, I am afraid those young students are not living in this new reality.

When people ask me what they should do, I recommend they travel to France, then fly to New York and Los Angeles, then fly to Hong Kong, Singapore, Shanghai, India, on to Dubai, to Prague, to London, and to Dublin, and then return home. It will be the best $25,000 or less you could have spent.

A friend of mine in Arizona always vacations in Europe and took my advice and went around the world. When he came back, all he said was, "Wow. Have my eyes been opened. I cannot believe how much faster the rest of the world is moving. Hong Kong and Shanghai blew me away. If American workers could see how fast Asian workers work, and for so much less, they might realize how hard they are not working. And in Europe, the rich are in great shape because they operate more globally than most Americans. But many other European workers are in the dark ages. Instead of going forward, many of them are going backward." So, travel and see the accelerating world of money, known as globalization.

Winning the Money Olympics

For people who are starting with nothing, yet want to be rich, I often suggest they imagine wanting to win an Olympic Gold Medal. Once you set the goal of winning a gold medal, the next question is, which Olympics—summer or winter? After that, the next question is, in which event? Do you want to be a gold medalist in the 100-yard dash, water polo, rowing, figure skating, downhill skiing, snowboarding, hammer throwing, or shooting? Once you choose which event, then study, train, hire a coach, enter smaller events, and dedicate your life to winning.

If you are not willing to dedicate your life to winning, I doubt you have a chance of winning the Olympics or becoming rich.

When I look back upon my life, the three subjects I failed in school were English, typing and accounting. Today, I am best known as a writer, I spend most of my time typing and I write about accounting. Although I am not great at writing, typing, or accounting, I am dedicated to winning.

Assess the Facts

If you are an adult, it is time to be truthful with yourself and ask, "Am I ahead of the world, or am I falling behind?" If you are falling behind and would rather keep falling behind, then begin to simplify your life. You may need to live below your means, as most financial planners recommend.

If you decide on joining globalization and becoming more complex, the following are some basic steps I recommend:

1. Find friends, new or old, or join a club with people who think the way you want to think.

2. Travel more. Take trips to learn and grow. See the world.

3. I recommend you read:

   The World Is Flat by Thomas Friedman
   The Dollar Crisis by Richard Duncan
   A Whole New Mind by Daniel Pink
   The Coming Economic Collapse by Stephen Leeb
   The America We Deserve by Donald Trump

If you are not up to speed, reading and studying these books as soon as possible will give you an interesting view of the world, a view very different from the one painted by our politicians and financial planners. By studying these books, preferably in a group, you will see beyond the problems of our world. You will see the brave new world that is emerging along with the abundance of opportunities to become richer beyond your wildest dreams.

Instead of living life like an ostrich, as most people do, you may want to soar like an eagle and enjoy a life that only 10 percent of the population will know.

Meet Like-Minded People

At The Rich Dad Company, we are thrilled that individuals have created their own CASHFLOW Clubs. A CASHFLOW Club is a group of people who get together to play the *CASHFLOW* game and invest time in their financial education. These clubs are independent of The Rich Dad Company and form on their own.

There are two kinds of clubs: commercial clubs and educational clubs.

1. Commercial CASHFLOW Clubs are often formed because the founder of the club uses the *CASHFLOW* game as a way of introducing the group to the game, but also to the products they are selling. For example, a real estate company uses the game as

an educational tool, but also to introduce people to the real estate company's staff and services.

It is important to remind you that these clubs are not affiliated with The Rich Dad Company. They are totally independent. All we ask of such commercial clubs is that they inform the new members of their commercial agenda up front, before people play the game.

At The Rich Dad Company, we realize that most of us have something to sell. All we ask is that it be done with respect and professionalism.

2. Educational CASHFLOW Clubs are formed primarily for the purpose of teaching friends and family the same principles of business and investing my rich dad taught me.

   You may recall from The Cone of Learning, introduced earlier in the book, that one of the best ways of learning and retaining what you have learned is via group study and playing games or simulations. This is what CASHFLOW Clubs do. It is a cooperative way of learning together. It is also a great way to meet new friends.

   We strongly recommend you invest time before you invest your money. We would rather you learn to fish before you turn your money over to people who sell fish. That is why CASHFLOW Clubs are formed in homes, at businesses during lunch hour, in schools, and in churches.

Those are the two basic types of CASHFLOW Clubs. We have new products that are especially designed to be guide and support materials for CASHFLOW Clubs.

In Conclusion

If you should decide to live in the more complex world of our global society, I strongly recommend you learn the following subjects:

1. **Fundamental investing:** This is the ability to read numbers. If you are going to invest in a business, real estate or a stock, it is important to be able to read numbers. They are an important part of financial literacy.

   CASHFLOW 101 was designed and created to teach the basics of fundamental investing.

2. **Technical investing:** Technical investing is essential in today's volatile world. Technical investing requires knowing how to invest when markets are going up and when markets are going down. A technical investor knows how to make money regardless of which direction the market is moving.

   More importantly, technical investing is essential for teaching investors to invest with insurance. As I have said many times, professional investors invest with insurance. Amateurs do not. One of my concerns with mutual funds is that besides not being able to borrow money to buy mutual funds, you generally cannot buy insurance against market crashes. That is extremely risky.

   CASHFLOW 202 was designed to teach you the ins and outs of technical investing.

I encourage you to seek out—or start—a CASHFLOW Club. Most of these clubs have both games as well as the electronic versions of our games so you can challenge, meet, and play against other like-minded people all over the world.

Most importantly, you will be investing only time, without risking your real money. Once you feel you have learned the basics of both fundamental and technical investing, then you may venture out and invest tiny amounts of your real money. Soon, if you study and practice diligently, you will be traveling the world, physically and electronically, playing the most exciting game in the world—the game of money.

Donald's Response

I suggest you take an in-depth look at your lifestyle and the kind of person you are. Do you like simplicity? Do you like complexity?

To me, money is like health. Health is very important to our wellbeing. You can have loads of money, but if you're not in good health, it's not so great. Money has its limitations. I say that in order to set you up to think about what you already have going for you.

If I had no money, but was healthy, I know I could make a fresh start of things by being diligent and patient. Due diligence is increasing your financial IQ daily by keeping up with world events and reading financial publications. Patience is realizing that things take time, effort and thought.

I would make sure that any ideas I had for making money were based on a reality check. The stakes get higher as we get older, and there's less leeway for making big mistakes. But hopefully we have a little more life experience to draw upon.

I was talking with Allen Weisselberg, my CFO, one day, and he mentioned how when he was a young teacher just out of college, he would introduce new lessons by starting with something known to the students before introducing the unknown. He was especially concerned that high school students had no money skills, which in his mind, meant their life skills were something to worry about. He finally figured out a way to get his point across by asking them if they liked to go shopping. They all did. Then he asked them to figure what a discount of 15 percent was off a pair of jeans. They said the cashier would figure it out for them!

> Due diligence equals increasing your financial IQ daily.
>
> – *Donald J. Trump*

Then he asked them, what if the cashier didn't give them the correct discount? Would they know what the correct amount was and be able to correct the cashier? Because if they didn't know, how would they know if they'd been ripped off or not? Well, the kids didn't like the idea of being ripped off, so they suddenly began trying to figure out the correct amount. He told them that this example was one step to being prepared, or at least alert to what was happening around them.

The same lesson applies to adults. We have to take the time to figure things out for ourselves, or we wind up being at the mercy of people who may intentionally or unintentionally have priorities other than our best interests in mind.

Review your skill set, your interests, your location, your inclinations, and put your mind to changing your situation. Remain open to ideas that you might not normally entertain. Realize that opportunity comes in different packages, and that some great things have come after wipeouts. It may not be easy, but it can happen.

Whatever you do, don't give up. Assess what you have going for you, and go with that. We all have something to offer, every person is unique, and as I've said before, I don't accept excuses.

When it comes to your life and the well-being of your loved ones, neither should you.

CHAPTER TWENTY-THREE

I AM A BABY BOOMER WITHOUT MUCH MONEY, WHAT SHOULD I DO?

Robert's Response

The baby-boom generation, that group born between 1946 and 1964, was, in many ways, a very fortunate group. They were born just as America became the dominant world power militarily *and* financially. However, they are now witnessing the decline of America, if not militarily, at least financially.

The baby-boom generation is the *last* generation of the Industrial Age and the first generation of the Information Age. They are a transitional generation, and this transition is causing an even greater divide between boomers who have money and boomers who do not.

Aging may not be easy for boomers who followed the rules and values of the Industrial Age. Upon leaving school, many of these boomers went to work in Industrial Age businesses such as the auto industry and the airline industry. There are significant financial challenges facing boomers in these industries today, just as they prepare for retirement.

The boomers who made the transition to Information Age rules and values will have a better chance of aging with grace and retiring with affluence. While many boomers in the auto and airline industry are suffering, boomers who went to work for companies like Microsoft and Apple have done extremely well.

As this group grows older, this division of wealth between Industrial Age boomers and Information Age boomers will become even more apparent. How they will fare in the next few years may depend upon which rules of money they followed—the rules of the Industrial Age or the rules of the Information Age.

Just as the first wave of baby boomers was leaving college, the world started changing. First we had the Vietnam War—a costly war that divided and nearly tore our country apart. Then in 1971, the United States came off the gold standard. In 1973, the first gas crisis hit. And then in 1974, ERISA was enacted.

In 1971, just as many of the first baby boomers were getting out of college, gold was $35 an ounce. Today, gold has hit $700 an ounce. That is an example of how much the dollar has lost in buying power.

In 1971, many of the baby boomers were getting married and buying homes. Back in 1968, my father paid $50,000 for his home. Today, the same home is worth nearly $2 million. While this increase in value is good for the baby boomers, it makes it tough on their kids and grandkids to be able to afford a home of their own. Some baby boomers now have a tough time getting their kids to move out of the house.

Many baby boomers do not have pensions due to the changes that began in 1974. Many boomers do not have the Defined Benefit Pension plans their parents did, and if they do, many of those DB plans are in trouble. Having received no financial training in school, they didn't understand the difference between a Defined Contribution plan, a savings plan and their parents' pension plan. Millions simply turned their money over to "financial experts" and had no idea what was happening with their money. In 2000, the stock market crashed and woke many of those boomers up to the reality that their retirements may not be that secure. Many found out that their "experts" had less financial training than they did.

In 2006, after buying huge gas-sucking SUVs, boomers were once again hit with an oil crisis. This time it is a real one, not a politically contrived one. Back in 1973, oil was about $3 a barrel. It is now expected to go over $100 a barrel, maybe even higher in the near future.

The increase in the price of oil means those counting on living on fixed incomes will find those fixed incomes will not buy as much. What will happen to their retirement savings if the price of gasoline goes to $10 a gallon?

And we already know about Social Security and Medicare. I hope none of you reading this book are counting on the government to take care of you.

It is estimated that 80 percent of the baby boomers are not going to be able to afford a comfortable retirement. Many are in trouble simply because they followed their parents' financial plans.

I'll Just Keep Working

Some of my boomer friends say they will just keep working. While I think work is an excellent way to stay active and alive, thinking you can work forever is a little shortsighted. What will happen when you cannot physically work? The cost of nursing home care is staggering. And what if your kids do not have a spare bedroom for you?

Health, Wealth, and Happiness

When I was in school at the academy, I realized that my dad had truly been a successful man. After all, he was the head of education, was recognized for his service and was well-respected by his peers. But he did not have health, wealth, or happiness.

My dad's health was deteriorating because he smoked two to three packs of unfiltered cigarettes a day. He eventually died of lung cancer.

He had no wealth. He made a lot of money, but he spent as much as he made. He tried to save and did not invest. I believe he was counting on a teacher's pension, Social Security and Medicare to take care of him.

He was also not happy. The more successful he became, the more the pressure of his work took its toll. He was rarely at home. Although I played sports most of my life, he never made it to any of my games. He was always working. He was always on the road, traveling to schools all over the state and attending PTA meetings—but not available to attend his own kids' PTA meetings.

Health and Wealth Are Measured in Time

While it is possible to measure health and wealth, happiness is less quantifiable. When we go to a doctor, the doctor will take blood samples, measure your blood pressure, and today, put you through an MRI. So health can be somewhat quantifiable. The same is true with wealth. When a banker wants to know if he or she should lend money to you, the first thing they ask for is a credit application or a financial statement.

Health and wealth are also measured in time. For example, if you are ill, the doctor may say, "You have six months to live." This means you are definitely not healthy. If the average life expectancy is 75 years of age, and you are 60, then you are running out of time.

Forbes magazine once defined "rich" as $1 million in income a year. So, rich is measured in money. Wealth is measured in time. For example, if you have $10,000 in savings and your monthly expenses are $1,000 a month, then your wealth is 10 months.

Many of us allow fear to run our lives, not love. For example, many people work, not because they love what they do, but out of fear of being fired or not making enough money. Many people invest out of the same fear— not having enough money. And many people are unhappy because they are not in love.

– Robert T. Kiyosaki

Definition of a Poor Person

While I was watching *CNBC*, the popular financial television station, the commentator reported that he had come across an interoffice directive from a well-known financial institution. While he mentioned the name of this well-known stock brokerage firm, I will not, simply because I did not personally see the memo. Anyway, the commentator said, "The company memo defined a poor person as a person who did not have at least $100,000 in cash to invest."

Imagine that. That means most of America can be defined as poor people by the standard of that company's memo.

When I asked a friend who once worked for this firm, he verified the comment and added, "Not only do they use that criteria before taking you on as a client, they also use that $100,000 criteria to hire you." He went on to say that the company did not really care about your college education or work experience. Before they hired you, they wanted you to write a list of people you personally knew who had more than $100,000 to invest. If you had a long list, you got the job. If you did not, you were not hired.

Back to Health, Wealth and Happiness

I mention the relationship between health and wealth and time because there are many people who have more health than wealth…and that may not make them too happy. If you are fortunate to have wealth and health, you might not only live longer, you may live longer and better than those without health and wealth. With the advances in research, there is no telling what impact future medicine will have on health, if you have the wealth to afford it.

What Is Your Answer?

Of the three, health is, in my opinion, the most important. If you're dead, wealth and happiness may not matter that much. The problem is, many people sacrifice one for the other. For example, many people sacrifice their health for wealth, or their happiness for wealth. We all know people who are working hard and are wealthy, but are not taking care of their health. Or, like my dad, worked hard for money and title, but sacrificed health, wealth, and happiness.

All three are important, especially if you are a baby boomer without much money and running out of time.

So these are my suggestions:

1. **If you are not doing what you love, then start doing it, even if it is only part-time.** For example, a friend of mine is a civil servant and hates it, but is passionate about golf. Every Saturday, he goes by the local golf course and volunteers his time for free. He works

in the local pro shop, teaches and helps out with tournaments. He has only a few more years before retirement, but because he has made so many friends at the golf course, he has opportunities to go full-time in golf once he retires.

2. **Start investing in things you love.** Notice again the word love. I know most of you have heard that you should work at what you love. Well the same is true for investing. Too many people invest their money in things they know nothing about, things they are not interested in and things they do not love.

    I invest only in what I love. I love real estate. My wife, Kim, says, "You've never gone past a building or piece of dirt you did not love." I also love oil because I worked in the industry when at the academy. I understand it. I also love gold and silver. If you've read *Rich Dad Poor Dad*, you may recall my attempts, at the age of nine, at making silver coins out of lead (aka counterfeiting).

    If you love what you're investing in, you're more likely to study the subject, know the pros and cons and understand the ins and outs. And the more informed you are about your investments, the more likely you are to choose ones that will make you money.

3. **Hire a coach.** In 2005, I looked at a picture of Kim and me in Hawaii. I was shocked at how fat I had gotten. I looked like a balloon. I had known I was heavy, but I always deceived myself that I was not as heavy as other people and that I could easily go on a diet and get back to fighting weight. I have been telling myself those lies for about 25 years.

Looking at that picture shocked me into action. It was not the fear of dying that got me to take action. It was the fear of losing time with Kim that hit me in the head. It was not fear, it was love. I had a lot to live for.

I also knew that I did not have the willpower to do what I needed to do on my own. I had been lying to myself for 25 years. I needed a coach, a mentor—someone who was going to hold me accountable and have me do what I did not have the discipline to do on my own.

A year later, I was over 50 pounds lighter. But more than weight, my percentage of body fat went from 36 percent to 20 percent. To get here, I had to reinvent myself.

Change starts in the head. Look at the diagram below once again:

I knew I had to change my thoughts and be reeducated about health.

Today, when people ask me how I've lost the weight (what kind of diet I'm on, what type of exercise I do), I try to explain that it is not as much because of what I did, as it is because of how I've changed my thinking.

I now eat more than ever. It kind of tickles me to see my friends gasp when they see me eat so much.

If you're a baby boomer without much money and you're running out of time, it's time to make a change in your life. If you can, hire a coach to assist you, someone with the expertise to help you reinvent the part of your life that needs attention.

Happiness Is the Key

Love is the key to a life of health, wealth and happiness. It is easier to be healthy if you are happy. It is easier to be wealthy if you are happy. And it is easier to be happy if you are in love with what you are doing.

Many of us allow fear to run our lives, not love. Make a commitment to yourself to let love dictate what you do next. You are far more likely to have the results of health, wealth, and happiness if your thoughts and actions are rooted in love.

Love Does Not Make It Easy

Some people think that doing what you love or investing in what you love or becoming healthy out of love means things should be easy. Love is not easy and it can sometimes be painful. Many people give up loving (whether it was a job, a person, a place—it could be anything) because it was painful. How many of us have heard someone say, "I'll never love again."

Love may not make life easier, but it does give meaning to life.

Love is spiritual, although sometimes painful. Every time I'm in the gym in agony and wanting to quit, I simply think of my sweetheart, Kim, and I find the will to carry on. Two hours of pain makes for a longer and happier life with the person I love the most, so I put up with the pain. The same is true with work and with investing. If not for love, I could not get through the pain and frustration that often comes with work and investing. Anyone who thinks love is easy is obviously someone who has never loved.

A Word on Coaching

The Rich Dad Company has a team of well-trained professional coaches. If you are looking for someone to assist you to get clear on your financial goals and hold you accountable, then go to richdad.com and find out more about our coaching program.

A Final Word to Baby Boomers

For most of us baby boomers, it is an exciting time to be alive, and there are even more exciting times ahead. May you have many more years of health, wealth, and happiness.

Donald's Response

I'd worry. Things aren't looking really great for people at the age of 60 in this country unless they're well off enough to care for themselves for another 35 years, counting in inflation and rising fuel and medical costs.

It's not that the baby boomers have been an indolent group they've been big achievers—but as Robert said, unless they entered the Information Age at mid-life, they have been left behind in many ways. I would become very serious about thinking about the future. You may be thinking, "But we've always done that" which is most likely true. It's just that the future has changed dramatically from what it was a few decades ago.

Having said that, and keeping in mind what Robert has suggested, I have to say that renewed diligence is of utmost importance. Starting over isn't always easy, but if you see it as a challenge that you are more than capable of meeting, you've already done half the work.

Very often it helps to remember situations that are worse than what we may be facing as individuals and citizens. You may be facing difficult times, but it is not a wipe out. My 'blip vs. catastrophe' theory comes to mind. In other words, keep it in perspective and you will keep your equilibrium.

A positive take on the age situation is that you have already survived for 60 years. That in itself is an achievement. Wisdom accompanies experience, so you've got an advantage right there. Your strategy will have to include seeing the future from a different perspective now as compared with when you were 20 or 25 years old.

Here's where your creativity comes in. We all know that opportunity can be hidden within disappointments or so-called setbacks. If you will see your situation that way, and focus yourself to look for those opportunities, your problems can be turned into a future that might be better than what you had planned on to begin with. It can happen. But I emphasize the importance of keeping your focus on the positive side of your situation for good reason: That is the number one reason you will come out winning.

There was a couple I knew who had lost their business when they were in their early 60s, for a variety of reasons. It represented their life's work, and their retirement. Needless to say, they were concerned about their situation and decided they'd return to the ski resort where they had enjoyed many wonderful vacations, both in the ski season and in the off season. They had always hoped they might be able to retire to this area someday. They stayed at the same inn where they'd stayed before, and were discussing what they should do about their situation when a situation arose with the owners of the inn. They had to leave town due to a family emergency, and they asked the couple if they wouldn't mind watching it for them, in return for a free stay. The couple agreed to do so and, long story short, they were asked to stay on as full time managers and eventually bought the inn for themselves. They wound up with a new business that they loved and they were living where they'd hoped to retire! This was better than what they had planned on, and they had great financial success as well.

That's just one example of opportunity being hidden within disappointment. There are millions of stories like that and there is no reason you can't become one of those stories. But notice that this couple went to a place that represented something that they enjoyed and already loved. It was a smart move for them to go to a place with positive memories in order to proceed with positive energy. If you have a place like that, keep it in mind. There could be a good reason why you think of it fondly, and it could be pertinent to your future.

It's also a good idea to ask yourself why you like a certain place. Sometimes it's obvious—it's beautiful, it represents holiday time, it's romantic, or whatever. But if you keep asking yourself the reasons why, very often you'll hit on something that could open a door for you to a new idea or career.

I also believe that retirement isn't always the best thing for people. My father used to say "To retire is to expire" because he got so much energy from his work. Remaining active and plugged in seems to prolong life in a lot of cases. Maybe your so-called 'setback' is a good tiding for a longer and happier life. Maybe you have more to do, and maybe doing more will bring you the satisfaction that retirement never could. Sometimes our plans are disrupted for good reason.

We've all heard stories of people who have missed flights and been very upset that their travel plans were messed up, only to find out that the plane had crashed. We've heard stories of people who have narrowly missed disaster in many different scenarios. Don't be one of those people who narrowly misses success or a second chance because they refused to take the time to consider alternatives.

> Don't underestimate yourself or your possibilities.
>
> *– Donald J. Trump*

Goal re-orientation is a good thing to do whether it's thrust upon us or not. Both Robert and I are firm in our belief that you have to love what you do in order to be very successful at it. He also advises to invest in what you love—which is exactly what ended up happening to the couple at the inn. They had the prescience to visit a place they loved for reinforcement, and reinforced they were. That's walking the talk.

If you are a baby boomer without much money today, be thankful for the life you've had, and know that life is still waiting to show you some great adventures. Don't underestimate yourself or your possibilities. Whether you're six or 60, there are still a lot of great opportunities out there. The good life isn't over until you give up on it.

I'd like to give you a statement from Steve Forbes that says it all. Steve wrote this a few years ago in his book *A New Birth of Freedom* and it remains insightful and pertinent: "The real source of wealth and capital in this new era is not material things—it is the human mind, the human spirit, the human imagination and our faith in the future. That's the magic of a free society—everyone can move forward and prosper because wealth comes from within."

CHAPTER TWENTY-FOUR

WHAT IF I'M ALREADY RICH? WHAT ADVICE DO YOU HAVE FOR ME?

Robert's Response

If you are rich, then count your blessings. But always remember that money can be both a blessing and a curse.

For most people in the world, making enough money is a problem. If you have a lot of money, hanging on to it can be the problem. Lottery winners, movie stars, professional athletes, and heirs to fortunes lose their money because hanging on to money and preserving it can be as hard a job as making money. You become a target for people who want your money.

When you look at the *CASHFLOW* game board, you can see the three different levels of investors. They are:

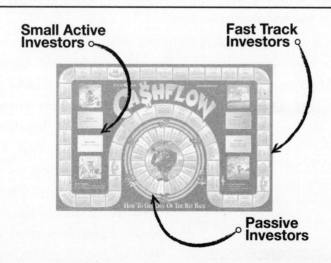

Small Active Investors

Fast Track Investors

Passive Investors

1. **The Rat Race.** The rat race is where most people are. Again, these people, if they invest, invest primarily in paper assets such as savings, stocks, bonds and mutual funds.

2. **Small Deals and Big Deals.** These small deals and big deals are where most people get their financial education and some actually make it out of the rat race.

3. **The Fast Track.** The fast track was created in 1933, by Joseph Kennedy, father of President John Kennedy.

   The fast track was created for rich investors with financial education and experience. The problem is, many rich people do not have the financial education and many lose their fortunes to unscrupulous promoters who prey on people with money.

So there are basically two kinds of rich people: 1) people who made their money and have the required financial education and experience to invest on the fast track, and 2) people who have a lot of money, but little-to-no financial education and experience.

Self-made people are less afraid of losing their money because they know they can make it back. People who came into their money by other means have two choices, the same two choices people who do not have money are faced with—get educated or turn their money over to a competent and trustworthy professional.

Every year, you will read in the paper about a sports star or movie star who lost everything to an unscrupulous promoter. You will also read about a rich, old person who has his or her money stolen by a relative or trusted caregiver. It is a very common story. And we have all heard of people who marry and then lose their money. One of the more infamous stories of late is Anna Nicole Smith who, at 26 years of age, married a man 63 years her senior. It had to be love! Also, Paul McCartney, after

> If you are not doing what you love, then start doing it, even if it is only part-time.
>
> – Robert T. Kiyosaki

four years of marriage, is getting a divorce, without a prenuptial agreement. That may prove to be a very expensive four years of bliss.

Investing on the Fast Track

For the average investor, the SEC scrutinizes investments and investment promoters. There is less protection for people who invest outside the rat race.

For small deals and big deals and the fast track, education, experience, trust, and integrity are essential. If you or your advisors lack education, experience, trust or integrity, stay with SEC-supervised paper assets.

But if you have the qualifications, investing on the fast track can be the most exciting, profitable, and fun. The fast track is where Donald and I invest. It is the only game in town.

Examples of Fast Track Deals

The following are examples of fast track deals I have done:

1. When starting a business, as an entrepreneur, and seeking funds from investors, it is a fast track deal. I need to be very careful that the investors I talk with are qualified, accredited investors.

    The definition of a qualified, accredited investor is:

    A person who individually (or jointly with a spouse) has a total net combined worth in excess of $1,000,000. A person who has an income in excess of $200,000 for the two most recent years with an expectation of such income in the current year or a person who has joint income with a spouse for such periods in excess of $300,000.

    My gold-mining company in China is an example of such an investment. That investment has made many of my investors millionaires.

    As you know, I also started an oil company that never found oil. My investors lost most of their money. The good news is that some of those who were in my oil company were also in my gold-mining company in China.

2. **Real estate partnerships:** Kim and I are partners in several large real estate projects—projects such as 300-unit apartment houses, commercial buildings and office buildings. Kim and I are not real estate developers like Donald Trump. We simply are the money partners to developers. We have never lost money in any real estate partnership…knock on wood.

The key is to have honest and experienced partners.

3. **Oil and gas partnerships:** There are many reasons I personally like oil and gas. They are:

Cash flow: If you strike, you get paid every month just as you do with real estate.

Tax advantages: If I invest $100,000 into an oil and gas partnership, the IRS allows me to deduct approximately $70,000 from my taxes. At the 50 percent tax bracket, that is almost the same as receiving $35,000 from the government in cash flow or to apply to my investment.

The other tax advantage is that for every dollar I receive from oil and gas, the government allows me to deduct an additional 15 percent (known as depletion allowance). That means I pay taxes on only 85 percent of the income I receive from oil and gas.

4. **Private equity funds:** These are mutual funds for the rich. Generally, a private equity fund is built around an investment group with an excellent track record. They invest in all manner of things, such as businesses and large real estate acquisitions.

Generally, the cash requirements are much higher than those for mutual funds. One I invested in required a million-dollar commitment. We got our money back plus a 40 percent return in less than three years. The dollar requirements and returns vary with the investment group you entrust your money to.

5. **Hedge funds:** Hedge funds are different from mutual funds in that they use leverage (borrowed money) and are not restricted in investments and investment methods as mutual funds are. I have had varied luck when investing in hedge funds. Again, most of the success of a hedge fund depends upon the management.

6. **Derivatives:** The world of derivatives is a world few people know about. Yet, they are a concern to all of us. Warren Buffett refers to derivatives as "weapons of mass destruction."

I do not know much about this investment class. Yet, I do know what a derivative is. A derivative is something that is derived from something else. For example, orange juice is a derivative of an orange. A mortgage is a derivative of real estate. So I believe the reason Warren Buffett is concerned about the world of derivatives is that many people, even those involved with them, probably do not fully understand them, and they are leveraged instruments on steroids. If there is a glitch, the whole world of money might collapse like a house of cards.

A friend explained it this way to me. He said, "It is like being unemployed and borrowing money to invest in something, using borrowed money as collateral to borrow the money." That sounds like people who refinance their homes to pay off their credit card debt but continue to use their credit cards. If that is what the shadowy world of derivatives is, then maybe this world of global high finance really is a house of cards—credit cards.

In Conclusion

If you are rich, your job is to hang on to your money and hopefully multiply it. Regardless of what you do, it is very important to have the following:

1. A will
2. An estate plan
3. A plan if incapacitated
4. A prenuptial agreement if you get remarried

Donald's Response

First of all, I'd say to be grateful if you are already rich. Then I'd say, be careful. Then I'd say, have a lot of fun.

That's what I'm doing. Right now, I'm in Los Angeles at the Beverly Hills Hotel with my beautiful wife, Melania, and our baby son, Barron, and we are having a wonderful time. The weather, accommodations, and food are fantastic here, and Alberto del Hoya takes good care of us.

I'm here to shoot the sixth series of *The Apprentice*. Mark Burnett and his wife, Roma, live in Los Angeles, and my daughter, Tiffany, will have a graduation ceremony this week, so while I'm a New Yorker, this is a pretty nice way to live and a wonderful place to be.

Not too far away is Palos Verdes, on the Pacific Ocean, which is where my spectacular new golf course, Trump National Golf Club/Los Angeles, is. I'll be making regular visits and playing some golf, and the new estate homes overlooking the golf course and the ocean are just about ready. These are exceptionally beautiful residences.

I have a lot of projects going on, and that's one of the reasons I am rich. I make the most of my wealth. There's nothing like it if you want to get things done. I'm not happy unless I'm busy making deals and learning new things. We are setting up a Trump Productions office in Los Angeles while I'm here, too. So there is never a dull moment. Life can, and should, be exciting.

That doesn't mean I'm not careful. It's too easy to become careless when things are going well, so I keep myself focused. I have children growing up and coming up into the business world, and I don't want them walking into any disasters, for one thing. It's important to remain responsible for what you have.

I keep in daily contact with everyone at The Trump Organization to see what's happening there, and

> Philanthropic efforts are among the best rewards you can have for a life well lived.
>
> – Donald J. Trump

Rhona keeps me on track with what's going on with my schedule. My two eldest children, Don Jr. and Ivanka, have been out here with me for the *Apprentice* finale and for some new episodes, so it's been a celebratory time.

If you are rich, I hope you can say the same thing about your life. Life is something to celebrate, especially if you have the means to do so.

Never underestimate your good fortune, and remember that philanthropic efforts are among the best rewards you can have for a life well lived. That's my best advice for rich people.

Donald, Melania and Barron

Donald and Barron

Don Jr. and Ivanka

CHAPTER TWENTY-FIVE

WHY DO SOME PEOPLE WHO WANT TO BE RICH... FAIL TO BECOME RICH?

Robert's Response

Obviously, there are many reasons why people fail to become rich, even though they want to be rich. Some of those reasons are:

1. Laziness	6. Bad attitude
2. Bad habits	7. Bad influence from friends and family
3. Lack of education	8. Lack of focus
4. Lack of experience	9. Lack of determination
5. Lack of guidance	10. Lack of courage

But there is one reason I would like to write about—a reason rarely discussed. And that reason is the person fails to find an environment that supports him or her becoming rich.

In *Teach To Be Rich,* I discuss the possibility that we are all born geniuses. In that package, consisting of two workbooks and three DVDs, I state that a person needs to seek the environment that is best for his or her genius to flourish. The example I use is that Tiger Woods' genius comes out on golf courses. If he were a jockey, he would not be successful. Also, Mick Jagger, who went to school to be an accountant, found his genius on stage as a Rolling Stone.

My poor dad was a genius in school. My rich dad was not. My rich dad's genius came out in the environment of the street. In my particular case, I did not do well in school. For me, school was the wrong environment. Like my rich dad, the street is the environment where my genius comes out. If I had stayed in the world of academia, I would not have thrived there.

The right environment is essential to developing your genius. When I was in Navy flight school, some of my fellow pilots found their genius piloting planes. One went on to become a general and others became senior pilots for the airlines. I was an average pilot. In football, some of my friends found their genius on the field. I was average in football. When I worked for the Xerox Corporation, one of my friends found his genius in the corporate world and climbed the ladder quickly.

Every gardener knows that plants need good soil, water and the right temperatures. If all of the right elements are there, the plant will flourish. The same is true with people. Each person needs certain elements to thrive. If the essential elements are not there, the person may not grow and blossom.

Rich Person In a Poor Environment

My rich dad used to say, "There are many rich people in poor environments." As I grew older, I began to better comprehend what he was saying.

My Home Environment

One of the first things I realized was that I was born into a family with a financially poor environment. Now, this does not mean we were not a loving family; we were. The problem was that the environment was not conducive to becoming rich. In my family, to desire wealth was taboo. As a family, we valued education, public service, and low pay. Although it was not spoken out loud, there was an underlying belief that the rich were evil and exploited other people.

There was never a discussion about investing. Investing in my family was gambling. Living below our means and saving money was the accepted way of life.

In my home environment today, money is not a dirty word. Getting rich is fun, and investing is a game. Rather than living below our means, we constantly work on expanding our means, increasing our income, building assets, and serving as many people as we can. Also, we keep financially negative people out of our lives and surround ourselves with like-minded people who challenge and support us. Our friends are also a part of our environment.

My Work Environment

When I got my first job, with the Xerox Corporation, I quickly found that it too was not an ideal environment in which to get rich. While my bosses wanted me to work hard and make a lot of money, their primary focus was to make the shareholders happy...not the employees. Whenever I talked about starting my own company, my managers above me let me know that it was against company policy to be working on my own business.

This does not mean I did not love working for Xerox, because I did. It was just not an environment designed for me to get rich in. In addition, even though I did make a lot of money, the tax schedules for high-income employees would not have allowed much in the way of wealth creation.

In The Rich Dad Company, every weekly meeting focuses on our staff becoming richer. We encourage them to attend financial seminars, to start their own businesses, and to invest—not through a company retirement plan, but through their own investment plans. Several employees have left because they did not like the pressure I put on them to become financially educated and eventually financially free. I am glad they left because they will be happier working in a different environment.

Environments for People Who Are Afraid of Losing

Many people who want to become rich fail to become rich simply because they are rich people in a poor environment. For example, if you are an employee, you are probably working in an environment designed for people who are working not to lose—people who want job security and a steady paycheck. Owners who create such environments usually have no problem attracting and keeping good employees—employees who are happy working not to lose and turning their money over to financial experts rather than learning to be their own financial expert. Obviously, government service is such an environment.

> Find the environment where you thrive. We would probably never have heard of Tiger Woods if there were no golf courses.
>
> – Robert T. Kiyosaki

Environments for Winners

There are organizations that provide environments for winners—people who want to become rich. Examples are professional sports, Hollywood and the music industry. The challenge with these environments is that you have to be exceptionally talented, driven and tenacious. In these industries, the 90/10 rule of money applies. There are definitely more losers than winners.

Other winner-driven environments are Wall Street investment firms, real estate sales, network marketing, and other high-performance businesses.

A Dying Tree

Recently, a young tree I planted began to die. This disturbed me greatly since I love trees. I called in tree specialists and experts who fertilized the tree, but the tree kept dying. Finally, I took a garden hose and soaked the roots twice a week for a month. Suddenly, leaves and new growth exploded from the dying branches. All it needed was a little more water. (Upon further inspection, I found the drip line that took water to the tree was clogged.) Today, that tree is healthy and vibrant. All it needed was an environment it could grow in. The same is true with people. Many people do not grow rich because they are in poor environments.

Powerful Environments

Taking this idea of environments a little further, consider the following ideas:

1. **If you want your intelligence to grow:** go to a library, a bookstore, or to school.

2. **If you want your health to grow:** go to a gym, ride a bicycle, or play more.

3. **If you want your spirit to grow:** go to a church, find a quiet spot and meditate or pray more.

4. **If you want your wealth to grow:** go to a place where people are getting rich (like a real estate office or stockbroker's office), join an investment club, or start a study group and meet new friends who also want to grow richer.

5. **If you want to expand your world:** go to places you've never been before…do things you've been afraid of doing before.

In other words, sometimes the fastest way to change and improve yourself is simply to change your environment.

Final Questions

I believe we are all born with a special genius, a unique gift. The problem is that not everyone finds his or her genius simply because he or she does not find the environment where his or her genius can blossom. Just remember this: We would probably never have heard of Tiger Woods if there were no golf courses.

So my final questions are:

1. Is your home and family life an environment that develops your financial genius? Yes or No?

2. Is your workplace an environment that encourages the development of your financial genius? Yes or No?

3. Do you have any idea what your genius might be? Yes or No?

4. Are you working with people who want you to develop your genius? Yes or No?

5. If you found your environment, would you be willing to work hard to develop your genius? Yes or No?

I ask this last question because just because you have a genius does not mean life is easy. We all know people who are talented. The problem is, some people do not work very hard at developing their talents. Always remember, Tiger Woods (or any great person for that matter) has worked very hard at developing his genius.

As my rich dad would say, "Laziness is the assassin of genius."

These five questions are important questions, so you may want to think about them as well as the answers before turning the page.

Donald's Response

Environment

I realize my great fortune in coming from the family I did, with my parents being supportive and being great believers in education. I often call it the lucky sperm club. But I've known people who have been in environments that were not conducive to achievement, yet they prevailed and became very accomplished and successful anyway.

As Thoreau said, "I know of no more encouraging fact than the unquestioned ability of a man to elevate his life by conscious endeavor."

You may have to work harder and longer, but that is preferable to making excuses and letting your goals slide. My father had very little to begin with and he just went about making ends meet and then kept moving forward with his work ethic and natural intelligence to eventually become very successful. I have great respect for people who have found their success the hard way.

The correct environment, as Robert points out, is necessary to nourish your particular talents. Part of our responsibility is to find the right environment so that we can flourish, or at least use it as a stepping-stone to the next level. Life experiences can be likened to school, as in when we reach fifth grade, we expect to go on to the sixth grade, provided we do what is required. Reaching a place in adult

> Keep your focus intact, and focus on the solution.
>
> – Donald J. Trump

life that remains the fifth grade for a few decades isn't really progressing. It might be comfortable, but it shouldn't be acceptable for the long term.

A very good way to deal with environments that are not ideal is to maintain your focus. Rarely is everything perfect, so if you are in a home or work environment that is not conducive to your success, you will have to put more effort into keeping your focus intact.

Above all, do not begin to focus on the negatives of your situation—focus on the solutions!

There are many examples of people who have risen above great hardship and profound disadvantages to become amazingly successful. That is always a possibility, and you could be that example. Remember that you are in some worthy company if you are in an environment that isn't great. Keep your focus on your goals, be willing to go the extra mile or miles and know you have just as much right to be successful as anyone else does.

I say that because I've seen people who seem to think they're asking too much if they want to be successful. It's almost as if it's a territory that belongs to someone else, but not to them. I don't know if they were raised to believe that success means you're greedy or selfish or whatever, but it's definitely a mind-set that needs to be worked on.

There is no advantage to being poor. In fact, poverty becomes a burden to everyone in the long run.

No healthy person wants to be a burden to someone else. Creating an environment that can help others requires money. Being in a position to be charitable is definitely more desirable than becoming a charity case. That alone can be a great motivation for paying attention and working hard.

Heredity and environment are two important factors that influence what we are and what we become or what we do not become. But they are not the only factors. The other factors are your responsibility—and your choice. That in itself should be an empowering thought.

You are in a position to override your disadvantages. We've all heard the term "environment-friendly," and it can apply here, too. Be friendly to your situations, learn from them, but keep progressing forward. For example, Robert learned from both of his environments, and they both served him well in the long run.

Keep your focus on success and elevate your life to where it should be.

Your View

Take some time to further analyze your environment.

1. Is your home and family life an environment that develops your financial genius? *If it is, how so? If not, what can you do about it?*

2. Is your workplace an environment that encourages the development of your financial genius? *If it is, how so? If not, what can you do about it?*

3. Do you have any idea what your genius might be? If so, what is it? Are you developing it? *If you don't know what your genius might be, how can you find out what it is?*

4. Are you working with people who want you to develop your genius? If so, how do they support you? *If not, what can you do about it?*

5. If you found your environment, would you be willing to work hard to develop your genius? *Why or why not?*

Next, review the CASHFLOW Quadrant and do the following exercise...

From which quadrant do you want to receive most of your income?

_____

List the six people you spend the most time with:

_____ ____   _____ ____

_____ ____   _____ ____

_____ ____   _____ ____

Now list which quadrant from which each of these six people derive their income.

Are they active in the quadrant that you want to be active in?

If not, you may want to change your friends and seek new friends who derive their income from the quadrant you seek.

If so, your environment may be supportive for you reaching your goals.

Robert and Donald walking through the entry of
Trump International Golf Club/Los Angeles

PART FIVE

JUST GET STARTED

Every day is filled with defining moments. From the moment we wake up, we define ourselves when we decide to get up and exercise or sleep an extra half hour. We define ourselves when we call in sick even though we could go to work. We define ourselves when we watch television instead of reading a book on business or investing. And we define ourselves when we turn our money over to a salesperson to invest for us instead of learning to invest for ourselves.

In Part Four, Robert and Donald shared their advice for people in specific situations. Now, in Part Five, they share more detailed recommendations for investing in real estate, network marketing and business ownership. Most importantly, they end with a commentary about the need to develop leadership skills. If you cannot lead yourself, you will not be able to lead others.

Robert and Donald are both frequently asked, "Do you think real estate is a good investment?" or "Do you think stocks are a good investment?"

Their reply is, "It depends. How good are you?" It has a lot less to do with real estate, stocks, gold, or anything else you might be investing in. Whether something is a good investment has everything to do with how committed you are to be good at what you do. Asking if real estate is a good investment is like asking if the diet someone is on is a good diet. Or if the person someone is marrying will make them happy.

They would also add, "Real estate is not a good or bad investment. People are good or bad investors." Investing is not risky; people are risky.

Robert's rich dad used to say, "There is no such thing as a bad investment, but there sure are a lot of bad investors."

Ninety percent of the investing public wants to be given the magic formula, the answer that will make them rich. There are three problems with this. First of all, there are millions of ways a person can attain great wealth. With the birth of the Internet, even more billionaires, millionaires, and rich people have and will be created. So the first problem is: Each person needs to find the magic formula that fits him or her best. The second problem is: People who look for a magic formula often fall prey to people who sell magic formulas—formulas such as, "Turn your money over to me for the long term, and I will invest it for you." The third problem is: Most people cannot follow a formula for long which is why, for example, there are so many different diets being sold, generally to the same people.

If you choose to be one of the many people who are not committed to being part of the 10 percent, then you know what advice to follow: "Save money, get out of debt, invest for the long term, and diversify." However, Robert and Donald would caution you to start as early as possible and save as much as you can because you will need a lot of time and a lot of money to do well using that formula. They would favor 'investing' over 'saving'... building or acquiring assets.

If you are committed to being one of the 10 percent of people who earn 90 percent of the money, then it takes focus and commitment—*your* focus and *your* commitment!

You will need to find your own magic formula.

Chapter Twenty-Six

Why Do You Invest in Real Estate?

Robert's Response

Why do I invest in real estate? The answer is found in one word, and that word is *control*. There is no other investment I know of that gives me so much control over the many aspects of making money and keeping my money. As a result, it gives me control over my life.

As stated often in this book, many feel investing is risky because they do not have control over the asset in which they invest. There is very little control over savings, stocks, bonds, and mutual funds. Always remember the following:

People worry about job security because they lack control over their jobs. Few employees have any control over the ownership of the company, how much they earn, how much they are taxed, or the future of their job.

In addition to control, real estate offers many other advantages. If a piece of real estate is purchased at the right price, is financed well, is in a good area, and is well managed—then some of the advantages of real estate are the following:

1. **Cash flow:** Checks come in every month.

2. **Leverage:** Bankers will line up to lend you money for investing in property. Ask your banker if he or she will lend you money to buy mutual funds.

3. **Amortization:** Tenants pay off the debt.

4. **Depreciation:** The government offers tax breaks for real estate because it goes down in value. Real estate can go down in value, but it tends not to. In reality, the reason why governments offer depreciation incentives is because real estate investors provide housing.

5. **Creativity:** The value of the property improves through creativity. For example, if I buy a piece of raw land, I can change the zoning. Or I can buy an old house and fix it up. Or I can convert an apartment house to condominiums.

6. **Expandability:** Once I learned how to buy single-family homes, I expanded into multiple units. Today, when my wife and I buy a property, it needs to be at least 250 units.

7. **Predictability:** It takes about a year after purchase to stabilize an apartment complex. After a year, the management is able to get rid of bad tenants, make the cosmetic repairs that good tenants want, and we can sometimes, slowly, raise the rents.

Once a building is stabilized, the checks come in every month like clockwork. This certainly beats watching the ups and downs of the stock market…feeling good when prices go up and feeling bad when prices come down. I like getting those monthly checks in the mail.

The key to good real estate is great management. As stated earlier, the reason many stock, bond, and mutual fund investors do not do well in real estate is because they are either poor managers or do not want to be managers.

In our investment plan, Kim and I worked hard to begin investing in apartment buildings with more than 100 units simply because with more than 100 units, we could afford better managers.

Since management of real estate is the key to success, some of the best investment opportunities are buying properties that were owned by poor managers.

8. **Tax-deferred money:** One of the great advantages of real estate is tax-deferred money. There are many ways a real estate investor can avoid paying taxes ever—legally. One way is known as the 1031 tax-deferred exchange. Last year, Kim and I sold a small apartment house and made over a million dollars in capital gains. By following the rules of the 1031 exchange, we were able to reinvest that money without having to pay taxes.

This tax-deferred treatment is not available for people who invest in stocks, bonds, and mutual funds. You'd be surprised how fast you can get rich if you reduce or eliminate taxes.

9. **Appreciation:** Because the dollar is going down in value, real estate tends to increase in value. Also, as our population increases, demand increases, which also drives up prices.

Most investors invest for appreciation (capital gains). In the stock market, most people invest low hoping to sell high. This is investing for capital gains. In real estate, these investors are known as *flippers*. Flippers also buy low and hope to sell high. The problem with a capital gains strategy is that the strategy generally only works in an up-trending market. If the market trends down (aka a bear market), many paper-asset investors and flippers are toast.

Investing for cash flow is better than investing for capital gains in real estate because the tax laws favor the cash-flow investor.

Why Appreciation Is Last

There is a reason I put appreciation last on my list. Yet for most people, appreciation is first. Many people buy a house to flip it, which means they buy it to sell it at a profit. People who flip properties have to work harder and pay a significantly higher tax rate. While I do occasionally flip properties, I prefer the first five reasons for investing in real estate. My favorite strategy is to buy a property, then buy another and another. In the long run, I work less, make much more money, and pay less in taxes.

I put appreciation last because it *is* the *last* reason. I don't really count on appreciation. In my opinion, to buy a piece of property or a stock and hope it goes up in value is speculation (or gambling), not investing. While I do like appreciation, I do not count on it. Investing for appreciation is especially tragic when the real estate market crashes, which it does on a regular basis.

The Secret Reason

There is another reason why I like real estate. And that reason is because real estate is slow; it does not change rapidly. As I stated earlier, the baby-boom generation is the last generation of the Industrial Age and the first generation of the Information Age. My problem with the Information Age is that I am obsolete—I am an old guy. I do not have an e-mail address, and I do not want one. I don't really know how to use the Internet very well, or the tech gadgets that the Information Age has spawned.

My companies do have Web sites, and I earn millions of dollars from the Web. I have a computer, but I use it like a typewriter—it makes me millions of dollars as a word processor, but not as a computer.

Not only am I obsolete, I am becoming rapidly more obsolete with each new technological change that comes along. I once bought an iPod but could not figure out how to put information into it or how to get anything out of it. In fact, I know exactly when I became obsolete. It was when I tried to program my VCR in the 1980s. That's when I realized I was not a techie.

So that is why I focus more time on real estate than attempting to keep up with technology. As best I can tell, we all need a place to live and a place to work, for a long time. As our population grows and our dollar declines in value, real estate should do nicely, as long as I buy the right properties, in great locations, at the right price, well-financed, and with good management.

> People with vision master the ability to see through to the heart of issues and investments. They value transparency.
>
> – Robert T. Kiyosaki

The real problem with being obsolete is still coming. The young people born after the year 2000 will radically accelerate the rate of change of technology by the year 2015. Just as high school kids of my generation began building souped-up cars, the kids today will take today's technology and soup it up.

The Web has only been around since 1989. Kids born after the year 2000 will experience a completely different reality than I do. They no longer watch television or read the newspapers. They do not know what world borders are. They know they can do business online and globally.

I was in elementary school when television first came into our homes. By the 1960s, the kids were rioting in the streets. Why? They were rioting because television brought the Vietnam War straight into our homes. It was real war. It was not the war as portrayed by John Wayne and Hollywood. My generation saw the realities of war, bodies of women and children blown to bits. That is why my generation rioted—at least some of them did.

It will not be long until this new generation makes their presence felt. They may ask tough questions like, "Why are we not seeking alternative energy resources?" Or, "Why not focus on reducing global warming?" Or, "Why is there poverty?" Or, "Why are there different tax laws for different people?" Or, "Why don't we teach kids about money in school?" Hopefully they will take on the challenges my generation has swept under the carpet.

Blue-chip companies that millions of investors are counting on may not be blue chips for much longer. New companies, run by kids with different minds, will bring down the blue-chip companies of today. Just as GM was the powerhouse when I was a kid and is an aging monstrosity today, maybe Microsoft or Dell or Google will be the GMs of tomorrow.

When I invest in real estate, I do not care if the tenant is GM or Google or an old baby boomer or a new kid on the block, just as long as the bills get paid.

And this is the secret reason why I like real estate: It will take some time before real estate becomes obsolete.

Who Owns Your Real Estate?

Just as a side note, I thought you might be interested in who really owns real estate.

The term *real estate* comes from the Spanish word *real*, which means royal. So real estate literally translates into *royal estate*. That is because during the Agrarian Age, there really were only two classes of people, royalty and peasants. As mentioned earlier, the royals owned the land, and the peasants lived on and worked the land. As payment for living on royal land, the peasants paid a tax, in the form of a percentage of their crops, to the royals.

Today, we still do not own our real estate. The government owns our land. We all pay a tax, known as property tax, to the government. If we do not pay this tax, we soon find out who really does own the land.

As you can tell, not much has changed.

How Many Ways Do You Get Rich?

The following is an article about some of the other reasons why Donald and I invest in real estate. It has to do with a favorite term of Warren Buffett, the term *intrinsic value*.

Warren Buffett is famous for talking about the intrinsic value of a stock. While many people parrot or mimic Mr. Buffett's words on intrinsic value, very few people know what he really means. In this article, I will do my best to explain intrinsic value, as simply as possible. If you would like a more sophisticated explanation, then you may want to read the plethora of books written about him and his methods of investing.

Once you understand intrinsic value, you may better understand why some investors make much more money than others. You will also realize that you can find intrinsic value in investments other than stocks. I will explain intrinsic value using real estate as an example. Why do I use real estate? Because real estate is more tangible than stock, meaning more people will be able to understand intrinsic value.

When the average investor thinks about making money, he or she usually thinks about buying low and selling high. For example, an investor buys a stock for $10 and sells when and if it reaches $20. He gets up every day and checks the stock price.

Many investors are addicted to watching the market go up and down. Their day gets off to a good start if the price goes up and to a bad start if the price goes down. That is not what Warren Buffett does and neither do I. While the price of an asset is important, it is not something we watch on a daily basis, as many investors do. Warren Buffett pays close attention to price when he buys a business. After that, he really is not concerned if the share price is going up or down. Nor does he care if the stock market is opened or closed. He does not play the stock market, as most investors do.

First of all, Warren Buffett does not just own stocks. He owns businesses. Secondly, in very simple terms, what Mr. Buffett looks for in a business is a well-managed business that will grow more valuable over time. He often refers to business value compounding, in other words accelerating in value.

Shifting to Real Estate

Let's shift to using real estate as an example, because I believe it may be easier to explain intrinsic value from a real estate perspective.

When I buy a piece of real estate, I am only concerned about price at the time of purchase (the same as Mr. Buffett) because price determines returns. What I am looking for when I purchase a property are the following four streams of income (or cash flow):

1. **Income (cash flow):** This is ideally called positive cash flow— the money you have left after all expenses are paid, including my mortgage payment and taxes.

2. **Depreciation (phantom cash flow):** Depreciation appears as an expense when it really is income that comes from a tax break. This confuses many people who are new to investing in real estate. It is cash flow or income you do not see.

3. **Amortization:** This is income to you because your tenant is paying down your loan. When you pay the mortgage on your personal residence, this is not income to you, but an expense. When your tenant pays your loan down, it's cash flow.

4. **Appreciation:** This is really inflation that appears as appreciation. If your rental income goes up, you as an investor can refinance and borrow your appreciation out as tax-free cash and have your tenant pay for the amortization of the new loan amount. In other words, it could be tax-free cash flow.

This is an example of the intrinsic value of a well-financed real estate investment, purchased at the right price, and well-managed. As a real estate investor, this is what I invest for. I invest for increased value and cash flows.

Investors who buy property to sell are often called *flippers*, but I call them *speculators* because this is not really investing. They are focused on capital gains, but those gains are often taxed at higher rates when they do not reinvest their money but spend their gains instead. Unlike such speculators, I invest for cash flow and increased value.

Warren Buffett also does not like to sell because selling shares triggers a tax and a tax reduces his wealth. For those of you who know Mr. Buffett's formula, he is into compounding his returns and not sharing his returns with the government.

One reason I recommend people play our games *CASHFLOW 101* and *CASHFLOW 202* is so that people will become better investors by training their brains to see what their eyes cannot. In other words, to see the real value or lack of value in any investment, regardless of whether it is a stock, bond, mutual fund, business, or real estate. I also recommend you play it at least 10 times because the more you play it, the more your mind will be able to see—see what most investors miss.

In this simple schematic diagram, you may better understand what I mean by allowing the brain to see what the eyes often miss. The following is a diagram of a financial statement:

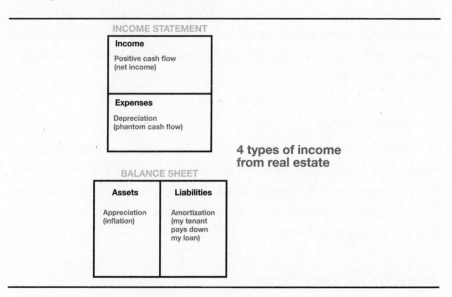

This is an overly simplified example of what a real estate investor looks for. They are looking for the intrinsic value most amateur investors miss.

When Warren Buffett mentions intrinsic value of a company, he is referring to many of the same things. The vocabulary he uses is sometimes different, but I believe you may have a better idea from this real estate example of intrinsic value.

The average stock investor often refers to *P/E ratios*; the average real estate investor speaks of *cap rates*. While these are important indicators to note, they hardly are a measure of intrinsic value—and professional investors are looking for value, not the price.

If you would like to experience playing our *CASHFLOW* games, without risking any money, there are CASHFLOW Clubs all over the world. You may want to join one and expand your mind to be able to see what your eyes cannot.

In conclusion, the average investor only knows one way to make money, and that is by buying low and selling high. A professional investor would rather buy low, realize gains from other arenas, and let the asset grow forever.

The Power of Vision

Financial literacy allows a person to see with their brains what the human eye cannot see. This is what I refer to as *vision*. Donald and I invest in real estate because we can see the cash flow and value. People with vision master the ability to see through to the heart of issues and investments. They value transparency.

No Transparency

Mutual funds have no transparency. A mutual fund company is not required to be financially transparent. They do not have to accurately disclose expenses. Why anyone would invest in an entity that does not disclose expenses is beyond me. That is more than just being an amateur—that is choosing to be blind.

Invest for the Long Term

Because mutual fund investors cannot see the true numbers, they cannot see how much money the mutual fund company is taking from them. When a financial advisor recommends you invest for the long term, this is the reason why:

Over More than 40 Years…

Mutual Fund Company	You
80% of the returns	20% of the returns
0% of the risk	100% of the risk
0% of the capital	100% of the capital

The mutual fund company may receive up to 80 percent of the returns because the mutual fund company is always collecting fees over the life of the relationship between the fund and investors. The investor takes 100 percent of the risk and puts up 100 percent of the capital. Now do you understand why banks do not lend money to buy mutual funds and insurance companies do not insure them against losses?

Not All Investments Are Equal

The job of a leader or a teacher is to teach people to *see*. Since our school system does not teach much about money, most people, even those who are well educated, cannot see why some investments are better than others.

Now that you have seen the differences between real estate and mutual funds, you should be better able to decide which investment is best for you.

Donald's Response

When I am asked why I like investing in real estate, I always feel like answering, "Because I like breathing." To me, real estate is like oxygen. It keeps me going when I'm awake, and it keeps me going when I'm asleep.

Aside from the fact that I was raised around the real estate business, I probably would have found my way to real estate investment and development anyway because I like so many things about it. I'm a builder by nature. I remember building very tall structures with my building blocks as a child. I would borrow my brother's blocks to make my buildings even taller (which I would have returned had I not glued them all together). I guess it was just in my genetic code to build things, and the bigger the better.

As an investment, real estate is one of the safer places to put your money. It doesn't go completely bust like many other industries do. Real estate may have ups and downs but, as Robert pointed out, it rarely if ever becomes obsolete. The earth has become more valuable as the centuries have passed. The original price of Manhattan was around $24. That's just twenty-four dollars—with no zeros added on.

When Robert mentions that he isn't fond of gadgets, I have to admit that I'm the same and that I agree. I don't even use an intercom in my office. I'd much rather yell—it's effective, and it saves time. It also creates an energized environment for everyone to work in, and as long as people yell back loud enough for me to hear them, all is well. As I've said, I'm not always a one-way street.

Real estate offices are not known for being quiet. Media people who have come to visit have called them "war zones" among other things. That's OK. Business is like combat sometimes. The fact that I expect it to be combative means I'm prepared for reality.

Which brings me to more reasons I like investing in real estate: It's exciting. It's complex. It's multi-dimensional. And it's tangible. You can actually go and see what you've invested in. It evolves and becomes bigger and better as time goes by, provided you know what you're doing.

Trump Tower hasn't been built for very long as far as landmark buildings go, but it's already considered a landmark building. It was built in 1983. That's an accomplishment I'm very proud of and another reason real estate can be rewarding. It has also been rewarding financially, as an investment.

> I'm passionate about real estate, and that's what works for me.
>
> – Donald J. Trump

If I am going to invest my time and money in something, I have to be proud of it at the end of the day. A lot of people invest in things they don't know one thing about or in things they don't care about. That's OK, to each his own, but I have to be passionate about something first. I'm passionate about real estate, and that's what works for me.

What are you passionate about?

Your View

Is real estate investing for you?

_____

_____

_____

_____

_____

_____

_____

_____

CHAPTER TWENTY-SEVEN

WHY DO YOU RECOMMEND NETWORK MARKETING?

Robert's Response

When I first heard about network marketing, I was against it. But after opening my mind, I began to see advantages that few other business opportunities offer.

Long-term success in life is a reflection of your education, life experience, and personal character. Many network-marketing companies provide personal development training in those key areas.

Most schools train people for the E- or S-quadrants, and that is great if those are the quadrants in which you want to spend your life. Most MBA programs are training students for high-paying jobs in the corporate world as an E, not a B.

What if you're in the E- or S-quadrant and you want to change? What if you want to be in the B-quadrant? Where do you find the education that trains you for that quadrant? I recommend a network-marketing business. I recommend the industry for people who want to change and get the necessary skills and attitude training to be successful in the B-quadrant.

Being an entrepreneur and building a B-quadrant business is not easy. In fact, I believe building a B-quadrant business is one of the toughest challenges a person can take on. The reason there are more people in the E- and S-quadrants is simply because those quadrants are less demanding than the B-quadrant. As they say, "If it was easy, everyone would do it."

Personally, I had to learn how to overcome my self-doubt, shyness, and fear of rejection. And I had to learn how to pick myself up and keep going after I failed. These are some of the personal traits a person must

> An important personal skill required for any B-quadrant business is leadership. Are you able to overcome your own fears and have others overcome their fears in order to get the job done?
>
> *– Robert T. Kiyosaki*

develop if they are to be successful in a B-quadrant business, regardless of whether it is a network-marketing business, a franchise, or an entrepreneurial startup.

An important personal skill required for any B-quadrant business is leadership. Are you able to overcome your own fears and have others overcome their fears in order to get the job done? This is a skill the Marine Corps taught me. As Marine Corps officers, it was imperative that we be able to lead others into battle, even though we were all terrified of dying.

I meet many people in the S-quadrant, the specialists or small business owners, who would like to expand, but they simply lack leadership skills. No one wants to follow them. The employees do not trust their leader or the leader does not inspire the employees to better themselves.

As mentioned earlier, *Forbes* defined a big-business owner, a B-quadrant business owner, as a person who controls a business with more than 500 employees. This definition is why leadership skills are vital for the B-quadrant.

Where could you find a business that will invest the time in your education, your personal development, and building your own business? The answer is: most network-marketing businesses.

Building a B-quadrant business is not an easy task. So you need to ask yourself, "Do I have what it takes? Am I willing to go beyond my comfort zones? Am I willing to be led and willing to learn to lead? Is there a very rich person inside of me, ready to come out?" If the answer is "Yes," start looking for a network-marketing business that has a great training program. I would focus less on the products or the compensation plans and more on the education and personal development program the company offers.

A network-marketing business is a B-quadrant business because it meets several criteria I look for in a business or investment. Those criteria are:

1. **Leverage:** Can I train other people to work for me?

2. **Control:** Do I have a protected system that belongs to me?

3. **Creativity:** Will the business allow me to be creative and develop my own personal style and talents?

4. **Expandability:** Can my business grow indefinitely?

5. **Predictability:** Is my income predictable if I do what is expected of me? If I am successful, and keep expanding my business, will my income increase with my success and hard work?

Isn't Network Marketing a Pyramid Scheme?

I am often asked if network marketing is a pyramid scheme. My reply is that corporations are really pyramid schemes. A corporation has only one person at the top, generally the CEO, and everyone else below.

The following is an example of a typical corporate pyramid:

Compare that to a network-marketing business system:

Purpose of Network Business

To pull you up

A true network-marketing business is the exact opposite of a traditional business model. A network-marketing business is designed to bring you up to the top, not keep you down at the bottom. A true network-marketing business does not succeed unless it brings people up to the top.

Additional Points Worth Mentioning

The following are some other points worth mentioning:

1. **Tax breaks increase.** By starting a network-marketing business in your spare time and keeping your regular job, you begin to gain the tax advantages of the rich. A person with a part-time business can take more tax deductions than employees can. For example, you may be able to deduct car expenses, gasoline, some meals, and entertainment. Obviously, you need to check with a CPA for exact rulings on your situation. And the cost of your CPA is tax-deductible. In most cases, an employee cannot deduct CPA expenses. In other words, the government will give you a tax break for advice on how to pay less in taxes.

2. **Meet like-minded people.** One of the advantages I had is that my friends also wanted to be in the B-quadrant. When I first

started out, most of my E-quadrant friends thought I was nuts. They could not understand why I did not want a steady job or steady paycheck. So an important part of becoming a B is to surround yourself with other people who are Bs and want you to become a B.

3. **Give yourself time.** It takes time to be successful in any of the quadrants.

Just as it takes time to climb to the top of the corporate ladder as an E, or become a successful doctor or lawyer in the S-quadrant, it takes time and dedication to become successful in the B-quadrant. It took me years before I built a successful B-quadrant business.

So give yourself time. I would allow at least five years to learn and develop into a B-quadrant person.

4. **Network-marketing companies are patient.** One of the beauties of a network-marketing business is that it will invest in you, even if you are not successful.

In the corporate world, if you are not successful in six months to a year, you are often fired. In the network-marketing world, as long as you are willing to put in the time, most companies will work with you in your development. After all, they want you to get to the top.

5. **Leverage the systems that are already in place.** These systems are already tried and proven, which allows you to hit the ground running instead of trying to build the internal systems of a new company.

In Conclusion

After opening my closed mind, I could finally see some of the unique benefits the network-marketing industry offers people who want more out of their lives.

Generally, it costs much less to get started in a network-marketing company than to build a business on your own.

Donald's Response

Like Robert, I did not know much about network marketing or the direct sales industry. But when a friend told me that it was one of the fastest growing business models, I had to open my mind and look into it. What I found surprised me.

Years ago, many businesses were opposed to a business model known as franchising. Many people questioned the legitimacy of franchising. Today, everyone in the world knows about McDonalds. Network marketing, being a new business model, is experiencing the same opposition franchising experienced years ago.

Looking into this new industry, I was surprised to find many major Fortune 500 companies have added a network marketing component to their business. Today many banks, telecom companies, real estate brokerages, credit card companies, and major consumer brands are committed to this new form of people-to-people marketing and distribution. So, my recommendation is to keep an open mind, and if you are looking to start your own business, a network marketing business might be for you.

Marketing is a powerful tool, and network marketing can increase that power, provided you are self-motivated. In a simple visual, see a product and then remove the advertising agency from it. It is up to you to do the marketing and advertising.

That's a big job, but it can be done if you are passionate enough to get it going on your own and to keep the momentum and motivation going at a high level. It requires an entrepreneurial spirit, and that means focus and perseverance. I do not recommend network marketing to people who are not highly self-motivated.

> Make sure the product is worth your energy.
>
> – Donald J. Trump

Another important aspect of network marketing is that it is inherently social, so if you are not a social or outgoing person, I'd think twice about going into it. Sociability is a requirement.

Just like in advertising, there's no point in having a fantastic advertising campaign if the product isn't equally fantastic. Also keep in mind that if you decide to become a distributor, you will be legally responsible for the claims you make about the product, the company, and the available opportunities. But above all, make sure the product is worth your energy and total devotion. Otherwise, you could be energetically spinning your wheels.

Robert mentions the importance of going beyond your comfort zone when it comes to network marketing. He also mentions giving yourself enough time. These are good points to consider. I would also agree that having leadership qualities is critical for success. You definitely have to have a take-charge, can-do attitude.

As with any other undertaking, know everything you can about what you're doing before you begin. Network marketing has proven itself to be a viable and rewarding source of income, and the challenges could be just right for you. There have been some remarkable examples of success, and those successes have been earned through diligence, enthusiasm, and the right product combined with timing. As with so many issues we have discussed before, there are tangibles and intangibles involved, but success is not a total mystery, and that applies to network marketing as well.

Most people have heard of focus groups, a research tool that advertising agencies use when they are testing a new product. They will go out to different locations and simply ask everyday people what they like and don't like about a new product. It's best if you can keep the focus group idea close at hand when you are deciding about a product. Just because you like it doesn't mean everyone else will. Finding a common denominator in product appeal will matter.

My nutshell advice about network marketing is to do your research and then put everything you've got into your product. Genuine enthusiasm is hard to beat, and the odds will be with you.

Your View

Is network marketing for you?

_____

_____

_____

_____

_____

_____

_____

_____

Chapter Twenty-Eight

Why Do You Recommend Starting Your Own Business?

Robert's Response

Take a look at the CASHFLOW Quadrant below again:

The big differences between the quadrants are the different values. My poor dad did not succeed in the S, B or I quadrants simply because, having been trained as a teacher, he was trained in the values of the E quadrant. He did not have the survival skills or survival instincts required for success on the street. He was not trained for the other three quadrants. So when the governor banned him from government service, my dad found out who was in control of his life.

The good thing about having a rich dad who made his fortune in the B and I quadrants was that my rich dad guided me mentally and emotionally from the E and S quadrants to the B and I quadrants—the same way Donald's dad guided him. While there were several failures along the way, it was my rich dad's wisdom and mentorship that got me through the rough spots.

I Love Being an Entrepreneur

Even though it was a tough road at the start, today I love being an entrepreneur. I love starting new businesses. I love the creativity, the people I meet, the challenges, and the rewards. The price for gaining the education and the experience was high, yet in retrospect, the journey was worth it.

I did not go back to sailing tankers or flying planes because most of the excitement of learning those professions was over for me. It was most exciting when I first took the wheel of an oil tanker and when I landed my first plane. Once I mastered those tasks, the learning curve got easier— and eventually ended. As an airline pilot or a ship's officer, today would be too much like tomorrow.

I love the new challenges I go through every day as an entrepreneur. I love the excitement of the startup and then the development. Once the business is up and running, I love the challenge of the expansion and growth. Once the business is growing, I love the challenge of bringing on new team members to add stability and grow the business, which makes the business predictable and profitable.

As an entrepreneur, every day is exciting, new, and educational. I am always learning something new, even on bad days. Donald says the same thing, which is why he has so many business projects going on. He is a true entrepreneur. To be a true entrepreneur, you need to be smart and love to learn. If you do not love learning, chances are your business will not grow…because you are not growing. Whenever I find a business that is declining or stagnant, it is often because the owner is declining or stagnant.

Looking in the Mirror

Your own business is the best mirror you can look into. Your own business is like the game of golf. It gives you instant feedback every time you swing the club. If you are good, your business will make you richer than Tiger Woods. As you know, successful entrepreneurs are the richest people on earth. And if you are bad, they won't let you join the country club. I know that personally. Today, I am offered many honorary country club memberships. A few years ago, the same country clubs would not have let me in the door.

Putting You Back in Control

One of the reasons so many people feel insecure today is because school never taught them about the importance of *control* in their lives. For example, if you are an employee, you have very little control over how much you earn, if you get the promotion, if you receive a raise, when you go on vacation, and sometimes even when to eat lunch.

In 1974, when ERISA was passed, the Act that led to the 401(k), many employees in the E quadrant were forced to become investors in the I quadrant. The problem, again, was a lack of education and experience. Since most employees, even though highly educated, have very little financial knowledge, they often invest in paper assets such as savings, stocks, mutual funds, and bonds. Again, the problem is the same—as investors, they have no *control* over those assets.

The other thing employees have little control over is taxes. Those in the E and S quadrants, in most cases, pay much higher taxes than those who are professionals in the B and I quadrants.

Again, the reason is *control.* The IRS and the tax code of a country offer more control to those in the

> One of the reasons so many people feel insecure today is because school never taught them about the importance of control in their lives.
>
> – *Robert T. Kiyosaki*

B and I quadrants because the people in these quadrants are important for the economic growth and strength of a nation. The true Bs provide jobs and the true Is provide the capital to fund the businesses, infrastructure, exploration, energy, and real estate.

Many people feel uncertain about their futures simply because they have very little control over their jobs, their investments, and their taxes.

Often I meet people from different countries, and they attempt to tell me that the laws in their country are different. That is not my experience. I know this because I have businesses in China, Japan, Korea, Canada, Australia, South America, Israel, the Middle East, and Europe. I have found similar tax advantages for the B and I quadrants to be available in most developed or developing countries. There are some differences, but the Golden Rule that states, "Those who have the gold make the rules," seems to prevail all over the world.

Learning to Take Control

Today, it is easier than ever to gain access to the B or I quadrants. We have technological tools that make it very easy to leverage and expand one's base of operation all over the world. For example, the computer and the Internet make being a national or international entrepreneur much easier and less expensive. For a few hundred dollars, I can buy a computer and access the world markets as a business owner or an investor. The question is, do you have the education, experience, mind-set, and core values to be a national or international entrepreneur?

How to Get the Education and Experience

Since our schools do not teach a person much about entrepreneurship or investing, the question is, how does a person get the education and experience to be successful in the S, B, or I quadrants?

My answer and Donald's answer are very similar. We both recommend going to business school or finding a mentor with whom you can work as an apprentice. As you already know, he and I both had rich dads who guided us through the developmental process.

In the previous chapter, Donald and I wrote about the benefits of network marketing. In my opinion, the biggest advantages of a network-marketing business are the training and the low cost of entry. If you are serious about becoming an entrepreneur, I would suggest you find a network-marketing company with a great training program and dedicate at least five years of your life to learning the core values of the B quadrant.

The Power of Franchises

If you have more money and are ready to make a bigger commitment, then you may want to look into buying a franchise. Again, if it is a good franchise, the owners of the franchise will focus a lot of time and energy training you to run the business and the business systems.

We all know about McDonald's. It is by far one of the most well-known franchise systems in the world. There were many times I thought about buying a McDonald's franchise, not necessarily for the money, but for their training programs. You may have heard of Hamburger University. It is a highly acclaimed business school that trains people for the real world of business. But one of the problems with a McDonald's franchise is the high cost of entry, which is often over a million dollars.

The Power of Mentors and Coaches

Personally, I understand the challenges, frustrations, rewards of the journey from the left side of the quadrant, E and S, to the right side of the quadrant, B and I. That is why we at The Rich Dad Company have more advanced programs for people who want to be successful in the B and I quadrants. We offer the following programs:

1. **Rich Dad Coaching:** We have a team of professionally trained coaches whose only goal is to keep you focused and on track to achieve your goals in personal finance, investing, starting your own business, or growing your business. This is a one-on-one program that has produced phenomenal results in participants' lives. I believe the magic of the program is that the goals you set are your goals: your own goals that are beyond your current reality,

your own goals that demand you bring out the best in you, and your own goals that you know—when accomplished—will change your life.

2. **Rich Dad Education:** While most investment advisors recommend diversification, diversification, diversification, we at Rich Dad recommend focus, focus, focus. All people who have achieved greatness have been very focused people.

In the near future, Rich Dad Education will be offering college-level courses and seminars for people who are ready to focus on specific areas of business or investing. For example, a course I am very excited about is learning to be a raw-land developer. Or you may want to become an expert in stock options or foreclosures. As you know, there are many ways a person can become very rich—if he or she is focused.

In Conclusion

There are two kinds of people in the world. There are those who seek security and those who seek freedom. As some of you know, security and freedom are exactly the opposite. That is why those with the most security have the least freedom. Those people are in the maximum security section of prison. If you seek freedom, I can sincerely say that maximum freedom exists in the B and I quadrants.

Donald's Response

Oddly enough, I don't always recommend that people start their own businesses. Some people simply are not entrepreneurs, and I feel it's bad advice to tell everyone that they, too, can be wildly successful when in fact it's probably not in the cards for them. This doesn't go over so well with the groups that ask me to speak on motivation and success, but I have to be honest. I don't ever want to give the wrong advice if I can possibly help it.

About a year ago at one of my speeches, I realized this when a man in his 60s came up to me and asked me some direct questions about becoming an entrepreneur. I had to tell him that it's not always the best thing to do—there's risk involved. The thought of advising a man who might lose everything at that stage of his life gave me something to think about beyond the usual sound bites of solid success advice I normally might offer. Every case is different, and I would feel personally responsible if he were to follow my advice and fail. I had a feeling he wasn't a natural entrepreneur, and it wasn't just because he wasn't a young guy just starting out. I'm a cautious optimist, but the cautious part comes first.

I have recommended that people start their own businesses when the situation warrants it—I've seen their work ethic, their drive, their passions, and their tenacity, and I know they've got what it takes. Some people think they have it, but they don't. The people I have advised to go into business for themselves have all succeeded. But I haven't told every person to do it.

I told a young woman in real estate that she should go into business for herself, and she did—the next day! Kim Mogull has become very successful in New York City with her own real estate company, and she still tells people the story of how she got started. She didn't spend more than 24 hours getting to it. Another person I knew was in the wrong business for him, which was on Wall Street, and I finally told him he was beginning to look like a loser because he wasn't very good at it and he was miserable. I asked him what he liked to do and his answer had to do with golf. It took a few years of coaxing, but he finally made the change and has become very successful with his own golf business—and very happy at the same time.

These two examples show that 1) you have to be good at what you're doing, and 2) you have to have the courage to take the leap and go for it yourself. We all have different timetables, but the inclination has to be there.

One of the first things I tell people is that being an entrepreneur is not a group effort. You have to be willing to go it alone for a certain amount of time—and sometimes for a long time. Robert did not have an overnight success, but he kept at it, learned along the way, and look where he is now. If you have the determination, believe me, it is worth it.

The pride of ownership doesn't have to be explained. It probably starts with our first bicycle. When something is yours, there's a built-in loyalty factor to making it work well. In my case, my name is on a lot of things, and my responsibility is to make sure the product represents the highest quality possible. Those are my standards, and I work and live accordingly. It's an integrity of purpose that is hard to equal unless you have your own business.

I've heard people say of certain employees they meet or may have, "They work as if the business were their own." They work with such singleness of purpose, it's as if they were the owners. Singleness of purpose is required if you want to have your own business—there are no time limits to your work week, for one thing. It can be 24/7, and ultimately, the responsibility is yours.

> "You will reap what you sow," rings true again. And you will be reaping it. A good thing to think about.
>
> – Donald J. Trump

I like having that responsibility because I find it empowering. It also gives me energy instead of enervating me. Some people will find this pressure to be less than enjoyable, and if that's the case, I urge them to remain employees.

The rewards of having your own business are certainly there to be seen by all. That doesn't have to be explained. Once you've had your own business, it's hard to go back to working for someone else. It's just not the same, by any stretch of the imagination. It can be a good incentive for working that much harder to remain the captain of your ship. You can say each and every day, "The buck starts with me—now, here, today!" It's a great feeling.

Having your own business is like growing a tree—it's a living organism that goes through seasons and storms and beautiful summer days and winter blizzards, but it keeps on growing and is literally an expression of yourself. That's one reason I'm so careful with the quality controls of what I do. If something represents you, you want it to be the best representation you can possibly find or achieve. Then you can even raise the bar on yourself and, believe me, you will never be bored.

That's another great thing about having your own business. If you are bored, you will have no one to blame but yourself, and that situation won't last long. Some jobs are boring, and there's not much you can do but leave them. With your own business, you are in control, which equals more freedom.

Freedom is an interesting word because freedom comes with a price. Most business owners will work many more hours than their employees, but I've never heard an entrepreneur say they'd rather be working for someone else! Ever!

We've all heard about expressing yourself, especially when it comes to art or the arts. That also applies to business, which I see as an art form as well. There are many things in common, including discipline, technique, perseverance, and so forth. But it's that freedom of expression that makes being a business owner especially great. If I have a vision of what I want to do, I go about making it happen. I don't have to ask anyone for permission, for one thing. It's my ball game. Granted, I have to follow the laws of the area, zoning and so forth, but the idea and the power to get it done resides with me. That's a terrific feeling.

People feel inspired for a reason—inspiration is a motivator. Frustration occurs when their inspiration is not attended to. If you have the inspiration and are able to combine it with diligence and focus, I would advise you to think about owning your own business. The rewards are greater, and the old saying, "You will reap what you sow," rings true again. And you will be reaping it. A good thing to think about.

Your View

Do you want to own your own business?

Why or why not?

_____

_____

What does "freedom" mean to you?

_____

_____

Chapter Twenty-Nine

Leaders Are Teachers

Robert's View

There are many challenges ahead. Instead of followers, we need more leaders.

Too many people have an entitlement mentality—people expecting the government or their company or their family to handle their problems for them. This book was written with the hope that you will become a leader.

What does it mean to be a leader? The following are three definitions to consider:

1. **Leaders are role models.** When I was at the Academy and in the Marine Corps, much of my training in leadership focused on being a role model—being someone my troops would look up to, being someone who lived his life according to a higher standard.

   Donald Trump certainly fulfills those criteria. In writing this book with Donald, I was able to get to know a person I have respected and looked up to for years. Just being in his presence has been a lesson on how I want to live my life—to live life according to higher personal standards.

   My poor dad advised me to live my life below my means. My rich dad advised me to continually work to expand my means. Being around Donald has inspired me to expand my means beyond what I thought was possible for my life. And that is what true leaders do.

   They inspire you to go beyond what you think is possible for you.

I trust this book has inspired you to go beyond what you think is possible for you, to live your life according to a higher standard.

2. **A leader inspires you to be bigger than your doubts and fears.** My rich dad used to say, "Fear is the great divider. Fear is the line between people who are cowards and leaders, failures and successes."

In my final days of preparation at the Marine Corps base at Camp Pendelton, California, just before we were shipped to Vietnam, the instructor pilot who trained me to shoot guns and rockets said, "School days are almost over. Soon you will be in Vietnam. You will soon be facing the toughest task a leader can face. You will soon be asking your men to give up their lives so others may live. My question to you is: Are you willing to do the same?" After letting my copilot and me think about his statement, he said, "If you are willing to give your life, you will find life. In a strange way, you are being given an opportunity to face a point in life most people spend their lives running from. You will enter a realm of life beyond life and death."

There were several times during my year in Vietnam that I faced the moment my instructor talked about—the moment in time when I faced one of my greatest fears and went beyond life and death.

Obviously, business and investing are not life-and-death events. Yet, to be successful, you often need to choose between the death of the old you and the birth of a new you. Many people stop growing because they are afraid of dying, the old identity refusing to commit ego suicide, so life remains the same as the world moves on.

> True leaders inspire us to be bigger and do things we are afraid of doing.
>
> – Robert T. Kiyosaki

True leaders inspire us to be bigger and do things we are afraid of doing.

Looking back on my life, I realize that for the new me to have emerged, the old me had to die.

For example:

When I decided to become a *rich* person, the *poor* person inside of me had to die.

When I wanted to become an *entrepreneur*, the *employee* inside of me had to die.

When I wanted to become a *thin and healthy* person, the *fat and lazy* person inside of me had to die.

A friend of mine often says, "Everyone wants to go to heaven, but no one wants to die." Spending the past two years around Donald has inspired me to go beyond the old me and seek a life few people experience.

Back in the 1980s, when Kim and I were going through the roughest financial times of our lives, we both read Donald's book, *The Art of the Deal*. As some of you know, in 1985, Kim and I were so broke we were living out of a car for a few days. In 1987, when *The Art of the Deal* came out, it was Donald's willingness to share his wisdom that encouraged us to keep going, even though many of our friends and family said we should quit going for our dreams.

In 1987, when the stock market crashed, it was Donald's words of wisdom that allowed us to recognize opportunity instead of disaster. Instead of become poorer, as many people did, we took the stock market crash, the crash of the savings and loan institutions (S&Ls), and the real estate crash as an opportunity to get ahead and become financially free.

Donald has been a lighthouse in the darkness for Kim and me and we owe a lot to him because of his willingness, over the years, to share what he knows.

3. **Leaders have vision and teach others to see.** I once read that Winston Churchill could see 200 years into the future. I also read that Dr. R. Buckminster Fuller could see 1,000 years in the future.

Whether this is true or not, we all know people who cannot see past tomorrow. We also know that Donald Trump can see tall gleaming skyscrapers where others see only blighted, burned-out buildings. That is what makes Donald a leader and a very rich man. He can see what others cannot.

My rich dad taught me to see what others could not see. Repeating an important lesson from this book, my rich dad taught me to see the four different forms of income a real estate investor receives.

INCOME STATEMENT

Income	
Positive cash flow	
Expenses	
Depreciation	

BALANCE SHEET

Assets	Liabilities
Appreciation	Amortization

As a young man, once I could see these four incomes with my mind, I was then able to see how I could become a rich man. By teaching me to see what others do not see, my rich dad gave me vision—a vision of my future.

When you compare that vision with the reality of investors who are investing for the long term in mutual funds, you are empowered to see a very different future.

Repeating a very important lesson from this book:

**Investing from Age 25 to 65 in Mutual Funds,
the Investor's Returns May Look Like This:**

	Over 40 Years Mutual Fund Company		Investor
Returns	80%		20%
Risk	0%		100%
Capital	0%		100%

Letting the Fox into the Hen House

As you can see, it is very profitable to sell investments to people with very little financial education. To make matters worse, many schools, organizations, and businesses, in their attempt to bring financial education into the organization, actually invite the very people who sell these high-risk, low-yield investments to "educate" them. In other words, it's the classic case of the chickens inviting the fox into the hen house.

The following is an example of foxes in a big hen house. In the May 2006 issue of *Money Magazine,* it was disclosed that the brand of mutual funds sold by the powerful, 36-million-member AARP, the American Association of Retired People, to its members are some of the worst performing funds available. In spite of all its money and political power, the organization sells its members funds that are not in the top 20% of the fund's asset class for performance. Its biggest and most popular fund is not even in the top 40%. The good news is that AARP is making changes to rectify this situation.

In the September 22, 2006 issue of the *USA Today* a headline blared, "Bill Would Shield Troops From Bad investments." The article begins:

> *"Service members would be protected from people pushing overpriced financial service and insurance packages."*

Later the article states:

"It also would ban discredited financial products that are no longer available on civilian markets but are still sold to people in the service."

As an example of a victim, the article quotes Representative Geoff Davis, R-Kentucky who said, "As a former combat arms officer, he was among the service members losing thousands of dollars from deceptively advertised investments." He goes on to say, "It was not until I got out of the Army and into the business world that I discovered how uncompetitive these products were when compared to other investment opportunities...My wife and I lost nearly half our life savings on this so-called investment."

Restating my point, it can be very profitable selling to people with very little financial education and who believe that investing is risky. It is not investing that is necessarily risky...but being financially uneducated is.

Do you want to be an investor who blindly turns your money over to a mutual fund company to invest for you, or do you want to be an investor who takes control of your future by taking control of four different types of income?

"But executive character has not gone unnoticed. CEOs are now close to the bottom of the barrel in public trust. One survey showed that while 75 percent of the general public trust shopkeepers, 73 percent trust the military, and 60 percent trust doctors, only 25 percent trust corporate executives—slightly above the 23 percent that trusted used-car dealers."

–John C. Bogle
Founder and CEO
Vanguard Mutual Fund Group

CEOs are running the companies that the mutual fund managers invest in. My rich dad said, "Mutual funds are like french fries. They fill you up but they are not good for the long run."

If you like stocks and mutual funds, I highly recommend *Battle for the Soul of Capitalism* by John C. Bogle.

Leaders Are Teachers

Years ago, my rich dad did not give me money. Instead, he gave me the power to see. That is what financial literacy is: the power to see with your mind what your eyes cannot see.

As mentioned earlier in the book, in the world of money, you often hear the word *transparency.* Transparency means being able to see into something. When a banker asks you for your financial statement, he or she wants to look inside you or your company. Your financial statement is your real-world 'report card.'

My rich dad, by being a great leader and teacher, gave me a vision of my future, yet left it up to me to determine my future. That is what great leaders and teachers do. Great leaders can see and teach others to see.

– Robert T. Kiyosaki

Donald's View

In Summary

Robert and I have outlined and addressed some of the problems we face as individuals and as a nation. We are both believers in looking at the solution and becoming a part of the solution. I hope we've been transparent enough to allow you to see how you might become part of the solution as well.

As teachers, we know that we can offer you insights and some guidelines, but that, ultimately, you will be responsible for yourself. In fact, that's one of our goals.

I've always been big on focus, because focus is one of the mainstays of effectively dealing with a problem, just as awareness is the first step to progress. How can you fix a problem if you can't see it to begin with? Our focus has been on what the problems are so you might more clearly see what the solutions might be, individually and collectively.

> We've realized the situation will not change so the answer is for us to change.
>
> – Donald J. Trump

In the course of writing this book, we've seen some headlines that underscore the value of this endeavor. We've seen some giant philanthropic endeavors and gifts, Enron principals being brought to court, and the constant gas and oil turmoil remaining in turmoil. More than ever, we've realized the situation will not change—so the answer is for us to change.

I once said, "Without passion you don't have energy; without energy you have nothing." I said that a long time ago, but it is still very true today, and it's a thought that has kept me going in getting this book done. These are not the times to withdraw from the world arena. If anything, we all need more passion and energy in order to deal with what's going on. A thought to consider from Winston Churchill:

> *"We make a living by what we get,*
> *but we make a life by what we give."*

Robert and I sincerely hope all of you will someday be in a position to give, because that will mean you have become part of the solution, and our efforts will have been worthwhile.

In the interim, know that being aware is a big step in the right direction, and just keep working on remaining in that condition. Let's keep our blind spots to a minimum when it comes to financial responsibility as well as global responsibility.

I know that Robert will continue on his path of excellence as a great teacher, and I hope all of you will continue to listen to what he has to say. Empowerment comes with enlightenment.

I hope we have empowered you to succeed.

– Donald J. Trump

CONCLUSION

SELF EVALUATION

Throughout this book, we have asked you to share your thoughts, your experiences, your goals, and your dreams. The reason we have done this is found in the Cone of Learning. As you can see "Reading" is at the bottom of the Cone and "Doing the Real Thing" is at the top of the Cone. By participating and reflecting on how the issues apply to your own life, you are operating in the middle of the Cone of Learning, close to where it says "Participating in a Discussion." By engaging in these activities, we hope that you will recognize and internalize opportunities for positive change in your life.

Cone of Learning		
After 2 weeks we tend to remember		Nature of Involvement
90% of what we say and do	Doing the Real Thing	Active
	Simulating the Real Experience	
	Doing a Dramatic Presentation	
70% of what we say	Giving a Talk	
	Participating in a Discussion	
50% of what we hear and see	Seeing it Done on Location	Passive
	Watching a Demonstration	
	Looking at an Exhibit Watching a Demonstration	
	Watching a Movie	
30% of what we see	Looking at Pictures	
20% of what we hear	Hearing Words (Lecture)	
10% of what we read	Reading	

Source: Cone of Learning adapted from Dale, (1969)

It is time for you to review and evaluate yourself. Did you leave any or all of these areas blank?

If so, what does that tell you about your level of commitment and focus?

In completing these sections, review your comments. Do they have a negative tone (I couldn't, I can't, I don't know how)? Or do they have a positive tone (I could, I can, I will)?

Negative answers tend to shut you down and depress you. Positive answers tend to motivate you and give you confidence. If your answers were negative, do you have some more work to do? If your answers were positive, are you ready to change your life?

How much time and money do you currently allocate for investing?

Have you made a commitment to spend more time and money on your financial education and investment plan? If you haven't, you may not see any improvement. If you have, spend your time and money wisely in an area of interest to you.

Have you selected an area to focus on, such as real estate, network marketing, stock options, or starting your own business?

If not, have you come up with another financial plan for yourself? No matter what you decide to focus on, continue to educate yourself and make a commitment to yourself to succeed.

Do you have a supportive environment and people around you who will push you toward success?

Or do you have an environment and people around you who will hold or pull you back? Do you need to make some changes in your environment? If so, then do it.

Only you can answer these questions. Only you can change your life.

Thoughts—Actions—Results
We want you to be rich.

Donald's Acknowledgements:

Working with Robert Kiyosaki and the Rich Dad team has been a tremendous experience and an enjoyable one. Robert's team has been gracious as well as rock solid in our collaboration on this book and I thank them for their help in weaving Robert's and my similarities and differences together. Not an easy job, and a job well done. Mona Gambetta has done a great job coordinating the launch of the book. Robert, thank you for a wonderful experience—you're one of a kind, and a very gifted teacher.

I'd like to thank my co-author, Meredith McIver, for her attentiveness as well as her good humor. With a schedule like mine, she needs it. Rhona Graff is always there to help us, and I'd like her to know it's greatly appreciated.

To Michelle Lokey, thank you for your hard work on this project from the beginning, and to Allen Weisselberg, thank you for your insight and help with the educational impact of this endeavor. Many people don't know you were a high school teacher at the start of your career before you became the CFO of the Trump Organization. They will now. To Keith Schiller, your vigilance and your thoughtfulness is appreciated by everyone. Kacey Kennedy, thank you for your help with the photo coordination.

To William McGorry and Cevin Bryerman at Publisher's Weekly, and their entire team, thank you for your enthusiasm and support from the very beginning of Robert's and my collaboration. You've been terrific.

And to my readers, it's been great spending time with you. Keep learning, keep moving forward, and keep thinking big.

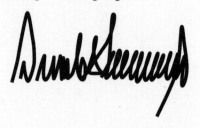

Robert's Acknowledgements:

It has been an honor and a dream come true to work with Donald Trump and his team. He is indeed an icon of our times. While demanding excellence in all he does, his graciousness and respect for those who work for him is paramount. I have learned so much from him, expanding my own reality of what is possible in the process. His team is a reflection of him in their dynamic attitudes and tremendous support.

Getting to know Meredith McIver and working with her has been a true pleasure. Her classic elegance is matched only by her talent and creativity. Michelle Lokey has been incredibly supportive in moving this joint venture along. Powerful women in their own right, I thank both Meredith and Michelle for taking a personal interest in this project.

I also want to thank Keith Schiller and Rhona Graff for their ongoing enthusiasm and kindness throughout this past year. In addition, it was a pleasure meeting Allen Weisselberg, CFO of the Trump Organization, and learning of his shared passion for the need for financial literacy for young people.

A special thank you to everyone on the Rich Dad team who supports our book projects for, once again, adding their insights and structure to my thoughts and delivering a clear and compelling text. Their talent in combining my style with Donald Trump's makes this book unique in its style and impact.

Mona Gambetta has been a tremendous help in driving the production and promotion of this book. Her enthusiasm is only surpassed by her never-ending dedication to excellence. And then there are those who make it all come to life.

I would also like to thank the team at *Publishers Weekly* for their guidance, wealth of knowledge and experience and, most importantly their enthusiasm. William McGorry, Cevin Bryerman, Hannah Volkman and Rachel Deahl in particular have been instrumental in their support. A personal thank you to Cevin for his mentorship throughout this project.

And most importantly, I thank you for your interest in your own financial education and for reading this book.

Donald J. Trump

Chairman and President, The Trump Organization

Donald J. Trump is the very definition of the American success story, continually setting the standards of excellence while expanding his interests in real estate, sports and entertainment. He is a graduate of the Wharton School of Finance and started his business career in an office he shared with his father.

In New York City, the Trump signature is synonymous with the most prestigious of addresses, among them the world-renowned Fifth Avenue skyscraper, Trump Tower, the Trump International Hotel & Tower, Trump World Tower at the United Nations Plaza, 40 Wall Street, and Trump Park Avenue. His portfolio includes the historic Mar-a-Lago Club in Palm Beach, Florida and his ever expanding collection of award-winning golf courses which span the U.S. from Los Angeles to New York, New Jersey, Washington, D.C., and Florida and internationally from Scotland to the Grenadines. The Trump Hotel Collection has grown to include properties in Chicago, Las Vegas, Waikiki, and Toronto in addition to Trump SoHo/New York and the acclaimed Trump International Hotel & Tower on Central Park West which once again won the coveted Mobil Five-Star Award as well as the Five Star Diamond Award from the American Academy of Hospitality Sciences. The Trump International Hotel & Tower Chicago was awarded the #1 Hotel in the U.S. and Canada by Travel & Leisure Magazine. Recent acquisitions include the iconic Doral Hotel & Country Club (800 acres) in Miami, the historic Old Post Office Building in Washington. D.C. and the Kluge Estate in Virginia.

Mr. Trump is the Emmy-nominated star and co-producer of the reality television series, "The Apprentice" which quickly became the number one show on television, making ratings history and receiving rave reviews and world wide attention. "The Celebrity Apprentice" has met with great success as well, being one of the highest rated shows on television, and 2013 marked the thirteenth season of this remarkable series. "You're fired!" is listed as the third greatest television catchphrase of all time. Mr. Trump also co-owns with NBC the Miss Universe, Miss USA and Miss Teen USA Pageants. The Miss Universe pageant is broadcast in 180 countries and the Miss USA Pageant won the ratings in the spring of 2011. In 2007, Mr. Trump received a star on the Hollywood Walk of Fame, and he is among the highest paid public speakers in the world.

The Donald J. Trump Signature Collection, which includes neckwear, business suits, dress shirts, cufflinks and more has met with great success, as has Trump Home, which includes a comprehensive collection of mattresses, furniture, lighting and room décor. In 2012, his fragrance, *Success*, was launched.

An accomplished author, Mr. Trump has authored over fifteen bestsellers, and his first book, *The Art of the Deal*, is considered a business classic and one of the most successful business books of all time.

DONALD J. TRUMP & ROBERT T. KIYOSAKI

MIDAS TOUCH

WHY SOME ENTREPRENEURS GET RICH–
AND WHY MOST DON'T

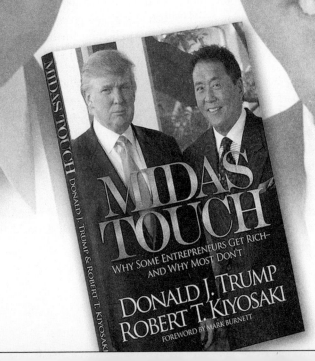

Robert T. Kiyosaki

Best known as the author of *Rich Dad Poor Dad*—the #1 personal finance book of all time—Robert Kiyosaki has challenged and changed the way tens of millions of people around the world think about money. He is an entrepreneur, educator, and investor who believes the world needs more entrepreneurs who will create jobs.

With perspectives on money and investing that often contradict conventional wisdom, Robert has earned an international reputation for straight talk, irreverence, and courage and has become a passionate and outspoken advocate for financial education.

Robert and Kim Kiyosaki are founders of The Rich Dad Company, a financial education company, and creators of the *CASHFLOW*® games. In 2013, the company will leverage the global success of the Rich Dad games in the launch of a new and breakthrough offering in mobile and online gaming.

Robert has been heralded as a visionary who has a gift for simplifying complex concepts—ideas related to money, investing, finance, and economics—and has shared his personal journey to financial freedom in ways that resonate with audiences of all ages and backgrounds. His core principles and messages—like "your house is not an asset" and "invest for cash flow" and "savers are losers"—have ignited a firestorm of criticism and ridicule...only to have played out on the world economic stage over the past decade in ways that were both unsettling and prophetic.

His point of view is that "old" advice—go to college, get a good job, save money, get out of debt, invest for the long term, and diversify—has become obsolete advice in today's fast-paced Information Age. His Rich Dad philosophies and messages challenge the status quo. His teachings encourage people to become financially educated and to take an active role in investing for their future.

The author of 19 books, including the international blockbuster *Rich Dad Poor Dad*, Robert has been a featured guest with media outlets in every corner of the world—from CNN, the BBC, Fox News, Al Jazeera, GBTV and PBS, to *Larry King Live*, *Oprah*, *Peoples Daily*, *Sydney Morning Herald*, *The Doctors*, *Straits Times*, *Bloomberg*, *NPR*, *USA TODAY*, and hundreds of others—and his books have topped international bestseller lists for more than a decade. He continues to teach and inspire audiences around the world.

His most recent books include *Unfair Advantage: The Power of Financial Education*, *Midas Touch*, the second book he has co-authored with Donald Trump, and *Why "A" Students Work for "C" Students*.

To learn more, visit RichDad.com

UNFAIR
advantage
THE POWER OF FINANCIAL EDUCATION

AUTHOR OF THE INTERNATIONAL BEST SELLER RICH DAD POOR DAD

UNFAIR advantage

THE POWER OF FINANCIAL EDUCATION

WHAT SCHOOLS WILL NEVER TEACH YOU ABOUT MONEY

ROBERT T. KIYOSAKI

True financial education is the path to creating the life you want for yourself and your family.

Robert encourages and inspires you to change the one thing that is within your control: yourself.

In *Unfair Advantage*, Robert challenges people around the world to stop blindly accepting that they are destined to struggle financially all their lives.

This book is about the power of financial education and the five Unfair Advantages that real financial education offers:

The Unfair Advantage of Knowledge
The Unfair Advantage of Taxes
The Unfair Advantage of Debt
The Unfair Advantage of Risk
The Unfair Advantage of Compensation

In true Rich Dad style, *Unfair Advantage* challenges readers to appreciate two points of view and experience how the power of real financial education is *their* unfair advantage.

www.richdad.com

BEST-SELLING BOOKS
BY DONALD J. TRUMP

The Art of the Deal
Donald J. Trump with Tony Schwartz

The Art of the Comeback
Donald J. Trump with Kate Bohner

The America We Deserve
Donald J. Trump with Dave Shiflett

How to Get Rich
Donald J. Trump with Meredith McIver

Think Like A Billionaire
Donald J. Trump with Meredith McIver

The Way to the Top: The Best Business Advice I Ever Received
Donald J. Trump

The Best Golf Advice I Ever Received
Donald J. Trump

The Best Real Estate Advice I Ever Received
Donald J. Trump

Trump 101: The Way to Success
Donald J. Trump with Meredith McIver

Think Big in Business and Life
Donald J. Trump and Bill Zanker

Never Give Up
Donald J. Trump with Meredith McIver

Think Like a Champion
Donald J. Trump with Meredith McIver

Time to Get Tough
Donald J. Trump

Best-selling Books
by Robert T. Kiyosaki

Rich Dad Poor Dad
What the Rich Teach Their Kids About Money –
That the Poor and Middle Class Do Not

Rich Dad's CASHFLOW Quadrant
Guide to Financial Freedom

Rich Dad's Guide to Investing
What the Rich Invest in That the Poor and Middle Class Do Not

Rich Dad's Rich Kid Smart Kid
Give Your Child a Financial Head Start

Rich Dad's Retire Young Retire Rich
How to Get Rich and Stay Rich

Rich Dad's Prophecy
Why the Biggest Stock Market Crash in History Is Still Coming...
And How You Can Prepare Yourself and Profit from It!

Rich Dad's Success Stories
Real-Life Success Stories from Real-Life People
Who Followed the Rich Dad Lessons

Rich Dad's Guide to Becoming Rich
Without Cutting Up Your Credit Cards
Turn Bad Debt into Good Debt

Rich Dad's Who Took My Money?
Why Slow Investors Lose and Fast Money Wins!

Rich Dad Poor Dad for Teens
The Secrets About Money – That You Don't Learn In School!

Escape the Rat Race
Learn How Money Works and Become a Rich Kid

Rich Dad's Before You Quit Your Job
Ten Real-Life Lessons Every Entrepreneur Should Know
About Building a Multimillion-Dollar Business

Rich Dad's Increase Your Financial IQ
Get Smarter with Your Money

Robert Kiyosaki's Conspiracy of the Rich
The 8 New Rules of Money

Unfair Advantage
The Power of Financial Education

Why "A" Students Work for "C" Students
Rich Dad's Guide to Financial Education for Parents